Sonny Boy

AL PACINO

Sonny Boy

A MEMOIR

PENGUIN PRESS   NEW YORK   2024

PENGUIN PRESS
An imprint of Penguin Random House LLC
penguinrandomhouse.com

Image credits appear on pages 367–70.

LIBRARY OF CONGRESS CATALOGING-IN-PUBLICATION DATA
Names: Pacino, Al, 1940– author.
Title: Sonny boy : a memoir / Al Pacino.
Description: New York : Penguin Press, 2024.
Identifiers: LCCN 2024031097 (print) | LCCN 2024031098 (ebook) |
ISBN 9780593655115 (hardcover) | ISBN 9780593655122 (ebook)
Subjects: LCSH: Pacino, Al, 1940– | Actors—United States—Biography. |
Motion picture actors and actresses—United States—Biography.
Classification: LCC PN2287.P18 A3 2024 (print) | LCC PN2287.P18 (ebook) |
DDC 791.4302/8092 [B]—dc23/eng/20240708
LC record available at https://lccn.loc.gov/2024031097
LC ebook record available at https://lccn.loc.gov/2024031098

Printed in the United States of America
1 3 5 7 9 10 8 6 4 2

Book design by Daniel Lagin

To Charlie, to my granddad,
and to my mom

Contents

Sonny Boy

1

A Blade of Grass

I was performing since I was just a little boy. My mother used to take me to the movies when I was as young as three or four. She did menial work and factory jobs during the day, and when she came home, the only company she had was her son. So she'd bring me with her to the movies. She didn't know that she was supplying me with a future. I was immediately attached to watching actors on the screen. Since I never had playmates in our apartment and we didn't have television yet, I would have nothing but time to think about the movie I had last seen. I'd go through the characters in my head, and I would bring them to life, one by one, in the apartment. I learned at an early age to make friends with my imagination. Sometimes being content in your solitude can be a mixed blessing, especially to other people you share your life with.

The movies were a place where my mother could hide in the dark and not have to share her Sonny Boy with anyone else. That was her nickname for me, the one she gave me first, before everyone else started calling me Sonny too. It was something she picked up from the movies, where she heard Al Jolson sing it in a song that became very popular. It went like this:

Climb up on my knee, Sonny Boy
Though you're only three, Sonny Boy
You've no way of knowing
There's no way of showing
What you mean to me, Sonny Boy

It stuck in her head for a dozen years, and at my birth in 1940, the song was still so vivid to my mother that she would sing it to me. I was my parents' first child, my grandparents' first grandchild. They made a big fuss over me.

My father was all of eighteen when I was born, and my mother was just a few years older. Suffice it to say that they were young, even for the time. I probably hadn't even turned two years old when they split up. The first couple of years of my life my mother and I spent constantly moving around, no stability and no certainty. We lived together in furnished rooms in Harlem and then moved into her parents' apartment in the South Bronx. We hardly got any support from my father. Eventually, we were allotted five dollars a month by a court, which was just enough to cover our room and board at her parents' place.

Many years later, when I was fourteen, my mother took my father to court again to plead for more money, which he said he didn't have and which we didn't get. I thought the judge was very unfair to my mom. It would take decades for the courts to have some sense about a single mother's needs.

Sonny Boy

To find the earliest memory I have of being together with both of my parents, I have to go back to when I'm about three or four years old. I'm watching some movie with my mother in the balcony of the Dover Theatre. The story is some sort of melodrama for adults, and my mother is totally transfixed. I know I am watching something that's really meant for grown-ups, and I imagine there is a certain thrill in that, in being a little kid at my mother's side and sharing this time with her. But I can't quite follow the plot, and my attention wanders. I look down from the balcony, into the rows of seats below us. And I see a man walking around there, looking for something. He is wearing the dress uniform of an MP—the military police, which my father served in during World War II.

He must have seemed familiar, because I instinctively shouted out, "Dada!" My mother shushed me. I didn't understand why. How could you say shush? I shouted for him again. "Dada!" She kept whispering, "Shh—quiet!" because he was looking for my mother. They were having problems, and she didn't want him to find her, but now she had been found.

When the film was over, I remember walking on the dark street at night with my mother and father, the marquee of the Dover Theatre receding behind us. Each parent held one of my hands as I walked between them. Out of my right eye I saw a holster on my father's waist with a huge gun pouring out of it, with a pearl-white handle. Years later, when I played a cop in the film *Heat*, my character carried a gun with a handle like that. Even as a little child, I could understand: That's powerful. That's *dangerous*. And then my father was gone. He went off to the war and came back, but not to us.

Later in life, when I was acting in my first Broadway show, my relatives from my father's side of the family came to see me. I was this young, avant-garde actor who had spent most of his time in Greenwich Village and gradually worked his way onto Broadway. After the show, a couple of my aunts and a kid or two of theirs paid me a surprise visit in the hallway backstage. They started showering me with kisses, hugging me and congratulating me. They were Pacinos, and though I knew them from making the occasional visit to my grandmother on my father's side, I was somewhat bashful.

But as we made small talk, something came up in conversation that struck me to the bone. They said something about "the time that you were with us." I said, "What do you mean, when I was with you?" They said, "When you were with us, remember? Oh yeah, Sonny Boy, when you were hardly more than a baby, not quite a year and a half old, you lived with your grandma and grandpa—your daddy's mother and father."

I said, "How long did I live there?"

About eight months, they said, nearly a year.

And suddenly things started to come together in my head. I was taken away from my mother for eight months while my father was away in the war. But I wasn't sent to an orphanage or put in a foster home; I was mercifully given over to a blood relative—my father's mother, my grandmother, who was an absolute gift from God. I have had lifesavers throughout my time on this planet, and she was perhaps the first.

This realization knocked me over. I had a sudden clarity about the inexplicable things I had done in my life this far, at twenty-eight years old—the checkered way I lived, the choices I made, and the ways I dealt with things. It was a revelation to learn that I had been given away, at least temporarily, at the age of sixteen months. To have been totally dependent on my mother, knowing nothing else, and then sent off to a whole different life—that's a powerful rupture. Shortly after that, I went into therapy. I certainly had things that needed to be dealt with.

My dad's mother was Josephine, and she was probably the most wonderful person I've ever known in my life. She was a goddess. She just had this angelic countenance. She was the kind of woman who, in the old days, would go down to Ellis Island and wait for the new arrivals, Italians and anyone else who didn't know English, so she could help them. She cared and fought for me so much that she was given visitation rights to me in my parents' divorce settlement. Her husband, my grandfather and namesake, Alfred Pacino, arrived in New York from Italy in the early 1900s. They had an arranged marriage, and my grandfather worked as a house painter. He was a drunk, which made him moody and unpredictable.

I have no memory of that time I spent in their household, away from my mother. I imagine my mother had guilty feelings about the arrangement. She must have. Sure, I wasn't separated from my mother for a very long time, but at that young age, eight months was long enough.

When my son Anton was a little boy, not yet two years old, I can remember a time when we were together on Seventy-Ninth Street and Broadway and his mother wasn't there. He had a look on his face like he was completely lost. I thought to myself, It's because he doesn't know where his mother is. He was actually looking for her—looking past other people on the street to see if he could find her. He was close to the age I was when I lived with my father's parents. I never saw my son so lost at sea, before or since. I picked him up and told him, "Mama is coming, don't worry." That's what he needed to hear.

My mother's parents lived in a six-story tenement on Bryant Avenue in the South Bronx, in an apartment on the top floor, where the rents were cheapest. It was a hive of constant activity, with just three rooms, all of which were used as bedrooms. These were small rooms, but not small to me. Sometimes we would have as many as six or seven of us living there at a time. We lived in shifts. Nobody had a room all to themselves, and for long stretches of time, I slept between my grandparents. Other times, when I slept in a daybed in what was supposed to be the living room, I never knew who might end up camped out next to me—a relative passing through town, or my mother's brother, back from his own stint in the war. He had been in the Pacific, and like so many other men who had seen combat, he wouldn't talk about his experience in the war. He would take wooden matchsticks and put them in his ears to drown out the explosions he couldn't stop hearing.

My mother's father was born Vincenzo Giovanni Gerardi, and he came from an old Sicilian town whose name, I would later learn, was Corleone. When he was four years old, he came over to America, possibly illegally, where he became James Gerard. By then he had already lost his mother; his father, who was a bit of a dictator, had gotten remarried and moved with his children and new wife to Harlem. My grandfather had a wild, Dickensian up-bringing, but to me he was the first real father figure I had.

When I was six, I came home from my first day of school and found my grandfather shaving in our bathroom. He was in front of the mirror, in his BVD shirt with his suspenders down at his sides. I was standing in the open bathroom doorway. I wanted to share a story with him.

"Granddad, this kid in school did a very bad thing. So I went and told the teacher and she punished that kid."

Without missing a stroke as he continued to shave, my grandfather said to me simply, "So you're a rat, huh?" It was a casual observation, as if he were saying, "You like the piano? I didn't know that." But his words hit me right in the solar plexus. I could feel myself slinking down the sides of the bathroom doorway. I was crestfallen. I couldn't breathe. That's all he said. And I never ratted on anybody in my life again. Although right now as I write this, I'm ratting on myself.

His wife, Kate, was my granny. She had blond hair and blue eyes like Mae West, a kind of rarity among Italians, which sort of set her apart from all my relatives. She may have had some German blood on her side. When I was around age two, I guess, she would sit me on her kitchen table and spoon-feed baby food to me as she told extravagant, made-up stories in which I was the main character. That had to have made an impact. When I got a little older, I would find her cooking in the kitchen, peeling potatoes, and I would eat them raw. They had little nutritional value, but I loved the way they tasted. Sometimes she gave me dog biscuits and I ate those too.

My grandmother was known for her kitchen. She made Italian food, of course, but we weren't in an Italian neighborhood. As a matter of fact, we were the only Italians living in our neighborhood. Perhaps there was one across the street, a guy named Dominic, a jolly kid, who had a harelip. When I'd be going out the door,

Grandma would stop me right in my tracks with her wet cloth, which always seemed to be in one of her hands, to say, "Wipe the gravy off your face. People will think you're Italian." There was a kind of stigma against Italians when we first started coming over to America, and it only escalated when World War II started. America had just spent four years fighting against Italy, and though many Italian Americans had gone overseas to battle their own brethren and help bring down Mussolini, others were labeled enemy aliens and put in internment camps. When Italian Americans came back from the war, they intermarried with other groups at sky-high rates.

The other families in our tenement were from all over Eastern Europe and other parts of the world. You heard a cacophony of dialects. You heard everyone. Our little stretch between Longfellow Avenue and Bryant Avenue, from 171st Street up to 174th Street, was a mixture of nationalities and ethnicities. In the summertime, when we went on the roof of our tenement to cool off because there was no air-conditioning, you'd hear the murmur of different languages in a variety of accents. It was a glorious time: a lot of poor people from various ghettos had moved in, and we were making something out of the Bronx. The farther north you went, the more prosperous the families were. We were not prosperous. We were getting by. My grandfather was a plasterer who had to work every day. In those days, plasterers were highly sought after. He had developed an expertise and was appreciated for what he did. He built a wall in the alleyway for our landlord, who loved the wall he built so much that he kept our family's rent at $38.80 a month for as long as we lived there.

Until I was a little older, I wasn't allowed out of the tenement

by myself—we lived in the back, and the neighborhood was somewhat unsafe—and I had no siblings. We had no TV and not much
in the way of entertainment, aside from a few Al Jolson records
that I used to mime along to for my family's enjoyment when I was
three or four. My only companions, aside from my grandparents,
my mother, and a little dog named Trixie, were the characters I
brought to life from those movies my mother took me to. I had to
have been the only five-year-old who was brought to *The Lost
Weekend*. I was quite taken with Ray Milland's performance as a
self-destructive alcoholic, which won him an Oscar. When he is
struggling to get dry and suffering from the d.t.'s, he hallucinates
the sight of a bat swooping from a corner of his hospital room and
attacking a mouse going up the wall. Milland could make you believe he was caught in the terror of this delusion. I couldn't forget
the scene when he's sober, searching frantically for the booze that
he squirreled away when he was drunk but can't remember where
he hid it. I would try to perform it myself, pretending to ransack
an invisible apartment as I scavenged through unseen cabinets,
drawers, and hampers. I got so good at this little routine that I
would do it on request for my relatives. They would roar with
laughter. I guess it struck them as funny to see a five-year-old pretending to scramble through an imaginary kitchen with a kind of
life-or-death intensity. That was an energy within myself that I
was already discovering I could channel. Even at five years old, I
would think, What are they laughing at? This man is fighting for
his life.

My mother had a sensitivity for these things. I think it's why she
was drawn to these kinds of films. She was a beautiful woman, but
she was delicate, with fragile emotions. She would occasionally

visit a psychiatrist, when Granddad had the money to pay for her sessions. I wasn't aware that my mother was having problems until one day when I was six years old. I was getting ready to go out and play in the streets, sitting in a chair in the kitchen while my mother laced up my little shoes for me and put a sweater on me to keep me warm. I noticed that she was crying, and I wondered what was the matter, but I didn't understand how to ask her. She was kissing me all over, and right before I left the apartment, she gave me a great big hug. It was unusual, but I was eager to get downstairs and meet up with the other kids, and I gave it no more thought.

We had been outside for about an hour when we saw a commotion in the street. People were running toward my grandparents' tenement. Someone said to me, "I think it's your mother." I didn't believe it. I thought, How could they say a thing like that? My mother? That's not true. I started running with them. There was an ambulance in front of the building, and there, coming out the front doors, carried on a stretcher, was my mother. She had attempted suicide.

This was not explained to me; I had to piece together what had happened for myself. I knew afterward she was sent to recover at Bellevue Hospital, where people who did that sort of thing were kept for a while. It's a period of time that is kind of a blank to me, but I do remember sitting around the kitchen table in my grandparents' apartment where the grown-ups were discussing what they were going to do. I couldn't quite grasp it, but I pretended to be a grown-up with them. Years later, I made the film *Dog Day Afternoon*, and one of its final images, showing John Cazale's character getting brought away on a stretcher, already dead, would make me think of the moment I saw my mother brought out to that ambulance and taken away. But I don't think she wanted to die then, not yet. She came back to our household alive, and I went out into the streets.

)͙(♦)͙(

AS A KID, IT WAS THE RELATIONSHIPS WITH MY FRIENDS ON THE street that sustained me and gave me hope. I ran with a crew that included my three best friends, Cliffy, Bruce, and Petey. Every day was a fresh adventure. We were on the prowl, hungry for life. In hindsight I realize I might have had more love from my family than the other three did. I think that might have made all the difference. I made it out alive, and they didn't.

To this day, one of my favorite memories is coming down the stairs and out onto the street in front of my tenement building on a Saturday morning in the springtime. I couldn't have been more than ten years old. The street was empty and the day was bright. I remember looking down the block, and there was Bruce, about fifty yards away. I felt this joy inside me that has stuck with me forever. The day was clear and crisp, and everything was quiet and still. He turned and smiled, and I smiled, too, because we knew we were alive. The day was full of potential. Something was going to happen.

Every few blocks were the vacant lots where the Victory gardens had been planted at the height of World War II. Once Eleanor Roosevelt got her Victory garden built at the White House, they started popping up everywhere, even in the South Bronx. But by the time we got to them, after the war, they were wrecked, full of debris—the flowers had gone off to heaven. Along the edges of these lots were sidewalks. Once in a while, when you looked down at the sidewalk, you'd see a blade of grass growing up out of the concrete. That's what my friend Lee Strasberg once called talent: a blade of grass growing up out of a block of concrete.

These Victory gardens filled with rubbish became our assembly halls and playgrounds. They made pretty good baseball fields, if you gathered up the garbage to make your bases.

Often I'd be playing baseball in one of those lots, and at around five o'clock I'd spot Granddad in the distance, passing by as he made his way home from work. No matter where I was in that lot, as soon as I caught a glimpse of him, I'd zip across to meet him at the sidewalk just before he could pass by, to shake him down for enough loose change to get an ice cream.

He'd look down at me and reach into his pocket, his hand going way down to what felt like the bottom of his pant leg, finally returning with my big gift: a shiny nickel. I'd quickly say "Thanks, Granddad" and run off.

If I noticed him walking by as I was up at bat I'd yell out to get his attention, hoping he'd see me crack the ball and get on base. He'd stop and watch for a minute, and every time he was standing there I would strike out. Every single time. When I went home, I would tell him that after he left, I got a triple, and he'd nod his head and smile.

In the neighborhood, I seemed to cheat death on a regular basis. I was like a cat with many more than nine lives. I had more mishaps and accidents than I can count, so from that bundle I'll pick a few that stick out and have significance. One winter day, I was skating on the ice over the Bronx River. We didn't have ice skates, so I was wearing a pair of sneakers, doing pirouettes, showing off for my friend Jesus Diaz, who was standing at the shore. One moment I was laughing and he was cheering me on, then suddenly I broke through the surface and plunged into the freezing waters below. Every time I tried to crawl out, the ice wouldn't hold up and I kept falling back into the freezing water. I think I would have drowned that day if it wasn't for Jesus Diaz. He managed to find a long stick twice the size of himself, spread himself out as far as he could from the shore, and use that stick to pull me to safety. I was soaking wet and freezing, so he got me out of the cold and into the apartment he shared with his family, in the tenement where his dad was the superintendent. Jesus Diaz gave me his own clothes to wear.

At around the same age, I had one of the most embarrassing experiences of my life. I'm even squeamish to tell it now, but why not? That's what we're here for. I couldn't have been more than ten years old, and I was walking on a thin iron fence, doing my tightrope dance. It had been raining all morning, and sure enough, I slipped and fell, and the iron bar hit me directly between my legs. I was in such pain that I could hardly walk home. An older guy saw me groaning in the street, picked me up, and carried me to my Aunt Marie's apartment. She was my mother's younger sister, who lived on the third floor in the same building as my grandparents. The Samaritan threw me on a bed and said, "Take care, man."

It was customary for doctors to go to people's houses in those days, even though their offices were just down the street. While my family waited for Dr. Tanenbaum to come by, I lay there on the bed with my pants completely down around my ankles as the three women in my life—my mother, my aunt, and my grandmother—poked and prodded at my penis in a semipanic. I thought, God, please take me now, as I heard them whispering things to one another as they conducted their inspection. My penis remained attached, along with the trauma. To this day I'm haunted by the thought of it.

Our South Bronx neighborhood had a full complement of extreme characters, and most of them were innocent. We had a guy who appeared to be in his late thirties or early forties, with a mixture of red and black hair, who dressed in a suit and a collared shirt with a loose, tattered tie. He looked like he went to a Sunday service and ashes had spilled all over him. He would quietly walk the streets by himself and hardly ever spoke; when he did, the only thing he said was "You don't kill time—time kills you." That was it. If he would have come up to us even once and said, "How are you guys?" we would have been shocked. Sure, I was a little suspicious of him, as we all were. We were like a pack of wild animals and we knew he stood apart from our species. Our instinct told us he was separate, so we didn't inquire about it. We just accepted him. There was more sense of privacy back then compared to our world now, a certain propriety and distance that people gave one another. Perhaps it's still there in smaller towns, and it's something I've always carried with me in life.

But darkness could lurk around the wrong corner. One time, when I was around eight or nine, I was by myself on Bryant Avenue, throwing a ball against the wall of my tenement building. This kid I knew, let's call him Steve, was coming back from a big bus depot by the El station, where we used to play inside the empty buses and collect the colorful paper transfers and pretend they were money. Steve had a weird, blank look on his face, like he was really stunned. I said, "Hey, Steve, what's the matter?"

He looked straight through me and said, "Some guy peed in my mouth."

I said, "Why would somebody pee in your mouth?"

He said, "I don't know."

"He peed in your mouth."

"Yeah, down at the bus depot."

Steve didn't know what was happening, and at my young age, neither did I. I didn't have the nuance or experience. Later in life, I would understand what I think might really have happened to him. It was the kind of thing that could have happened on any street in any town, and it had happened here. I found a way to move on from it in my brain. There are things that we happen upon as we grow up, and though they strike us, we can't quite compute them, or remember much about them unless we are put into some hypnotic state. But we absorb them all the same. I knew at the time that something really wrong had occurred and that Steve seemed kind of broken by it, helpless.

All I knew was that with friends like Cliffy, Bruce, and Petey, I never felt helpless. When we got a little older, eleven or twelve, we formed gangs and explored the neighborhood, venturing out past the end of our block, seeking out new horizons. You went to one place and some gang beat you up. You went to another place, you got attacked by another gang. Pretty soon, you learned the boundaries of your own turf and you stayed put as much as you could.

We did anything fun we could afford to do. We spent hours at a time lying flat on our stomachs as we fished in the sewer gratings at the ends of our blocks, hoping for the gleam of something shiny down there in the grime that might be a lost coin. This was not an idle pursuit—fifty cents was a game changer. We'd scale to the tops of tenements and jump from one roof to another. On Saturday nights, when we saw guys just a few years older than us who had graduated to dating girls, and they'd be taking their dates out to the movies or the subway, we'd get up on the storefront roofs and pelt them with trash. Sometimes we'd split up a head of lettuce and toss it at them. A string bean thrown from twenty feet away could really sting. We opened up hydrants in the summer, which made us heroes to all the young mothers who let their small children play in the water. It would get pretty hot in the South Bronx in mid-July. We hitched to the backs of buses, jumped over turnstiles in the subway. If we wanted food, we'd steal it. We never paid for anything.

Making mischief and running away from authority figures was our pastime. We tried to join the Boy Scouts, but we knew we couldn't afford to pay for their uniforms or go to their summer camps. Their meetings were held in the local public schools, so we'd gather with them in a gymnasium where some scout leader would try to tell us what to do. We'd just break into laughter until we were made to leave. We could never have been Boy Scouts: we didn't know how to.

We lived and breathed the old street games like kick the can, stickball, and ringolevio. To play ringolevio, you'd split into two teams, and you'd chase your opponents and try to capture them by throwing your arms around them and saying, "Ringolevio, one, two, three," three times in a row. Then that person would be thrown into a jail, in a marked-off circle at the center of the schoolyard. But if you could stick one foot in your team's jail and shout out, "Free all!" then the whole gang would get sprung. It was the greatest feeling in the world if you somehow were able to accomplish it. Kids were known to jump off buildings just to try to get a foot in that circle and scream out, "Free all!"

Where I came from, we were always either being chased or doing the chasing. When we'd see cops, we'd yell out to one another, "Hey, what's a penny made out of?" And then we'd all scream, "Dirty copper!" Those cops would either yawn or laugh or take off after us, depending on whatever mood they were in. But we all knew the neighborhood cop on our beat; he walked with us, kept a watch on us, encouraged us to have fun. I don't know how much violence he stopped, but we grew to love him, and he got a kick out of us. I always thought the guy had a crush on my mother. He'd ask me questions about her, and even at age eleven, I sort of knew why.

In my little gang, in addition to me, Bruce, Petey, and Cliffy, there were a few others—Jesus Diaz, Bibby, Johnny Rivera, Smoky, Salty, and Kenny Lipper, who would one day go on to become a deputy mayor of New York City under Ed Koch. (I later did a film called *City Hall*, which I acted in with John Cusack and was solidly directed by Harold Becker, that was based on his experience.)

We also had a kid named Hymie in our group, who today would be described as special needs. He was older than us and very strong. Other gangs would think twice when they saw him. At night I'd walk home with him and together we'd sing "I Wonder Who's Kissing Her Now." That was an old World War II song about a soldier thinking of his girl back home. Hymie would follow me up all the flights of stairs in my apartment building, and then as he left, he would go down the stairs singing, "I wonder who's—" and I would sing back, "kissing her now." When Hymie turned sixteen, he became violent; he started attacking his mother, and they put him away in an institution. We never saw him again. We missed him.

There was a boy in our neighborhood named Philly, who was being bullied by another kid. There was a slang term at the time: if you wore your collar turned up, you were "rocky" or "a rock"—you were cool. The kid kept calling Philly a rock: he'd say to him, "You think you're a rock?" The bully did it so much that Philly just lost it. He started banging his head against a brick wall, over and over again, shouting, "I'm a rock, I'm a rock." After that, Philly got taken out of school and put into a place of rehabilitation. He was never the same after that. He'd sit in a chair and stare off in a daze, never speaking to anyone. His mother sat next to him.

Cliffy, Bruce, Petey, and me—we were the top four bananas. They called me Sonny, and Pacchi, their nickname for Pacino. They also called me Pistachio, because I liked pistachio ice cream. If we had to choose someone as our leader, it would be Cliffy or Petey. Petey was a tough Irish kid. But Cliffy was a savant, a true original, fearless, and even at thirteen never without a copy of Dostoevsky in his back pocket. This kid had the potential to be whatever he wanted in life. He had the talent. He had the looks. He had an IQ through the roof, which he used to boast about. And he had four older brothers who beat the shit out of him every day. He was full of trickery. You never had to ask him, What are we going to do today? He always had a scheme.

We would go up to the rooftops of the tenements when we wanted to hang out, and also because they offered us escape routes if we were being chased. Up on that roof were TV antennas mounted all along a twelve-inch ledge that ran the perimeter of the building. Sometimes we'd get up on that ledge like we were in a high-wire act and walk along it. We'd move like cats, five stories high, and when we'd come to one of those antennas we'd stop to steady ourselves before we went another stretch. Cliffy moved with joyful abandon, shouting, "See me?" He'd fly like he was a frenzied bird. I did it myself a few times but not the way Cliffy did.

We'd go over by the Bronx Zoo, to what they used to call Monkey Island, where we would go to a secluded area and climb up the giant ropes that had been tied around tree branches there by some distant ancestors of ours. We'd swing ourselves on those ropes out over the pond there, let go, and frolic in the water. Bruce came out of there with a leech stuck to his body, sucking his blood. Some of the guys who were older than us would stand on a large, flat rock that went out into the water and hold contests to see who could jerk off the farthest. Everything was a contest to them: "I'll bet you a nickel you won't eat that cigarette butt that's been lying on the ground, and the orange peel next to it." And sure enough, someone would take that bet. I would stay out of those games and let them do their thing. Somehow I always seemed to be observing things; only occasionally would I participate in them.

One time Cliffy saw a squirrel run up in a tree, so he threw a rock at it. The poor squirrel fell to the ground with a thud, dead, and Cliffy started crying. He didn't think he would kill it. We buried the squirrel and said prayers over it. Another time, I came home with an injured sparrow I had found and brought it to my mother, and we really took care of it. After a while this sparrow got used to us. It would fly around the apartment and land on our shoulders. We just had to make sure to keep the dog away from it. We all really took a liking to it. My mom used to kiss it, and we built it a little birdcage. She gave it food to build its strength back up, and she nurtured it, petted it, and loved it. Finally we had to let it go, because it needed to be free, we thought. We brought it back to where all the other sparrows were and set it loose. It was smaller than the other sparrows around, and we were later to find out that they usually rejected birds that had been domesticated. The idea that our friend had likely been killed by his own kind because of his time with us broke our hearts. I later read Tennessee Williams's *Orpheus Descending*, and when I came upon his line about the little birds that "don't have no legs at all and they live their whole lives on the wing, and they sleep on the wind," I thought of that sparrow.

)(✦)(

MY GRANDMOTHER'S METHOD FOR CLEANING OUR KITCHEN WINdow, the way of most tenement dwellers, was to open it up, sit on the windowsill, and wash the window from the outside, while her backside dangled precariously out of the window frame five stories above the ground. When I stood in the kitchen and looked out that window, I could see down into the alleyway, the one where my grandfather had built the wall that separated our alleyway from the alleyway of the building next to ours. If you climbed over that wall, there was a corridor that led to a whole system of exits and entrances, a world unto itself, full of passages connected to courtyards and circular spaces. When I started smoking cigarettes somewhere between age ten and eleven, I made sure I was in an alleyway where no one would see me, because I knew that smoking was not allowed. I would imagine tawdry things were done down there, whatever was forbidden. It had that feeling, but it wasn't frightening, it was inviting. The first time I kissed a girl it was down there in those alleys. I didn't know what I was doing, but I thought something spectacular had happened. I thought I lost my virginity. Sadly not.

Often when I looked down into that alley from my apartment window, I would see my friends—a pack of wild, pubescent wolves with sly smiles—looking up at me, calling out, "Come on down, Sonny Boy! We got something for ya!" One morning Cliffy showed up with a huge German shepherd. He yelled up, "Hey, Sonny, wanna look at my dog? He's my new friend, and his name is Hans!" I wanted to jump right out the window to get down there and have a look at this gigantic canine specimen, but I was all the way on the top floor.

Cliffy wasn't known for stealing dogs. Cars were more his thing. At around fourteen, he stole a city bus. Once, he stole a garbage truck. He still had that copy of Dostoyevsky with him when he did it. He also used to burglarize houses—he could no longer go to New Jersey because he was wanted by the police there. He would tease me because I never did any of the drugs that he was into. He'd say, "Sonny doesn't need drugs—he's high on himself!"

Sports were an area that divided me from the rest of the gang. My grandfather had instilled a love of sports in me: he was a lifelong baseball fan and a boxing fan. He grew up rooting for the New York Yankees before they were even the Yankees—they were called the Highlanders first, and as a poor kid he would watch their games through holes in the fence at Hilltop Park or the Polo Grounds, where the New York Giants played. Later the Yankees would get their own stadium, which would be known as the House That Ruth Built. That stadium is in the background of a scene in *Serpico*, which Sidney Lumet shot with such beauty, where Serpico meets with the crew of corrupt cops, all gathered like a den of thieves. The day that scene was shot was the morning Tuesday Weld and I broke up, and if you notice the look on my face, you can tell that guy looks pretty sad.

My grandfather always cheered for the underdog, and that seems to be my plight too. I always root for the losers, until they start winning, and then I say to myself, Oh man, I'm not rooting for them anymore.

When he could afford to, Granddad would take me to baseball games, and we'd sit way up in the grandstand—the cheap seats. We knew, of course, that there were box seats that cost more money and got you closer to the field. That was another thing entirely—we didn't belong to that class. I didn't think of myself as being disadvantaged—it was just another block in the neighborhood, another tribe. It might as well have been another country. The difference between Cliffy and me was that Cliffy would see those same box seats and want to go down there. If there was a line to get into a movie, he wouldn't wait—he'd cut in front of someone and just go right in. He was daring in that way. It was like nobody existed but him, a solipsist if I ever saw one. When I think about it, I might be on that continuum too.

I was an athlete myself at that age. I was fast and agile, and I bounced around when I moved. I played baseball for the PAL team in my neighborhood. Sports were of no interest to Cliffy and the guys, so it was almost like I lived two lives: my life with the gang, and my life with the guys I played ball with. For a time I thought I might grow up to be a professional baseball player, until I saw some of those guys go out for the farm team of the Yankees—they couldn't even get looked at, and they were far better than me, let me tell you. I'm in awe of professional athletes. You've got to climb a mountain to get there, and they have all summited Mount Everest as far as I'm concerned.

The guys in the gang were where my life was, but I would go without them, on my own, to play in my games. One day I was coming back from a game in a bad neighborhood when my glove got stolen from me. A group of four or five guys not much older than I was got the jump on me; they had knives and God knows what else, and they said, "Give us the glove." They knew I had no money, and I knew I was losing the glove. My grandfather had bought it for me, and I went home in tears and told him that they had stolen it and I didn't know what to do. I knew he couldn't afford another one, and that trying to find those guys who had taken it from me would have meant a war. If only I'd had Cliffy, Petey, and Bruce with me it never would have happened in the first place. It wasn't just comfortable for us to be together in our group—it was necessary, because otherwise we were vulnerable, defenseless.

At the edge of the Bronx River, about four blocks from our homes, sat the Dutch Houses. They were ancient buildings, built by the Dutch people when they settled in this country, now dilapidated but not quite abandoned. Herman Wouk talked about them in his novel *City Boy*, describing the surrounding territory as an area of "odorous heaps." When we felt really daring, we would venture out to the Dutchies. Their ruins were populated by wayward kids and runaways—Boonies, we called them, because they were on Boone Avenue. They lived down there in shacks, and they carried diseases, and the lore was that they had poison on the ends of their homemade weapons.

Wild, untamed plant life grew along the riverbeds: thick weeds as high as your head and bamboo trees that kids would cut down, chop up, and carve into knives, bows, and arrows. Rafts were run up and down the Bronx River, to move the kinds of products you couldn't sell in stores. We'd spy on shady merchants who slipped in and out to conduct their mysterious transactions, and men who showed up to do who knows what with the women they brought along.

You'd hear the occasional muffled gunshot, usually from a homemade gun fashioned from wood and rubber bands. It was a variation on a slingshot: if you added a .22-caliber bullet and ignited the shell, it would usually go sideways; if you were unlucky, it would fly up toward your head. You shot them at cans, bottles, and rocks, but they had a presence. If you carried one, it gave you the extra step you needed and it could get you in trouble. The whole place had danger written all over it, but that was fun for us.

One day I was on Bryant Avenue when I saw the rest of the gang limping back from the Dutchies looking defeated. Cliffy was covered in blood. When he noticed the shocked reaction on my face, he shouted, "It's not me! It's Petey's blood!" Behind him was Petey, whose blood was gushing like a geyser from a wound on his wrist. They had been deep in the Dutchies, making their way down a hill, when Cliffy suddenly screamed, "Look out, there's a Boony there!" He shouted out a name that was notorious in that area. Even now I can't bring myself to say it. Cliffy had only been kidding, but the other kids scrambled in every direction. Petey knew he had to move quickly, but unfortunately he stumbled and fell, and he hit the ground hard. He landed on something sharp and jagged that sliced through his left wrist. The cut was so deep that it went all the way down to the nerves. It was horrible.

The doctors were eventually able to fix him up, but they stitched him up in a botched way, so he couldn't move correctly. I would imagine if it happened today, that kind of injury could be taken care of properly—it would cost you, but they'd do it right. But there he was with a hand that he couldn't move anymore. The dark world of poverty had left him crippled. When Petey played ball with us, he'd have to take his glove off the hand he just caught with and use it to throw the ball back. Cliffy always blamed himself for what happened to Petey, all because of his dumb prank.

)X◆X(

IN THE EVENING I'M TAKING A BATH IN MY GRANDPARENTS' APARTment when I hear a rumbling in the alleyway downstairs. From five stories below, the voices are reaching up to my bathroom window:

"Sonny!"

"Hey, Pacchi!"

"Sonn-*ayyyyyyyyy*!"

These are the cries of my friends in the alley calling to me. They are gathering for another round of escapades—the late shift. I'm ten or eleven years old, but they want me to join in with them. They are howling like wildcats. There's no bell for them to ring and no phone they can call me on, so this is how they communicate. They are up to something—something exciting—and I want to be with them.

But something else is preventing me from leaping out of the tub, throwing on my clothes, and reuniting with them. I don't mean my conscience; I mean my mother. She is telling me I am not allowed. She says it's late and tomorrow is a school day and any boys who come to shout out in the alley at that time of night aren't the sort of boys I should be spending my time with, and anyway, the answer is no.

I hate her for this. She is cutting me off from my connection to the world. These friends are the source of my identity. They are everything in my life that means something to me at this time, and my mother won't let me be with them. I loathe her for it. And then one day I'm fifty-two, looking in the vanity mirror at my face, fat with shaving cream, racking my brains for someone to thank in an acceptance speech for an award I'm about to receive. I think back to that moment and I realize that I'm still here because of my mother. Of course that's who I have to thank, and I never thanked her for it. She's the one who kept a lid on all of this, who parried me away from the path that led to delinquency, danger, and violence, to the needle, that lethal delight called heroin that killed my three closest friends. Petey, Cliffy, Bruce—they all died from drugs. I was not exactly under strict surveillance, but my mother paid attention to where I was in a way that my friends' families didn't, and we all knew it. I believe she saved my life.

)X◆)X

I COULD TELL THAT MY MOTHER'S FAMILY DID NOT HAVE THE greatest image of my father, but my grandparents were careful not to say anything negative about him in my presence. My mother, however, let slip certain things from time to time that made it clear she did not respect him or feel that he took care of me. That kind of talk can hurt children. When you come from a split home, you already feel like an orphan. That point of view from an adult can lead to lasting prejudice—it can poison the well forever, and it's something we should be very careful of. And I'm sure that hearing it from her had some effect on me. But even at that age, I was determined not to let her influence my feelings about my dad. I wanted to form a picture of him myself.

When I was nine years old, my dad took me around the neighborhood where he was living in East Harlem. He and my mother had been divorced for a few years, and since he had gotten back from the war, he had made a new life for himself. He was in his late twenties and had gotten himself a college education on the GI Bill. He was working as an accountant and doing pretty well for himself, from what I understood. I would occasionally see him on holidays and birthdays, and he had a new apartment, a new wife, a new child. But he still wanted to have me in his life somehow. So he took me around his block, stopping at the storefronts and local hangouts, showing me off to his friends. "This is my son," he would say to them. "Hey, son," they would say back. But I didn't know who any of these people were. They were of a different breed. They were Italians, and they looked like relatives I had met, but they had a certain manner I wasn't familiar with. They were older and they sipped anisette out of tiny espresso cups at storefront cafés. They were cool and they liked me, but I just wanted to go home to the Bronx and be with my own friends. I felt like my dad was putting me on display.

I thought this was just supposed to be a daytime visit, but somewhere between the walk around the block and my father's house I learned it was now an overnight stay. I was going to be sleeping at his place, a long, narrow railroad apartment where I was put to bed at one of its far-apart ends. When I woke up in the middle of the night, I was completely disoriented. Everything felt wrong. I couldn't see the room they had me in. The bed they gave me to sleep on wasn't my own. The sounds coming up from the street were totally alien. I heard some sort of scratching in the wall that I thought had to be mice or rats.

I began creeping my way through the dark to reach my father. Every door I passed could have danger behind it. Every room I entered was full of obstacles. When I got to the rear of the railroad apartment, I found him sleeping in the bed he shared with his new wife. Its bed frame came up to my belly, and all I could make out in the darkness were lumps of different sizes under the covers. I couldn't tell which were his and which were hers, but I knew I didn't want to stir this woman who, based on how she had looked at me and talked to me during the day, seemed to regard me as some sort of pigeon that got separated from its flock and was sure to be carrying a lethal disease.

So I shook the sheets, which of course woke them both up. But I wanted more than anything to get out of there, and I didn't know how. I just stuttered, "Can I—can I go home?" And that weary man got up in the middle of the night and got me in his car. He actually had a car, which to me was like having an airplane. And he drove me back home, which was relatively far away by car. It would've been faster by subway.

When we pulled up at my family's tenement, my father shut off the engine and spoke to me as we sat there. He was trying to tell me his side of the story. He said, "I was trying to do my best, but your grandmother was always getting in the way." In his awkward, unrehearsed way, he was trying to reach out to me. But he was talking to a nine-year-old, and I just couldn't absorb it. I was so relieved when I got upstairs to my grandparents. I thought, My dad isn't such a bad guy. I mean, look what he did—he brought me all the way home when he didn't have to. But I honestly just wanted to get out. He was a stranger to me.

At school the teachers used to tell my mother, "Your son also needs a father." She was enraged. *You mean we've got to be together and suffer and fight and argue, and my kid hears all of that?*

I've since had friends throughout my life who liked their dads, or even had strong bonds with both of their parents. But others didn't have good relationships with their fathers. Some grew up seeing their drunken fathers beat the shit out of their mothers. I've even known people whose hatred for their father was so intense that they'd get physically sick being around them. I just never had a father. He was absent. I'm so lucky I had my grandfather. But when I think about it now, it must have been pretty painful that my father couldn't have a relationship with me. He was Italian, and I was his first and only son, so I know it must have haunted him. At the same time, I realized I was spared, in a way, not having that guy around. If I was brought up by that guy, I wouldn't be me. But I have three half sisters, his daughters, who I got to know, and all had good words about him. I could see how much they loved him.

I had other people in my life who were looking out for me and guiding me, even if I didn't realize it at the time. My junior high

teacher, an attractive middle-aged woman named Blanche Rothstein, selected me to start reading passages from the Bible at our
student assemblies. I didn't come from a particularly religious
family. My mother sent me to catechism class, and I wore my little
white suit for my First Holy Communion. But I was fearful that
maybe I was so good that the Virgin Mary would come down and
make me a saint. I said no, I don't want to be a saint. I actually got
scared by that, and that's the truth, so I never went back for my
confirmation. That, and because the nuns beat you for no reason.

But when I read from the book of Psalms in a big, booming
voice—"He that walketh uprightly, and worketh righteousness,
and speaketh the truth in his heart"—I could feel how powerful
the words were. Because words can make you fly. They can come
to life. Like my friend Charlie used to say, the word made flesh, to
borrow another biblical phrase. That's what I thought acting was,
just saying beautiful words and trying to entertain people with them.

Soon I was performing in school plays like *The Melting Pot*, a
little pageant celebrating the many nations whose people had contributed to the greatness of America. I was one of the children
chosen to stand in front of a huge melting pot in the middle of the
stage. I was there to represent Italy, along with a ten-year-old girl
with dark hair and olive skin. I looked across the melting pot at her
and I thought, Is that what Italians look like?

When our class did *The King and I*, I played Louis, the son of
the heroine, Anna. Another kid who played the young Prince of
Siam and I sang a song together about how we were puzzled by the
ways that grown-ups behaved.

I didn't take acting very seriously—it was just a way to goof
off, get out my energy, and especially get out of classes. But I

somehow got a reputation for being a guy that you simply had to have in these school productions. I guess I must have been okay at it, because a guy came up to me after one performance and said, "Hey, kid, you're the next Marlon Brando!" I looked at him and said, "Who's Marlon Brando?"

At the end of the year, our junior high class held an assembly to vote on various student prizes, and I was chosen Most Likely to Succeed. I was disappointed because I wanted to be Most Handsome. But this guy Willy Rams won it—he was one of those guys who used to do one-armed push-ups and walk around on his hands. He was a nice kid. But Most Likely to Succeed, which they gave me, was just a popularity contest. All it meant was that a lot of people had heard of you. Who wants to be heard of anyway?

Blanche Rothstein, my junior high school teacher, had bigger plans for me. One day she scaled the five flights of stairs in our tenement to reach our apartment because she wanted to speak to my grandmother. She was there not to discipline me but to embolden me: "This boy must be allowed to continue to act," she told Granny. "This is his future." It was such a simple gesture, and so rare. No one else ever made this kind of effort, at least not on my behalf. What this great, devoted teacher was doing was an honorable thing, what all teachers can offer, which is inspiration and dedication to their position. Encouragement—the greatest word in the English language. My grandmother didn't quite pick up on what this teacher was doing, but my mother did, and she was troubled by it. As she understood it, we were poor people, and poor people don't do acting.

This didn't discourage my progress at school. When I was thirteen and we did our class play, *Home Sweet Homicide*, I was chosen to play one of the kids who helps their widowed mother solve a murder in the house next door. Before I went on, someone told me backstage that both of my parents were in the audience. My mother and father in the audience. Oh no. It threw me off, and I didn't give as good a performance as I hoped I would. To this day, I still don't want to know who's in the audience on opening night or any night.

But aside from that, doing the play was wonderful. I always felt at home on a stage. I felt this is where I belong. I mean, I liked being on a baseball field, too, but I couldn't play baseball as well as I could do this other thing called theater. I just enjoyed it. I felt free. I felt happy. I felt people were paying attention to me. And I enjoyed being with the other actors.

Right after the show, my mother and my father took me out to Howard Johnson's and we all toasted my success. Howard Johnson's was just a diner, like Denny's, like the kind you see in the beginning of *Pulp Fiction*. It's nothing fancy. Simple people go there. You don't get a big fat check at the end of the meal. But a feeling of such warmth and belonging came over me. It was the first time, probably in my entire life, that I saw my parents sitting next to each other. I mean, can you imagine that? This was something I had been wishing for all along, only I didn't know it consciously. Every child grows up wanting to be together with their mother and father. That's security. That's family.

I was discovering something that I had been missing, that sense of connection. I could see that they were talking to each other pleasantly, not arguing about anything. My father, at one point, even touched my mother's hand with his own—was he flirting with her? It just felt so natural and so easy, I wondered why did they ever separate? The play had united them, however briefly.

Whatever had been hanging over me was lifted, because in this moment, these two humans would take care of me. Acting in this play had brought my mother and father back together again, had made me part of something again. I actually was whole. I felt that sensation for the first time in my life. And then it was gone.

2

A Change

For years, the old Elsmere Theatre on Crotona Parkway in the Bronx was one of the places I went to watch films. They called these buildings movie palaces for a reason: they were ornate beyond belief. Sculpted faces stuck out of the walls and chandeliers dangled high above your head. The curtains and carpets gleamed with red and golden hues. Just setting foot inside such a place for a few hours was enough to take you away from drab daily life. And then when I was fifteen years old, I saw something there I'd never seen before. As if they arrived straight out of some bygone century, a troupe of actors came there to put on a production of *The Seagull* by Anton Chekhov. The theater seated nearly two thousand people, and an audience of about fifteen came to see the play, maybe twenty if I'm being generous. But two of those audience members were my friend Bruce and me.

I thought it was wonderful. I had nothing else to compare it to at that age. It just hit me like a lightning bolt out of the clear blue sky. I don't know how much of it I really understood, with all its unrequited romances and the tragic character of Konstantin, so frustrated in art and in love, so unsatisfied by the renown that his work brings him that he can see no way out but suicide. But I was riveted by the performances. Before this, I thought poets were people with beards down to the floor. Now here I was, watching this Russian play that could have seemed so alien to me, but I felt its power—the sense of being transported into a world that I was not familiar with and seeing myself in the lives of these fictional people.

I was stunned when Konstantin took his life at the end. The other characters and the audience heard a gunshot from offstage, and at fifteen, I must have been so shocked that I missed the line explaining that the women are being led away so they don't enter the room where Konstantin has killed himself. His suicide just seemed to not register with these characters in the play—I thought they were oblivious, when they hadn't been told at all—and it affected me deeply.

I had never questioned what I wanted to be—I never had a goal. Things either stuck on me or they didn't. And that stuck on me. I heard something. I started reading Chekhov myself, carrying his books around with me, amazed at the idea that I could have his writing whenever I wanted it. Chekhov became a friend of mine. I had just recently passed my audition to get into the High School of Performing Arts in Manhattan, and so had Cliffy. In the mornings we'd ride the train together from the Bronx and emerge at Forty-Second Street and Broadway. For the four blocks we walked up to PA on Forty-Sixth Street we were mesmerized by all the people, tourists and gawkers and gadabouts, trying to get wherever they were going, while movie marquees blared their latest offerings and a sophisticated man on a billboard blew smoke rings from his Camel cigarette onto all of us. One day as we turned a corner I saw Paul Newman, the movie star, go past us, and I thought to myself, Wow, he's a real person. He actually walks and has friends he talks to when there are no cameras around. Cliffy missed him entirely. His mind was elsewhere.

On another morning's train ride, Cliffy's thoughts were focused on the woman who taught our voice and speech class. She was an intelligent and sophisticated woman, not very tall but quite beautiful and well endowed. Her claim to fame was that she had dated Marlon Brando. Cliffy said to me, "I'm going to feel her breasts." From the way he said it, it was clear this was not just some fleeting impulse. This was something he had been thinking about for a while. I said, "*What?*" He said, "Watch. You'll see." It was an impossibility. That's a teacher! You can't do that!

The class began that morning as it normally did, with the teacher giving us our lesson in her deep, resounding voice. Before long, Cliffy got up in front of her. He said something to her, some provocation that started a spat between them. The teacher started chasing Cliffy around the room, haplessly swinging her fists at him to no avail. What he said to produce this reaction I'll never know, but I couldn't believe this was happening right in front of all of us, and that he had actually told me he would do it. They caught each other in a clench, like wrestlers, and as the two of them were tussling, Cliffy reached his arms around her from the back, turned her around to face the class, and there he was, behind her, with both hands on her breasts. He looked at me and smiled.

This was the act of someone with no propriety, no limitations, and no conscience. It was so strange and diabolical. Where did that come from? Was it in the Dostoyevsky he was reading? Most of the students were silent. I broke into laughter, as did another classmate, a boy by the name of John Wilson. I'm not sure why we laughed. It was just our automatic, involuntary reaction to a shocking sight. I loved Cliffy, and I was genuinely horrified by this trespass. The lack of respect for our poor teacher was depraved. Our shocked laughter was enough for me and John to get tossed out of the classroom for the day, a day I spent in exile in the principal's office until my mother came down and apologized on my behalf. The hammer came down much harder on Cliffy. He was thrown out of school altogether, and then he got thrown out of his house. After that, he seemed to disappear from my life for a while, though I would occasionally hear about him around the neighborhood in snippets of stories about the antisocial life he was now leading.

On another day I was on my meal break from Performing Arts and I went out for lunch with the money that my mother gave me. I stopped into a Howard Johnson's around the corner on West Forty-Sixth Street, and there taking orders behind the counter was one of the actors from the performance of *The Seagull* that I had seen up in the Bronx. I was a little bit starstruck, and I said, "I saw you the other night! Oh my God, you were so great!" I couldn't believe I was talking to him. He seemed pleased to have a doting fan. He was looking at me like, this kid is giving me a little bit of hope here. He was this actor I had seen onstage, and I was comfortable talking to him. I felt connected to him somehow. By day, he wore a waiter's outfit while he served people their meals and drinks, and by night, he performed in a play. One was a job that supplied him with the means to keep going, and the other was his artistic calling.

This was how I came to understand acting as a profession. You did the work that paid you while you did your acting, and if you could find a way to get paid for the acting, all the better. He was an actor moving from role to role and theater to theater, like actors have done for hundreds of years. Actors now are embraced and celebrated by society; there are prestigious dynasties of acting families, and actors can even become presidents. But it wasn't always a reputable occupation. The great French playwright Molière was disowned by his family. Theater people are vagabonds, wandering gypsies. We are people on the run. That, too, is our heritage.

)X◆)X(

THINGS BETWEEN MY MOTHER AND ME WEREN'T LIKE THEY USED to be. I wasn't her little Sonny Boy anymore. I had entered my teenage years. I was always naturally protective of her, and it drove me crazy to see her mistreated. At the age of three or four, I can remember walking down the streets with her and yelling at the construction workers who whistled at her. My mother was quite a beauty, and she would sort of smile at it, but I would get really mad that they would look at her that way. The construction workers would just laugh at me—"Oh, tough guy!"—and my mother would say, "It's okay, Sonny, everything will be all right." I just didn't like to see my mother objectified like that. But now I was an adolescent, and my mother didn't know how to deal with me.

She continued to follow all the screen idols of the day, who could never disappoint her. She loved the vulnerability of Monty Clift and the virility of Marlon Brando. She was one of millions who felt an intense connection to James Dean and experienced real pain when he died. It hit her so hard, it hurt me too. No one who had seen his work could let go of the unanswered questions his death left behind. What would have happened if he hadn't gotten killed in that crash? Where else would he have gone with that great gift he had?

When I was around sixteen, my mother started seeing a new suitor, the first one who seemed like a serious boyfriend since she and my father divorced. Their relationship became so serious, in fact, that they began making plans to get married. I was gleeful, and I saw that she was acting more secure than I had seen her in years. My entire life I've had a sensitivity to the way people feel, and I would see little things in her—inflections in how she acted or spoke. I thought she sounded like some other person, like a schoolteacher or the principal of a high school.

She would even say to me, "You know, we may live in Texas or Florida," meaning her and her new husband-to-be. I was relieved in a way, but I didn't see how I belonged in this arrangement. This man was around fifty, and she was a beautiful woman with a teenage son. She was trying to say, this guy probably doesn't want you around. Meanwhile, I was in our apartment with her, and I couldn't do anything. By now, my grandparents had moved farther uptown to an apartment on 233rd Street, which they felt was a somewhat better neighborhood, so it was just me and my mother living in the old place on Bryant Avenue. I thought she was better off going with this guy. I needed her to get out of there. It would make me free.

Then their engagement was abruptly canceled. The guy didn't even have the decency to tell her in person that he was calling it off. He sent her a telegram saying that he couldn't go through with it anymore. When she received that telegram, she was sitting at our kitchen table, and I was leaning against the arch of the hallway that led to it. Four feet away was the door to leave, which I was always aiming for. My mother gave me the news that the engagement was off. She was shattered.

Nasty boy that I was, I actually said to her, "I knew that was too good to be true." Those were ugly words. It was one of the most terrible things I ever said to her. How could I say that? I was disappointed that it was done to her in the first place, and it bothered me that she was hurt. But it also bothered me that she wasn't going to get out of the house and leave it to me.

My mother did not react well to the breakup. It just about crushed her. She was a Tennessee Williams character, fragile and uncontrollable. She was diagnosed by doctors with what they called anxiety neurosis. She was spiraling; she needed electroshock treatment and prescriptions for barbiturates. These were costly things. I was encouraged by my mother to quit school and go to work. We didn't have the money.

I stayed in school a little while longer, at least until I was sixteen, when I was legally allowed to quit. Quitting school might have seemed like a devastating setback in my life, but I was comfortable with it. Actually, I was ecstatic about it, which I realize was kind of a weird attitude to have. But I just never saw school as my place. When I started to get a little bit of renown for the good work I was doing in my acting classes in the school, PA picked me to represent the student body in a photo that would accompany an article being written about the school in the *Herald Tribune* newspaper. Can you believe that? Then at the last minute I was pulled from the story and replaced with another student who was studying to become a dancer. She was tall and had red hair; I had my dark complexion and Italian name. It crossed my mind that that could be why they made the switch, that she represented a more mainstream version of beauty than I did; when you looked around, you just didn't see people like me in detergent commercials or on soap operas. Losing this opportunity didn't bother me, and I didn't believe they were being biased. Performing Arts was trying to get more students to attend the school, and this was the status quo at the time.

So I left. I was feeling the need to get out into the world and start earning my keep. My mom needed the help. I went through various jobs, all fairly short-lived. I spent a summer working as a bicycle messenger, riding a bike around the city for eleven hours a day. When I was seventeen, I had a successful stretch working for the American Jewish Committee and their magazine, *Commentary*. When I got hired for the job, I said to the woman who interviewed me, "I love sitting around offices. I love the sound of typewriters. I love switchboards." I was giving her a spiel, and I'm sure she saw right through my bullshit, but she hired me anyway. I'd come into their offices first thing in the morning ready to jump over huge tables in a single bound. They would send me on errands and sometimes I wouldn't even come back. I had a lot of energy. It was a bustling office, full of activity, and I made friends with my coworkers. I learned how to operate a switchboard, and I would file things for them. The people who worked there—people like Susan Sontag and Norman Podhoretz—were intellectual heavyweights, and though they were very welcoming to me, I never felt like I fit in with them. But when I would be at an office party with a drink in my hand, I'd be able to talk to almost anyone.

)(◆)(

AT AGE EIGHTEEN, I WAS NURSING A FIFTEEN-CENT BEER AT Martin's Bar and Grill, on Twenty-Third Street and Sixth Avenue in Manhattan. I had been sitting there for as long as I could to keep out of the cold. The regulars who would come in were working people. They all appeared to be miners and lumberjacks. The bartender's name was Cookie—a big guy with glasses, he looked like the last person you'd call Cookie, but that's what they called him. The bar had a big picture window that looked onto Sixth Avenue, and across that avenue was a place called the Herbert Berghof Studio, an acting school I was trying to get into. This bar had free lunch sometimes, so I'd go in there and have ketchup sandwiches, which were two saltine crackers with ketchup in the middle, and I ate my share of them.

A friend of mine from the Bronx had told me about the Herbert Berghof Studio and a great teacher there named Charlie Laughton. I said, "The actor Charles Laughton?" He said, "No, no, different guy—his name is Charlie Laughton. He teaches sensory work." I thought, I'm lost already. I'd been pulling away from my old friends, pulled into the orbit of acting, taking it more seriously as a real thing. None of my friends had something like that to pull them onto another path. And past a certain age, being a juvenile delinquent becomes a grim business.

I was pondering things when suddenly Cookie got an angry look on his face. He got out from behind the bar and banged on the door of the men's room. The next thing you know, he had hold of two scruffy little girls by the collars of their leather jackets, and he was throwing them out. Something had been going on with the two girls in the bathroom that bothered him. As Cookie returned to his post where all the working stiffs, seven or eight of them, were lined up at the bar, the two girls stood in front of that big, wide window in broad daylight and began blatantly, passionately, embracing and kissing each other, in defiance of their eviction. They were doing their thing so that everybody in the bar could see them. There was a rift I was witnessing right there between these two separate worlds: the brazen girls outside who were the very essence of liberation, and the guys at the bar who were sitting there somewhat shell-shocked by something they'd never seen before in their lives. The sixties were coming, and the world was changing.

I was introduced to Charlie at that same bar sometime later. I saw him in a booth wearing a baseball cap, drinking with a few people. And the moment I set eyes on him, I thought, This guy is my kind of guy. He was about ten years older than me. When you lose your father, you're always looking for one in some way. When I met him, I knew. This guy is my teacher. I enrolled at the Herbert Berghof Studio. I had no money, so I cleaned the hallways and the rooms where they had dance classes, and they gave me a scholarship.

Charlie possessed a literary brilliance that I wish I had myself.

He turned me on to many novelists and poets I didn't know. He loved the poetry of William Carlos Williams, who came from Paterson, New Jersey, just like Charlie did. Charlie was a great poet in his own right. His poetry had a kind of fatalism to it and a natural feel for the rhythms and the texture of the city. One was called "Somehow I Got Through the Night Again." A part of it went:

> somehow I got through the night again:
> I tip toe up the dawn. safe!
> I look down. what a world!
> the huge disaster like a dark balloon
> goes soft right below my eyes—

Charlie had knowledge about the world and the ability to draw lessons from it that I could understand and relate to my own life. He told me this story once about a group called the Flying Wallendas, a family of performers who would do amazing tightrope walks, way up there, without a net. And they would sit on each other's shoulders while they walked across this high wire. Well, this one time they were doing it, and one of the guys said, "I can't do it." The whole group had been stacked on top of one another like a pyramid, and it collapsed. A couple of them fell from the high wire and died, and others were hurt or paralyzed. When the rest of the family recovered from this tragedy, they went out and did the act again. They asked Wallenda, the father, who was the leader of the group, Why? Why are you doing this? And he said, "Because life's on the wire. The rest is just waiting."

I understood immediately why Charlie was telling me this story. It stuck with me for a long time. Life's on the wire, man.

That's my acting, my life. When I work, I'm on the wire. When I'm going for it. When I'm taking chances. I want to take chances. I want to fly and fail. I want to bang into something when I do it, because it's how I know I'm alive. It's what's kept me alive. It's like I would say years later, when I would have other aspiring actors ask me from time to time, "How come you made it and I didn't? I always wanted to." I would tell them, "You wanted to. I *had* to."

After class, Charlie and I would go out together. We became faithful drinking partners. His wife, Penny Allen, was an actor, too, and they lived together in an apartment in the East Twenties. They never had any money either. One time Charlie came to the office at *Commentary* magazine and asked me for five bucks, and I gave it to him.

Later on, I lost the *Commentary* job, and I was a man without work. My mother had moved up to 233rd Street to live with her parents, and I had our old apartment to myself. All I was facing was $38.80 a month in rent. But I was broke. I had profited all that I could from cashing in the beer bottles I had cluttering up my apartment, and now I had nothing. So I made my way out to find Charlie, who was in Far Rockaway.

It was the summertime, and getting there from Manhattan was a journey: I took a bus to a train, to another train, switched trains at another station, until I reached the end of the line. It could take hours, and all the while I would read Balzac, Baudelaire, and Flaubert from pocket-size books with the tiniest type you've ever seen. It was a hot day, and when I got to Far Rockaway, Charlie and Penny were on a beach with their baby girl, Deirdre. I saw them by the surf, and I was walking on the sand, dressed all in black—shoes, pants, shirt, leather jacket—doing my Paladin thing. They were all smiles as Charlie gave me a fiver, and I said, "Great, love you guys." Then I got on the train and began my long and complicated return voyage to Manhattan, reading my little books all the way back.

Charlie and I worked together as moving men. We moved office furniture and a lot of books. You should try it sometime—just physically moving things from building to building, floor to floor. Not your own stuff, but doing it every day for someone else, in walk-up buildings with no elevators there to get you up a few flights, moving books, books, books, and more books, boxes of them.

Our friend Matt Clark, who was in Charlie's acting class, ran our moving operation. He had started off small with a little truck, moving pieces of art down in the Village, then went on to moving apartments, and got himself a bigger truck to handle bigger offices. He was good at this, as well as being an actor. How does an actor prepare? He carries a refrigerator up the stairs. Matt Clark looked at me like I was some guy from the Bronx, but he let me tag along and scrape together a few bucks, mainly because Charlie would vouch for me. I got on Matt's bad side when I dropped my end of a refrigerator going up a five-floor walk-up. Another time we were moving an office, and as usual I wandered off. I ended up in some sort of Christmas party on that floor. I was having a little food, sipping a Scotch, and flirting with a couple of girls. Our job had stopped for a bit and I figured I was due for a break.

When Matt found out, it really took him over the edge, and I got fired right there on the spot. I explained it all to Charlie, and somehow he talked Matt into taking me back again.

When I was growing up, we'd never had a telephone in the apartment, but now I finally had one. I got a call there from my father, who I had not heard from in months. His second marriage had gone bust just like the first, and he had moved out to Los Angeles, where he was once again indulging in life as a single man, and he wanted me to join him. His invitation to me was to say, in this phone call, "Why don't you come out here and take some of these girls off my hands?"

Can you imagine that? The poor man wanted to connect with his son, and he finally felt he had something to offer me. He probably thought, He's a regular kid, he's nineteen, he wants girls, doesn't he? He didn't know enough to understand that his son was some kind of aspiring poet, artist, and Chekhov wannabe. I didn't care about girls—I mean, I did, but I didn't understand them or realize that they were interested in me. It's taken me a lifetime to figure out that my father was just trying to reach me in a way he thought best. But at the time, it just made me feel like he didn't know me, so how could he?

While I lived alone, I had to make rent. I tried it as a busboy and I didn't make it. They caught me eating off the leftovers from the tables. That's how hungry I was. In my free time, I was a wanderer. I would walk the streets all day, and then I'd sit at the library, pretty much for warmth. But I became a voracious reader. I had no teachers and no homework assignments, so I followed my own passions. Charlie Laughton helped suggest various writers to check out, things to read, places to go, like the Forty-Second Street library for warmth and the Automat for sustenance.

At the Automat, I could make a single cup of coffee last all morning and sit there for five hours while I read my little books of the great authors. There was something so absorbing about that gift of reading. It could calm your mind and give you another world to be engaged in. Television was too distant; books were more intimate, like having friends and enjoying their company. I would be reading *A Moveable Feast* and thinking, I don't want to finish the pages, I like it here too much.

If the hour was late and you heard the sound of someone in your alleyway with a bombastic voice shouting iambic pentameter into the night, that was probably me, training myself on the great Shakespeare soliloquies. I would walk the streets of Manhattan, bellowing out monologues as I rambled. I'd do it by the factories, at the edges of town, where no one was around. Where else was I going to go? Where could I emote? That's what you do when you're obsessed.

In these side streets and passageways I didn't need anyone's permission if I wanted to play Prospero, Falstaff, Shylock, or Macbeth. I grew to love one of Hamlet's monologues so much that I started to use it at auditions. I would say to the director, "I know you have your pages that you want me to perform, but I have a little something that I've already prepared, if you don't mind." Usually they would give me back a look that told me they were already finished with me. And then I would hit them with this:

> O, what a rogue and peasant slave am I!
> Is it not monstrous that this player here,
> But in a fiction, in a dream of passion . . .

That would occasionally get me a nod from someone, as if to say, "Oh yes, very nice. See you in the next world." And out the door I went. Did I learn anything? I doubt it, but it felt good.

Hamlet says something that pretty much summed up my own

feelings about being taught how to act: "let your own discretion be your tutor: suit the action to the word, the word to the action, with this special observance, that you o'erstep not the modesty of nature . . . the censure of the which one must in your allowance o'erweigh a whole theater of others."

In other words, go to acting class. Have an audience. Show yourself that you can do the part. But don't listen to the teachers. You have to be careful. Take what they say and use only what you identify with; just use that. There are no rules, because when it comes right down to your performance, it doesn't matter what most people think. Your intuition should not be swayed by the audience, but by your own imagination and your willingness to go into yourself and express what's there.

When I was about nineteen or twenty, Charlie and I had finished one of our wanderings full of walking and talking and we came back to my Bronx apartment. As I looked in my mailbox, he was going up the stairs. He stopped on the stairway, looked back at me, paused, and then said, "Al, you're going to be a big star." And Charlie never talked like that. I mean never. As long as I knew him, he never said a word about that stuff. That was not his deal at all. It came out of nowhere.

I said to him, "I know, Charl. I know," and I meant it. Now I'm not religious or anything. But I feel there's a spirit. You don't even have to call it God. In A.A. they call it the Higher Power. Whatever it is, whatever you think it may be, that was mine. I believed it would happen, although it wasn't something I was preoccupied with at the time or really thought about at all. I just sort of assumed that was what was going to happen, and I accepted it. Whatever this acting thing was, I could do that.

Sonny Boy

ⵣⵣⵣ

ANOTHER YOUNG ACTOR IN CHARLIE'S CLASS WITH ME WAS A GUY by the name of Martin Sheen. In one session Marty did a monologue from *The Iceman Cometh*, and he blew the roof off—I said, this is it, this is a great actor we are witnessing. He was the next James Dean as far as I was concerned.

I got to be friends with Marty Sheen, and one day he said to me, "You know what my real name is, don't you? Estevez." He was half Spanish and he came from Ohio, out there in the Midwest, where he had a tough upbringing. He was one of ten kids in a working-class family that was always struggling for money. He had tenacity and grit and I could tell he was one of the best people I'd ever know, all grace and humility. I loved him. I still do.

Marty Sheen moved in with me in the South Bronx so we could split the rent. We worked together at the Living Theatre in Greenwich Village, where we cleaned toilets and laid down rugs for the sets of the plays they put on. The Living Theatre had been founded by Judith Malina and Julian Beck, two actors who happened to be true visionaries, who started it in their living room in the 1950s and eventually moved it to Fourteenth Street and Sixth Avenue. They did the kinds of shows that made you go home afterward and lock yourself in your room and just cry for two days, staring at the ceiling. They had that kind of impact. They created off-Broadway theater, and its success paved the way for off-off-Broadway. That made it possible for some of the shows I was doing off-off-off-off-Broadway, where actors performed in Village cafés for audiences drinking coffee and eating pastries. When I did *Hello Out There* by

William Saroyan, we would put on sixteen performances a week at Caffe Cino on Cornelia Street and pass the hat to what little audience was there, hoping to come away with a few dollars to have a meal. It was always passing the hat when you performed down there. That's how you ate and afforded your habit. It was our Paris in the early 1900s, our Berlin in the 1920s. A renaissance happening in our great city, New York. That was the spirit of the scene, the energy of Sartre, Ibsen, Bertolt Brecht, Leonard Melfi, Allen Ginsberg, Ferlinghetti, Kerouac, Sam Shepard. We inherited the world they created.

When the Living Theatre put on a play called *The Connection* by Jack Gelber, Marty and I would do our work and then stand in the back of the orchestra section of the theater and watch them do that play every night. We were teenagers, still sweaty from having put down the sets that the actors were now performing on. We did it for no pay, just to see where acting could take you, how far you could go with just a plank and a passion. One night Marty turned to me and said, "See that actor playing that role? *That* is a great role. I'm going to do it someday." And sure as there is a heaven and earth, ol' Marty Sheen landed that role for himself. He got it done. And he was great when he did it.

One summer I was sitting on a stoop on Tenth Street and Second Avenue. The heat had been bearing down on me all day, and I was enjoying the relief that came when the sun finally set and the city cooled down at night. I was wondering how I was going to eat that night. Marty came sauntering up the street like he was walking on air. He had something he wanted to tell me. "Hey, Marty!" I yelled out to him. He came right up to me and said, "Al, I met the girl I'm going to be with for the rest of my life. She's a painter and she's going to be my wife." I said, "That's a secret well kept, Marty. But we still got to eat." But sure enough, if you look at your calendar and you look at the year, he is still Marty Sheen and Janet is his wife, and she was the girl he told me about sixty years ago.

Before I gave up the Bronx apartment for good, other people would come and go. Sometimes one of Marty's brothers would stay over, or this guy Sal Russo from acting class who was going with this girl named Sandra. Her best friend was a musician with long dark hair and piercing eyes named Joan Baez, who would occasionally drop by the apartment, sit cross-legged in a corner, and play her guitar. She hadn't linked up with Bob Dylan yet, but we knew Joan was going places. I don't believe she and I even exchanged hellos. She was just part of the traffic that came and went in that apartment while the world spun around us.

Cliffy was back in the neighborhood again. Both he and Bruce had enlisted in the army. Bruce made it as far as his induction ceremony when he got second thoughts, pretended to flip out, and threatened to jump out a window, so they let him go. Cliffy, on the other hand, stuck around long enough to serve for a few months, but of course he got in trouble there and was thrown into the brig before being thrown out. I knew I had no risk of being drafted myself, because I was supporting my mother. But as Charlie used to say to me every day, "They don't want you in the army, Al." He knew how crazy I was, in terms of my strangeness and my high-pitched anxiety. That was why I drank. Could you imagine me, that boy that I was, going around saying, "Hup-two-three-four"? I can do it in a play.

Cliffy had come out of the army in even worse shape. He was on the needle now and doing and saying all kinds of crazy stuff.

He said he had been in the same platoon as Elvis Presley, and it turned out he actually was. He said he went to Canada, got a Catholic girl pregnant, and converted from Judaism so that he could marry her. Every time he stopped by my apartment he would go into the bathroom to shoot up, sometimes alone and sometimes in the company of other people he'd brought with him who just wanted to get their fix too. With a heavy heart I had to tell Cliffy he couldn't come around and get off in my bathroom anymore.

It was no surprise to anyone when he overdosed and died. It made me think of a story that he had told me. When he was in the brig, Cliffy said, he was watched by this guard, a southerner who carried a .45 pistol. He would hold out the pistol just so, to polish it or keep it in his lap. He would start saying ominous things about "the Jews," because Cliffy was still Jewish at the time. In his southern drawl he would tell Cliffy, "You know, I could just blow your head off and tell people you tried to escape. Would that be something to do?" He kept repeating it day after day until Cliffy finally turned to the guy and said, "Hey, man, you know what? You better kill me. Because if you don't, when I get out of here, I'm gonna come back and kill you." I can only imagine that when this guard looked into his eyes, he saw enough to know that Cliffy meant it. All I can say about that is Cliffy may not have been the toughest guy I ever met, but he certainly was the most fearless.

)(◆)(

WHEN I TURNED TWENTY-ONE, HAVING HARDLY STARTED WORK-ing as an actor, I was asked to do a reading with Elia Kazan, practically the biggest director in the world in both stage and screen, for a new movie he was casting. It was called *America, America*, and it was going to tell the story of a young Greek man's journey to the States. They were trying to find a young actor, relatively unknown, probably ethnic looking, to play the lead role. I thought I had a shot at it. I don't know if I would have excelled at it, but I felt I had a real chance because I fit the description.

But I was late and I missed the audition. I went there and they were gone and it was over. They got somebody else.

My first thought in that moment wasn't about me. Before I even got to that audition I had fantasized how I would help my mother. I would take her out of her destitution and her despondency, give her what she always longed for and needed. Not because it would mean I was successful. Not because she could have done things with the money. Because she would have engaged herself in it. It would have sparked a natural curiosity, because she was smart. It would have given her a jump-start. I think she would have survived.

It was Bruce who later told me when my mother was dying. I came back to my apartment in the Bronx late one night from my wanderings in the East Village to find a note he left at my door saying that he had an urgent message for me. He lived in the tenement next to ours, so I climbed onto the roof and over to his building, went down the stairs, and knocked on his door. Bruce lived with his parents, and he took me into the kitchen of their apartment. He said, "Your mom's in a lot of trouble. She's really sick. You better go, man." I said okay, scraped together whatever money I could, and jumped in a cab to my grandparents' place on 233rd Street.

Outside the cab I looked up and saw the lights on in their

apartment. It was a bit bigger than the old place. I went up the stairs, walked in the door, and there were my grandmother and grandfather, their eyes wet with tears. My mother was gone. You see, it was too late. I was too late. She had died like Tennessee Williams had died, choking on her own pills, on her regurgitation of them, like so many have.

A lot of people want to leave this world behind for one that's better, and she was in a state where she escaped by taking drugs. It was interpreted by some that she had committed suicide, which she had tried almost fifteen years earlier. But she left no note this time, nothing. She was just gone. That's why I always kept a question mark next to her death. When drugs are involved, people often die when they don't intend to kill themselves. I don't know that she did. I'd like to give my mother that benefit of the doubt, that dignity, to be fair to her memory.

The next morning, I'll never forget the image of my grandfather, sitting in a folding chair in the middle of the room, nothing around him, crouched over with his head in his hands, almost between his legs. He just kept banging a foot on the floor. I'd never seen him that way. I had never seen my grandfather so emotionally stirred. He didn't speak, but I knew what he was saying. *No. This was the wrong thing to do. She was too young. She could have been helped. What a waste.*

Maybe somehow I could have stopped this. My mother's tragedy was poverty. She was stuck in the mud of it and couldn't move. I knew she had the innate intelligence and sensitivity to understand our world, because she did have curiosity. She read books, and she had taken piano lessons in her youth, when her family could afford them. We went to the movies together, and we always went to the theater when we could. My mother took me to Broadway plays in Manhattan. When I was a teenager, I ended up on a popular TV game show called the *Wheel of Fortune*. The game show highlighted human-interest stories and I was there because I had helped save my childhood friend Bruce, who ended up dangling from a pipe twenty feet high after a ridiculous bet gone wrong. On the show, I won prizes and some money, and the first thing my mother did with that money was take me to see *Cat on a Hot Tin Roof* on Broadway. It was just like when I was three and four, only now I was fifteen, going out to dinner at a restaurant with my own mother after seeing *Cat on a Hot Tin Roof*. She had a gift of a sense of humor and a certain innate taste. That was what made her stand apart from the rest of the family. But she was a lonely woman. Therapy, moderation, security—these things could have helped her. I knew I was going to be able to supply her with that and more.

And I don't think I ever told her that. I don't think I ever said to her that I was going to succeed and was going to take care of her. What would I have said to her? "Ma, just wait, I'm getting there." It sounds like an Odets play, but it's true. I knew that in a few more years I was going to be able to help. It's one thing to think it, but how do you tell anyone that you're destined to be successful? Who would believe you?

How can you tell someone that you know this is going to happen for you when you're down and out, sleeping in hallways and on floors of theaters, borrowing friends' apartments to get a night's rest? My mother once said to me that she had a dream about me: I was standing on some cliff, like in *Wuthering Heights*, with the wind blowing my hair, my face pale and undernourished. I was skinny, and I looked so drained. I had no color in my face. That dream made her so sad. How do you go from hearing that to saying, Don't worry, I'm gonna make it?

I knew that I was going to get there. That was my blessing. Maybe I learned it when my grandma fed me baby food and made me the star of all the stories she told me. Maybe it was my friends in the street. Maybe it was Marty Sheen, or my great friend Charlie Laughton. When did it happen? Who was this kid, with this fierce energy that could light a schoolyard at night? Something was driving me. I had to make it, because that was the only way I would survive this world.

But first came a hard period of mourning, wandering around zombielike. I was in a state—I started missing my stops at the subway station, bumping into things, thinking about some things and forgetting other things. It seemed impossible to accept at that age, unfathomable, to lose a mother.

)X(◆)X(

I WAS WORKING AS AN USHER AT THE RIVOLI THEATRE IN TIMES Square. Some of the other guys who worked there were on the run, and some had families they had to support, and ushering was one of the three jobs they were holding down to feed their wives and children. They'd say to me, "Hey, kid, I gotta get some sleep— could you just cover for me?" I'd say okay, and they'd go take a nap in the balcony.

When the Jerseyites would come to the theater, you know the type, usually Saturday nights, the young pretty girls would come up to me and say, "This is for you," and press something into my palm, as though it were a tip. Then I'd look at what was in my hand and see that they had given me a used match from a book of matches. I had to laugh.

The theater had a candy counter with a four-way mirror. I would stand in front of it and marvel at the angles of my face, angles I never saw before in my life. Who is this guy I'm looking at in that mirror? I wondered. I saw my profile. I saw myself in three quarters. I saw myself head-on, and I thought, How could I be an actor with a face like this? The house manager there, a big old white guy, had his own perspective. He said, "I don't like those sideburns—makes you look like a Mexican." I thought, That's a rather obtuse comment. What does that even mean? Eventually he fired me for looking at myself in the mirror too much. I got fired in flight. It was a beautiful thing, like a ballet. The house manager was all the way up in the balcony, and as he made his way down the theater's colossal winding staircase, this elegant structure like something out of *Gone with the Wind*, he rounded past me on the second floor, pointed at me, and bellowed, "Now you're fired," and continued on his way to the lobby. He never broke stride. What a graceful way to get the axe. I almost applauded him.

At another job I delivered copies of *Show Business* newspaper to the newsstands along Seventh Avenue. It was published once a week: people in the business would buy it and read it for information about what plays were being performed and where they could audition. This was valuable information. I made twelve dollars for one day of work, and that was a huge payday to me. When I got paid, I'd hit the bar afterward with my bankroll of singles. I liked to roll my dollar bills into a big ball and peel them off one by one, like a big shot, then snap 'em down on the counter like I had more where that came from. When you're down and out like that, you try to sleep till 4:00 p.m., just to stave off hunger. If I could scrape together $1.19 and splurge on a steak and a baked potato at Tad's Steaks, it was like Thanksgiving dinner.

I had this little red wagon that I'd use to carry the papers, hitting various newsstands along Seventh Avenue, from Thirty-Fourth Street up to Fifty-Seventh Street. In the back of the wagon, I kept a bottle of Chianti wine. When it was pouring rain, they'd give me a head-to-toe poncho that didn't protect me much, but at least it protected the newspapers I was wheeling. I'd pull that wagon up Seventh Avenue, already loaded at 9:30 or 10:00 in the morning, and as I got soaked in the downpour, I made up a little song that I sang to myself as I strode up the street:

> I feel fiiiine
> With my bottle of wiiiine

Along with Charlie and Chekhov, I think drinking saved my life. I was able to self-medicate. It helped me through my pain, and it kept me away from the outpatient clinic at Bellevue. I would drink at night and pop pills the next day to calm down. I was always looking to be calm, because my mind was going wild, and alcohol had a calming effect. If I had cocaine I would probably levitate, so I used alcohol to ease the pain and emptiness and lower my energy. All I know is, it worked for me.

I experienced a separation from Charlie, I couldn't tell you why. I don't know what I did or didn't do. It wasn't because we'd had an argument. Suddenly he told me, "You have to move on," which was a very strange thing to say, and felt like a rejection. I think Charlie saw my potential, but he had a life of his own to deal with. He was in his midthirties, with a wife and a child, and he was headed toward something else. I was this kid in my early twenties, vulnerable and not fully developed. I was borderline hopeless. Maybe I called him too much, maybe I was too dependent on him. Maybe he thought that, after losing my mother, I needed something else. But my level of sophistication wasn't up to his. I was behind and he was ahead.

Our falling-out didn't last very long. There was no reconciliation; just somehow, by osmosis, we got back together. But I was sensitive to how he had distanced himself from me—it hit me hard.

I was feeling adrift and alone in the Village, caught up in my feelings about my mother and in a general malaise. Everything about my life was fading out. I got on a pay phone in a bar and called my granddad, up in the Bronx, to tell him what I was going through, and I started to cry. He just kept saying, "Come on. Come with us. Live with me. Come live with us." I was really bawling. He just said, "Come here. Come with me." I was stunned. But I didn't go. I stayed where I was. I had moved out of the Bronx by that time and found a low-rent rooming house in Chelsea for eight bucks a week.

Another time I called my grandfather after he had arranged to get me a job in construction. I had been up all night, the night before I was supposed to start, and I rang him up at seven o'clock that morning. And he picked up the phone and said, "You're not going to work, I know. That's okay." You know how difficult it is to get a job at a construction site? I'm sure he worked hard to do that for me. But I kept doing these other menial jobs. That's all I could do; I had no education and no desire to have more. I was interested in one thing. I believed I was an artist.

My grandfather passed away himself that year, which does happen when that kind of trauma hits, when a parent loses a child. My mother was his first child, and they had a great relationship; he loved her and she loved her dad—it was obvious. I was still doing the *Show Business* newspaper deliveries at that time, and I passed out on the route. It must have been from the lack of food and the trauma of losing my granddad.

He was a warm man with a soft heart, though he came from a merciless world. When his family moved to East Harlem, where many Sicilians had settled, they lived among the gangsters who had yet to become household names but were still notorious at that time. That world was there for my grandfather and easy to access, but though he was poor, he didn't want to go in that direction. As he once said to me, he never had the heart to go into that under-world.

My grandfather had trouble with his stepmother, so when he was nine, he quit school and ran away to work on a coal truck and didn't come back until he was fifteen. He was a wild kid who trav-eled with his fellow urchins around Upper Manhattan and the Bronx, back when it was all farmland. When he could, he'd do apprentice jobs or get work in the fields out there and live under the stars. This was in the early 1900s, when everyone mostly trav-eled by foot or by horse-drawn carriage, and he was living in the heart of this harbor town. It was a rough road he had chosen for himself, but it seemed like an adventure to him.

His town in Sicily had a tradition of skilled masons, and he became a plasterer, just as his father had been, becoming more and more skilled in his craft as he grew older. His expertise was what kept our family alive. People used to marvel at his work. His son, my uncle, used to say that if he had my grandfather's talent he would own New York. My grandfather would tell the story of when he was working in a fancy office building in mid-Manhattan, Katharine Hepburn happened to be there, and looked up at his ladder, watched him work, and smiled up at him. I said to him, "What was she like?" And he said, "Oh, she was nice, she had a lot of freckles." When I was a youngster, I watched him work on the building where we lived, and I noticed the focus he had. He was in a zone: there was no other world but that, nothing else existed. The movements of his hands were so decisive, so clean and clear, and fast and intricate. His focus alone would draw you in, it had a gravitas, like a painter absorbed in his canvas. I'm sure it affected me, because that's the way I would one day look at my own work. I don't talk about him much, but I was influenced by him, his humor, his intelligence. Charlie met him once and saw in an instant how he just lit up and how his kindness could reach people. He saw a man with a soul. I loved him greatly. I'm still here because of him, and I'll never forget it.

)(◆)(

I WAS FINALLY STARTING TO MAKE SOME ACQUAINTANCES DOWN-town in the Village, fellow artists or actors. One friend, Tommy Negron, who I grew up with in the South Bronx, was a piano tuner who I thought was going to be a great musician. He would let me sleep on the floor of his place, where he had a big jar of pennies that I would take a dip into from time to time. A handful of pennies could get you far back then. Alec Rubin was a longtime member of the Actors Studio, a part of their directors' unit and an occasional moderator there. I liked him, and he used to put on plays in a little performance space below his apartment on West Seventy-Second Street. I once took a bath in his bathtub, then went downstairs to join in his production of *Why Is a Crooked Letter*, which I was starring in. The space was so small that as I was smoking, in character, a woman from the audience reached in and gave me an ashtray. I did children's shows at Theater East, comic send-ups of fairy tales. In one, I was a blowhard hunter coming to rescue Little Red Riding Hood's grandmother from the Big Bad Wolf. In another, I was a frog who turned into a prince but wanted to go back to being a frog because his girlfriend was still a frog. It was a musical, and I sang songs in it. I would come in for afternoon shows on Saturdays and Sundays, still half stoned from the night before, and sing and dance in these plays and somehow get through them. They paid me real money to eat and to get through the rest of the weekend.

The Actors Gallery was a playhouse in SoHo, just a little room up a flight of stairs that sat maybe twenty-five or thirty people. It was run by Frank Biancamano, who had also been my dispatcher when I was a sixteen-year-old bike messenger. When I walked into my audition for him, he asked, "Don't I know you?" I was a little embarrassed to see him, now standing there as an actor when he knew me as a messenger. I stood there stooping awkwardly low and showing him various sides of my face, pretending to be sensitive, because I didn't want him to recognize me. But he liked my audition, saw something in me, and took me on.

He started to put me in plays like Jean Giraudoux's *Tiger at the Gates* and Thomas Mann's *Mario and the Magician*, heady stuff.

And then he cast me for a part in *Creditors*, a three-character play by August Strindberg. It was a strange piece about a woman and two men—one her ex-husband and the other newly married to her—that I wasn't sure I totally grasped. But now I was working with other experienced actors. They were giving great performances, and I was part of it.

And then, one night, onstage, just like that, it happened. The power of expression was revealed to me, in a way it never had before. I wasn't even searching for it. That's the beauty of these things. You're not looking for it. I'm opening my mouth and I'm understanding somehow that I can speak. Words are coming out, and they're the words of Strindberg, but I'm saying them as though they're mine. The world is mine, and my feelings are mine, and they're going beyond the South Bronx. I left the familiar. I became a part of something larger. I found that there was more to me, a feeling that I belonged to a whole world and not just to one place. I'm thinking to myself, What is this? It feels as though I'm lifting off the ground. I thought, Yes, this is it. It's right there and I can reach out and touch it. This is out there, and this is what I know now is possible. All of a sudden, in that moment, I was universal.

I knew I didn't have a worry after that. I eat, I don't eat. I make money, I don't make money. I'm famous, I'm not famous. It didn't mean anything anymore. And that's lucky, in this business, when you don't care about that. A door was opening, not to a career, not to success or fortune, but to the living spirit of energy. I had been given this insight into myself, and there was nothing else I could do but say: I want to do this forever.

3

A Tiger and an Indian

Herbert Berghof was not quick to anger, and he was furious with me. All it took was seeing me act.

It was a practice at HB Studio that every so often, all the acting classes would gather in a seminar room and each teacher would pick one or two of their students to perform a scene, with Berghof watching at the front. It was something of a distinction to be selected, and the level of work that was put on was usually pretty high.

Charlie had picked me and a classmate to do a short selection from a teleplay called *Crime in the Streets*, about a gang of street kids. I had worked on the scene before in other acting classes and with Charlie, so I felt I had a good handle on it. I put on a white tank top, which I thought suited the character, and I gave the scene the energy that I thought it required.

When the performance was over, I went back to my seat next to Charlie in the half-dark room. Charlie grabbed my arm and squeezed it and whispered, "You were great, Al. You were great."

I was happy to hear it, but there was something in Charlie's bearing he was trying to communicate, and he had to whisper because we were surrounded by others in the class. I immediately sensed that something was up.

From his own seat, Berghof began to discuss the scene. Berghof was a stern Austrian who had fled Vienna before the war. I watched his face turn red as he absolutely exploded at me. "Who do you think you are?" he said. "Who gave you the right to do—*things* like that?" He spoke with ferocity and bitterness. All the while, Charlie was still squeezing my arm and whispering, "You were great."

As an actor, your performance is always a reflection of how you feel about things. Not just what's on the page but whatever you are feeling in the moment—your issues, as we might call them today. And you don't always know what you feel until you're in the scene and delivering the lines. But what you're doing is always an expression of yourself. I was simply doing a scene that I thought expressed something in me, embodying a kind of person I had once known and a world I spent time in.

I couldn't figure what I might have done to make Berghof so emotional. He was a reputable actor and a major force in the theater—he had directed the original Broadway production of *Waiting for Godot*—and his opinion meant something. Perhaps he instinctively didn't like me or my type. I looked like I had come in off the streets. I had encountered that kind of bias in my life before. Did he think I was overdoing it? Was I exposing too much of my physique? Should I have worn some sort of cloak?

The uncharacteristic severity of his response stayed with me for a long time—I'm talking decades. When I was in my seventies and Charlie was deeply ill with multiple sclerosis, I would visit him at his hospital in Santa Monica and sit by his bedside and talk to him. One day I happened to bring up what had gone down in the classroom all those years ago.

I said to him, "Hey, Charl, remember when I did that scene that one time and Berghof went crazy?"

Charlie said, "Yeah, I remember that day. I thought about it too."

"What do you think happened there?" I asked him. "What was that about, really?"

And Charlie said, "I think he saw the future."

It was the early 1960s, and something was happening in acting. I wondered if it was alien to someone like Herbert Berghof. Perhaps he didn't like my choice of material, didn't relate to it personally or didn't like the way it was expressed. Not just my scene, but other selections he had watched other students perform that day were similarly outside the realm of his understanding. Or maybe it wasn't such a shock to him at all. Maybe people like him had seen this train coming in the distance for some time, and now it had arrived at his doorstep. It could have felt like a new chapter was about to be written and it wasn't going to include him.

It had started with Brando. He was the influence. The force. The originator. What he had created, together with collaborators like Tennessee Williams and Elia Kazan, was more visceral. It was threatening. Brando had become part of a triumvirate of actors, along with Montgomery Clift and James Dean. Clift had the beauty and the soul, the vulnerability. Dean was like a sonnet, compact and economical, able to do so much with the merest gesture or nuance. And if Dean was a sonnet, then Brando was an epic poem. He had the looks. He had the charisma. He had the talent.

There's that classic sequence from *A Streetcar Named Desire* where Brando completely loses it during the card game, until he's at the bottom of the stairs, yelling, "Stella! Stella!" It's an episode that builds gradually, which of course comes from Kazan's original staging of the play and Brando's memory of it as he had done it every night. But by the time Brando got this on film, he had become one with the elements. You experienced that sequence like you experienced a tornado or monsoon. It was that captivating.

But evolution always makes people nervous. There was anger toward Brando. People said he mumbled. They said his features were too soft, too delicate. They said he liked to show off his chest. If people disparaged his approach it was because they didn't see the technique that went into it. But he found whatever it was that opened the door to his expression, that allowed him to reveal himself and communicate it to audiences so that they identified with him.

Brando made possible the Paul Newmans of the world, the Ben Gazzaras, the Anthony Franciosas, and the Peter Falks, people like John Cassavetes, who was his own special kind of phenomenon. These were the idols of an era just before mine, actors who had already moved beyond the studios and had been out in the world for a decade or more by the time I arrived there. And then Dustin Hoffman just blasted open the door for actors.

Dustin was a student of Lee Strasberg's at the Actors Studio when I started to hear about him. You would pick up on other students discussing him with a strange reverence, like he was a ghost or a wanted criminal. There was such energy around his name you had to see him for yourself, to see if he lived up to his formidable reputation.

And then Mike Nichols got hold of him, all of him, for *The*

Graduate. The Graduate was contemporary and of the moment, a commentary on the world we were living in, and it fit him perfectly. It came along at the right time, right when we were ready for it. And its success made Dustin a movie star supreme.

I was working up in Boston when *The Graduate* opened, and I said, this is it, man—it's over. He's broken the sound barrier. The excitement for me was in seeing an artist doing something so well, something original, that you recognized had never been done before.

><+><

IN THE EARLY 1960S, WE ALL KNEW MARTY SHEEN WAS ON HIS way. He was still doing off-Broadway work when he saw me on the subway one day. I was standing on the platform waiting for a train, with a long coat that went down to my ankles. I looked like I was playing a part in a Charlie Chaplin film from the silent era. It had been about a year since we had roomed together, and our careers had gone in different directions. He was working regularly, and I was still down and out. My next move was to hold my hand out for somebody to put a coin in it. He said, "Hey, Al, man, how you doing?" I said, "I'm okay." And he looked at me in my dusty thrift-store coat, and my shoes that were ripped apart, and my toes poking through the holes, and he knew that maybe that was not the case.

But he looked past all of this and he said to me, "Al, would you do me the honor"—he actually said that, *honor*—"of understudying me in this part that I'm doing?" He was starring in *The Wicked Cooks* by Günter Grass, a real far-out and allegorical play that was very physical for him. He was constantly getting hit with props and thrown to the ground in it. Now we both knew I couldn't be an understudy—not to Marty, not to anybody. Not for any moral reasons. I was just incapable of it. I wish I was able to, because it was a way to make some money, but for whatever reason I'm easily distracted watching someone else do a performance that I would have to mimic. But this play was at the Orpheum on Second Avenue, which was practically like being on Broadway. And it was money in my pocket. So I thanked him and said, "Of course, Marty, I'll do it." I thought I was doing it for Marty, because he seemed so effusive about me. He loved me, and I was just so enamored of him.

Of course, the director hated my guts. He just seemed to have it in for me from the start. I had that anarchic look. No matter where I went, people looked at me as if to say, "Where does this guy come from? Who does he think he is?" Something was there in my bearing, whatever it was, that bothered people in certain situations, usually in the theater. When I encountered authority figures, there could be a little tension. The director was a guy named Vasek Simek, and he ran the play like he was a dictator. I saw an invisible whip in his hand. He would yell at me, "Method actor!" It was a taunt, a put-down. Then I found out I had to be in the play as an extra, a soldier just walking around the stage, when I wasn't playing Marty's part. I don't even know what I'm doing out on the street; what am I going to do on the stage? I would pretend that I was walking around, but I would leave the theater altogether. And Simek was getting madder and madder at me. I'm looking at this guy, thinking, there's no way this is going to work.

You know what had to happen next. There was only one way

for this to turn out. First, Marty Sheen had to get laryngitis. He came in one day, coughing and croaking. I was probably hiding out in some corner of the theater, sitting alone and reading Spinoza, when he grabbed me and looked me straight in the eye. He said, in his raspy voice, "Al, buddy, my friend, you have to go on for me. I've lost my voice. But you can do it." I said, "What?" I couldn't hear him—that's how bad his laryngitis was. He said, "You're going on." I was transfixed. I thought perhaps it was a practical joke, and that in a moment he would regain his voice and laugh at me. He wasn't joking. I didn't want to let down my friend, but I knew nothing about what he did or said in the play. It was like being caught in the vault of a bank and trying to explain that you didn't go there to rob it.

I said, "Marty, I can't. I don't know the words." He said, "You'll make it up." I said, "I can't do this, Marty." So I didn't, and Simek fired me. I only found out later that the production wasn't even paying me to be Marty's understudy in the play—Marty was paying me himself, out of his own salary. He just wanted me to have the money. I wanted to give it back to him, but he wouldn't take it.

I was sitting in a Jewish cafeteria in the East Village, lamenting how I'd let Marty down, and this other actor who was very good in the play was there. He came over to me and seemed to think I was in need of advice. He spoke with a bit of a lisp, which was unusual for an actor, and he said, "Let me tell you, if I was you, I'd be back there, learning those words." I was someone that the wolves threw out of their den. I had been exiled by a dictator director, so I was just grateful he didn't shoot me. This guy was giving me a pep talk about what to do? I thought, You know what

I'm doing? I'm going home and I'm never coming back. That was the end of that one.

)X◊X(

AT TWENTY-FIVE, I BECAME A BUILDING SUPERINTENDENT, THANKS to my childhood friend Bruce from the South Bronx, who gave me his job in a building on Sixty-Eighth Street and Central Park West. He was running off to get married and he knew I could use the work and a place to live, so now I had shelter in a great neighborhood. I was earning fourteen dollars a week and had my own place, rent-free, in the building. The apartment was a tiny room with just my bed; when you opened the door, all you'd see was a kitchen and a bathroom that was visible to all. The window in my apartment had bars on it, like in a prison—if there was a fire, you wouldn't be able to escape. I knew I wasn't qualified for the job. Outside my apartment door it said SUPER, so I took an 8 x 10 glossy headshot of myself and attached it above the sign with Band-Aids. I had gotten that picture from Michael Avedon, a relative of the photographer Richard Avedon, after Michael had seen me in *Creditors*. He had wanted to take photos of me so I had something to send to agents and casting directors. It was a pretty good shot of me, so I put it up there, not because anyone in the business would see it, but because anyone coming to visit me would get a good laugh.

Penny Allen, Charlie's wife, would come by the building and help me out by washing the hallway floors on her hands and knees, because she knew how badly I needed a place of my own. I was moving from one place to another, usually ending up on a friend's couch or floor. My super's apartment was barely big enough to be alone with your thoughts. One Sunday at around seven in the morning I heard a knock on the door, and a sweet old woman with her Sunday hat on, probably on her way to the Christian Science church up the street, was standing there looking at me. I said, "Can I help you?" She said, "Ah!" She was holding her tummy. She had cramps. So I gave her my bathroom to use, which was in the kitchen, which took up the other half of the apartment. After she finished her business, she said goodbye, no thank you and no tip, and when she left, she left me alone with a stench I had never experienced before. I'm telling you, I haven't smelled stuff like that in a zoo. I had to get out. The place was too small to take it. I sat on a bench on Central Park West, looking forlorn and getting over this experience. If anyone I knew had seen me they would have said, "My God, what happened to you, Al?"

Most of the time, I would sit in that apartment and play Mozart on an old phonograph. For a time, Charlie and Penny were on the outs, so every now and then, he'd come up to my place with his beautiful daughter, Deirdre, and she'd bounce around on the bed while Charlie and I worked on bottles of beer. Then around two o'clock, we'd all go to the bar around the corner on Sixty-Ninth Street and get little Deirdre a Shirley Temple to sip on while we proceeded to drink some more, spouting whatever we could remember from Chekhov, Dylan Thomas, and Eugene O'Neill. We couldn't stay too long because we couldn't afford much. Whatever work Charlie came to my place to do, it never, ever got done.

Sometimes the young women who lived in the building would see my photograph on the door of my super's apartment. They would see that I was an actor, and they would take a bit of an interest in me. I was a young guy and not in a relationship at the time, and here and there I would have little affairs with them. One of the girls I took up with was from the Midwest, a country girl. I don't know what had brought her to New York, but she was very sweet. After one of our flings, we lay there together in my bed. The space was so small that I could stretch my arms out from the bed and practically touch both walls; you had to climb in from the foot of the bed because there was no room on the sides. We were just lounging there blissfully, looking up at the ceiling that was all cracked and falling apart. The room was calm and quiet. And then suddenly, out of nowhere, she blurted out, in her Midwest accent, "Oh, if my mother could see me now. She. Would. Go. Into. *Orrrr*-bit."

)X◆X(

ONE DAY I WAS AT HOME IN MY SUPERINTENDENT'S APARTMENT, probably listening to Stravinsky with a Ballantine Ale in one hand and a lazy cigarette in my mouth, when a guy stopped over to give me a script by Israel Horovitz. It was a short one-act piece called *The Indian Wants the Bronx*, about an East Indian and two street toughs who have an encounter on upper Fifth Avenue. The Indian is looking for his son, whose address and phone number he has with him on a piece of paper, but he's come to the wrong part of town, and he speaks no English. The street toughs have no interest in helping the Indian, and instead they mock and abuse him. The play was unlike anything I had ever read before. It felt a bit mystical and even dangerous—you could sense that the Indian was way out of his league, and that something bad was going to happen the moment he crossed paths with those two young guys. But deep down it was really a story about how people talk right past each other and fail to connect. It was a beautiful and often funny play.

Israel had heard of me through Tullio Garzone. Tullio was a friend of Penny Allen's, and he had been my director when I did children's theater, like *The Adventures of High Jump*. Now he was directing the first run of Israel's play, and Penny recommended me for it. Without Penny, there would have been no Tullio; without Tullio, there would have been no *The Indian Wants the Bronx* for me, and a whole chain of events that led from it. But I, of course, didn't know any of that yet—I just knew that Israel and Tullio wanted me to play one of the toughs, a guy named Murph. He was a little bit out there, and there was an unpredictability about him. You watched him and you thought, He's capable of stuff that we haven't seen yet.

At this point as an actor, I had played my share of exotic and interesting stage roles: lowlifes, gamblers, artists, soldiers. In a sense your preparation for any part is always the same. You have to organize yourself in such a way that allows you to bring yourself to the role. You have to get to know someone else within yourself. And I guess there are a lot of me's in me.

What actors call their instrument is their entire being: your whole person, your body, your soul. It's what you play on, it absorbs things and lets them out. And when I feel a role is right, I don't have to do anything to get a nice sound on my instrument. It will play, and the notes will just come. Also, I will want to do it. I will want to go there. I want to play my instrument because it will just come out. I saw all of that in *The Indian Wants the Bronx*. It was like something I had actually experienced, and I could bring my whole life to it. I had the reins and I could ride the horse. Murph was practically the reincarnation of Cliffy and the rest of the guys from my crew, and maybe I'd have turned out like him, too, if I hadn't found acting.

We rehearsed the play at a loft on Bleecker Street, and I invited Charlie and Penny to come see it. They sat on the floor, leaning against a wall, and when it was over, Charlie looked at me with a grin on his face and said, "You've arrived, Al. This is it." And I said, "Really? You think?" All three of us—Charlie, Penny, and me, my adopted family—went out to a bar on Canal Street and had a drunken celebration for my future. Celebrating what? What future? I didn't have a pot to piss in. No offers, no agent, no nothing. But I loved it. Charlie's words made me believe that this was it. It was the real thing.

We did staged readings of *The Indian Wants the Bronx* in Connecticut and then put it on in Provincetown at the Gifford House, which was so small that the audience had to walk through the stage to get out. And they did, too, sometimes right in the middle of the play. They would walk so close to me that I could stick my leg out and trip them—though I never did. I remained in character. The play was only about an hour with no intermission, so why they were walking out, I'll never know, except they didn't like it.

Back when I was a messenger for Standard Oil in Rockefeller Center, I worked with another guy there named John Cazale. He was a few years older than me, lean looking, with a low-key manner. He had a modesty about him, but also a sense of reality, a groundedness about how the world really worked. He seemed to know something about everything. My grasp of the state of global affairs was that Hitler was gone and that was a good thing. Other than that, I had no idea what was going on. Johnny would be reading *The New York Times*, understanding every issue and making it comprehensible to me. At least, he tried.

To my great surprise, when I showed up in Provincetown to start rehearsals for the play, there was John Cazale, who had been hired to take over the role of the Indian. He was the sweetest man ever, but he had a unique way that he liked to rehearse. He did not just simply want to run lines. When you did a scene with John, you'd start talking through the scene, and he would question every line, every word choice. It was an interrogation. He'd say to you, "What am I doing? I'm standing here. What do I think of that? I don't know what I think of that." They call it the unconscious narrative. And this is how he was. Then before you knew it, as you kept talking and talking and talking, you'd just slip into the scene with him. There's a certain trust that comes with acting, like tightrope walking. With John, I knew that I had found a scene partner for life.

I had been doing *The Indian Wants the Bronx* on and off for about a year when they decided to bring it off Broadway to the Astor Place Theatre. But the producer in charge of transferring the play, a woman named Ruth Newton, said, "I don't know who this Al Pacino is. I have to meet him." I was no longer doing the superintendent's job. I don't think I got fired—I just left and I don't know why. I had so many wild times and adventures in that apartment, too many to tell. It was a period of awakening for me and I look back on it fondly. When I quit that job, I left all my stuff behind—all I had from it was a boiler permit, my first and only degree. I ventured into the provinces, this particular time in Boston, to join the circus of acting troupes and begin a life in repertory theater.

So when I came down to New York to interview with Ruth Newton, I put on the clothes of the character I was playing in Boston—a three-piece blue suit, a shirt, and a tie. I thought that was the way you did things, and I didn't know better. I met her, I said hello, and I left. She told Israel, "He's too clean-cut for the part. He looks like a prince. He's not this guy."

Israel went crazy and said, "Please, this guy has been great in the role. He will continue to be great in it. Believe me." He even gave her a review of our Provincetown production that read: "Remember the name Al Pacino. It's a name that we all will know one day." She still said, "No, he'll have to audition for it."

I was incensed. I have to audition for a part *I* created? It's like I wrote it. This is *my* play. I went to Charlie and said, "They want me to audition for this. Can you believe that? I'm not going." He said to me, "Al, you know, if you don't go, you don't get it. If you go, you *might* get it. Do you have a choice?" Charlie would have accepted if I didn't go. He knew my feelings were hurt. But we both knew what I had to do.

I had a beer and I went to the theater for my audition. I sat in a basement room below the stage, where all these other actors were waiting, even guys that I knew from the Actors Studio. As their names were called out one by one, they would go up to read with a stage manager. All the time, I'm thinking, how am I going to do this? This is humiliating. I heard my own name called out—"Al Pacino, for the part of Murph"—so I walked up the stairs and onto the stage, and I could feel myself on fire. My character is looking up at a building across the street. It's the home of his social worker, who he's forced to visit. Murph enters with another street kid from his group; they're messing around, singing a song, staring up at the social worker's open window, and then out came my first line of the play: "Hey, Pussyface!" I got about thirty seconds into the scene when Israel came bounding down the aisle, and he shouted, "Stop, stop! You got the part!"

The first critic from *The New York Times* who wrote about *The Indian Wants the Bronx* didn't especially like it, and actually didn't even mention the actors in the play, who were all unknown to him. But then came Clive Barnes, the *Times*'s lead theater critic, who was from Britain and was known for his taste and his refinement. He gave me and the play such an enthusiastic review that they started quoting it in the advertisements. More people began coming to see it, and word of mouth started to build. In the years since Julian Beck and Judith Malina had founded the Living Theatre, off Broadway had become much more fashionable and even a little bit profitable. It was never going to challenge Broadway, but you could make enough money to make a dent. Out of its beatnik, bohemian energy in the late 1950s and early '60s, off Broadway was becoming more formalized. John Cazale and I both won Obie Awards for the play—the equivalent of Tony Awards for off Broadway. We took *The Indian Wants the Bronx* to the Spoleto Festival in Italy for two weeks that summer. I'd still be in the play now if I hadn't quit it. For years and years after, I would still have recurring dreams that I was performing *The Indian Wants the Bronx* or putting it on somewhere. It made that much of an impact on me. It was my introduction to the world—before that, I always felt I was outside the world, looking in. *The Indian Wants the Bronx* was the culmination of a life that began when my mother started taking me to the movies as a kid, because after that play, everything changed.

And people had seen it. Faye Dunaway, who had just done the film *Bonnie and Clyde* and was one of the biggest stars of the time, came to see the play and told her manager, Marty Bregman, to check out this kid. Marty was already working with Judy Garland, Barbra Streisand, and an up-and-comer named Bette Midler, and he came to the play with superagent David Begelman. After the performance they came backstage to see me, and Marty told me he wanted me to come in for a meeting at his office.

He worked in a towering building on Fifty-Fourth Street between Lexington and Third. There was a security station in the lobby that you had to pass before you got to the elevators, and the guard eyed me up and down. It was a look I was used to, and it meant keep walking—you don't belong here. I've since developed a personality that is more open, but back then I was lacking a certain kind of social behavior. I was a nonconformist and not easily approachable. I told the guard that I had come to see Marty Bregman, and I could hear his end of the conversation as he phoned up Bregman's office: "Somebody here who says that he has a meeting with you? . . . I don't know, kind of shabby looking? . . . Okay, sending him up." What a start I was off to here.

Bregman's office shimmered with prosperity. He sat behind a well-polished wooden desk with a view from the windows that let him take in all of Manhattan at once. He represented a roster of celebrity clients that was honestly intimidating. I wasn't sure where I fit in. He stood up to shake my hand, and I thought I perceived something: the gleam of a pearl handle in the side of his jacket. I realized he had a gun. He had a license for it and kept it for his own protection because he walked around with a serious limp. He'd had polio as a child, but he never let that impede his life. I later heard that he was involved with bootlegging as a young man. That was the word anyway. I never asked.

Bregman had a bit of the Gatsby in him. He was a handsome man in his early forties, and he spoke with a very cultured voice, but he talked to me in a way that put me at ease. He said, "Look, I let Dustin Hoffman go by. I'm not going to do it again." He told me, "I want to represent you and I'll take care of any finances you need. I'll help you." I would never borrow money from him—not from this guy with a gun. I didn't want that kind of obligation. But when he said that, I knew that he was legitimate and that he'd put his money where his mouth was. This was somebody who had influence and was willing to exert it on my behalf. He would actually go the distance and back me up.

Bregman had grown up in an area of the Bronx close to where I came from, and I thought, This guy is a street person. He had been around, let's face it. I went back to Charlie and told him about our meeting. I said, "I trust him and don't trust him at the same time." But I knew Marty had a real sophistication that I didn't have; I didn't see what he saw. I wasn't looking for an equal—I was looking for someone who did their job better than I could do it.

)X◆X(

WHEN I WENT TO BOSTON TO DO REPERTORY THEATER, IT WAS A new world for me, and I started to gain a perspective beyond New York and the modest circle of off-off-Broadway influences that represented my understanding of theater at that point. I had parts to play. I was getting paid and could eat. And I was out there with other repertory actors who were around my age—twenty-five, twenty-six or so—but seemed privy to things I never knew about. I had my dog-eared Chekhov books and my classical albums, but it felt like I'd been let in on some great secret of the universe when they introduced me to the music of the Mamas and the Papas.

The Charles Playhouse had hired me to do *Awake and Sing!*, the Clifford Odets play about a struggling Jewish family during the Great Depression. I was kind of at sea, just didn't have a handle on it. I was backstage before one of the performances, and another actor in the play, John Seitz, was reading a newspaper. But when he saw me, he quickly closed it up and covered it with his hands. He got his cue to make his entrance and he went out to the stage. The newspaper remained behind.

Like Oedipus, I had to know. I opened up the paper, and I saw a review of our show. And it was practically glowing off the page. One after another, the lead actors were praised for their performances. The supporting actors too. And then it got to me and said, "If you can manage, somehow, to avoid Al Pacino, you're better off. He's the one thing that drags this play down." As I was reading this, I heard my cue from the overhead speaker on the ceiling. That meant I had to go onstage. So I went out in front of the audience, having read the most withering criticism of my young career, and I made my entrance laughing. A good chuckle helps sometimes. I stopped reading reviews after that one, but it stuck with me. I still remember how it stung. Another thought I had was very simple: This guy just must not like me. That does happen and that's the nature of the beast.

Sonny Boy

I fared better that season when I did *America Hurrah* at that same theater. Jean-Claude van Itallie had written these three short plays, and I was in two of them. In one segment, I played an effeminate gym instructor, really pretentious and full of himself, a very funny part. In the other segment, I played a nerdy TV ratings guy, once again with John Seitz and a young actress named Jill Clayburgh. It was an insane comedy piece, and I was enjoying the part, so I just flew with it. Every night I was going out with the gang, singing "Monday, Monday" whether it was playing on the jukebox or not. We were all drunk. Drunk every night. Happy drunk. Sad drunk. Always drunk. And that's the actor's life. Like Baudelaire said, "Be drunk, be continually drunk! On wine, on poetry or on virtue as you wish."

Around 1:00 or 2:00 a.m. one night, after the bars had closed, we went out to Gloucester, drunker than skunks, delivered by the charity of someone kind and sober enough to drive us there. There was a rock formation that overlooked the ocean, and at some pre-dawn hour I found myself drunkenly climbing my way up these rocks, risking my life because I knew that following just behind me, doing whatever I did, were Jill and her friend Jennifer Salt. The crevasses had started to become all twisty-turny, so I waited by a ridge that overlooked the ocean, wondering who would show up next. Water from the ocean was splashing me in the face as I waited. Would it be Jill or would it be Jennifer? Maybe if it had been Jennifer, I would have dated her for the next five years. But out came Jill, and she and I looked at each other. She came up close to me, and we had our first kiss overlooking the ocean with the mist falling on our faces.

I had been in relationships with women before, but none quite like my romance with Jill, our version of what we thought a romance looked like at that time. She was four years younger than me, but we were both in our twenties and both getting started in this world of professional acting. And in other ways, we couldn't have been more unalike—two natives of the same city who had experienced it in completely different ways. She was an Upper East Sider through and through, who had been educated at a private high school and at Sarah Lawrence College. So many things were about to happen to me, and she had so much to do with my happiness during them. I don't know if I was good for her, but she certainly was for me. Like with all things, the more distant you get, the more you see the value of people. And with her that's all I saw, was her value. She made me happy. And we knew we cared for each other.

We started living together in a railroad apartment on Fourteenth Street between B and C, really just a couple of rooms with a tub in the kitchen and a shared bathroom in the hallway. We were a playful couple, and we used to do private little comedy routines together, like we were Nichols and May.

A few times I'd come home and Jill would have a big pillow stuffed under her shirt. I'd say, "What's wrong with you?" She'd say, "Ah, nothing." That wasn't just a bit. She wanted to marry me. She wanted to have a baby. That was her way of saying, hey, man, let's go. But boy oh boy was I not ready. I knew that. She didn't.

Jill and I acted together in an episode of the TV cop drama *N.Y.P.D.* that was my screen debut. They actually chose me, of all people, to play a cornpone southerner who gets shot by a sniper in the opening scene. When I watched myself in it, I saw that I needed a lot more experience as a screen actor.

I don't think that I was a good companion to Jill. I was neglectful of her. I drank and drugged, and she didn't, and she had to deal with me when I did. I took her for granted. But Jill and I had a lot of fun together.

I once was called out to Los Angeles to meet with Franco Zeffirelli, the great director of *Romeo and Juliet*, who was casting for a new film. He was looking for young guys, but I was twenty-seven years old and surrounded by teenagers who were trying out for the same part as me. I may have looked young, but put me next to a seventeen-year-old and it's another story. Zeffirelli didn't know who I was, and he spent our whole conversation talking to me about Method acting in a way that gave me the impression that he didn't care for it, or for me—all while he was shooting film of me.

All my life I'd be asked what Method acting was and what the Actors Studio does and I never quite answered the question correctly. I could express what the Actors Studio is. It's not a school; it's a place for people who are already professional actors to come and develop their skills and not be charged money. To go on in front of a moderator—who could be anyone from Lee Strasberg to Paul Newman to Ellen Burstyn—and an audience of your peers and get their criticism without being lambasted or having it turn mean. A place for actors, directors, and playwrights to interchange with other artists. No one is asking anything of you except to discover. You could develop a scene from a play or movie, something no one else would let you do onstage, and eventually take it from the Studio out into the world. Or you could sit in there for years and not even perform, just attend. Imagine when you're out of work and you're pounding the pavement or you're alone in your room, you find something like this. And the spirit of what you're doing is kept alive by the very place itself.

There's no method at the Actors Studio. Everybody comes with their own method. Is there a method to writing? Yeah, you pick up a pen. You don't ask a violinist or a cellist if they use a method. They practice. But since I was a kid, I got criticized by people for being a Method actor when I didn't know what they were talking about. Method? I played a role in a play. How I observe it and bring it to life, that's my task, that's what I go after. Finding a way to bring something to life so it can go through me. But at that time, I didn't know how to express this to Zeffirelli or to anybody else.

I spent a few more days in LA, where I didn't know anyone. I wondered and wandered and found myself with half a pint of something in some hotel room, looking at the Hollywood sign, which, if I stared at it long enough, started to conjure up figures: Cary Grant dancing with Gina Lollobrigida, Boris Karloff eating a pumpkin, and Bette Davis and Greta Garbo singing a duet of "Hooray for Hollywood." I said to myself, I better get out of this place.

After a couple more days, I headed home to New York on the red-eye. Jill and I were now living on Ninety-First and Broadway in an apartment that was paradise to me. We had four rooms and a piano that I used to bang around on. Stumbling in from my flight, I slowly opened the door. Jill was sound asleep in our big double bed, and I crawled in next to her. She started to stir and said hi to me in a soft voice. I whispered to her, "Hi. I don't want to wake you, but I've written a song. You mind if I just sing it for you?" And she said, "Okay, go ahead." So I sang in this folk-song style as if I were the next Joan Baez:

Sonny Boy

Cal-i-forn-ia

Cal-i-forn-ia

Cal-i-forn-ia

I'm never going back

Caaaaaaalll-iii-forn-yaaaaaa

She smirked and fell back asleep.

)X◆)X

IN THIS BUSINESS, YOU'RE UP, YOU'RE DOWN, AND YOU'RE UP AGAIN.
I went to work for Joe Papp in a play called *Huui Huui*. Joe Papp
was one of my heroes. He did so much for Shakespeare in New
York with his summer program of Shakespeare in the Park. He
was the kind of powerhouse for theater that is so rare, and when
he died it created a void that to this day has yet to be filled. I
thought it was great to be working with Joe, who I admired, and
that the play was pretty good. However, I was taking too long in
his opinion to come to my part. Papp didn't have the patience. It
was getting to "we don't know what to do" time, and in the theater, that means somebody has got to go, and yours truly was
given the ol' boot. The great actor Charlie Durning, who was in
the play with me, begged Joe to let me stay on in it with him, but
no luck. So here I was, after my big success in *Indian*, getting fired
from the next thing I did. Talk about sobering up. In a way, it was
a break. I was getting used to the seesaw of show business. All actors experience it.

When he lowered the boom, Joe Papp took me aside into his
office and said, "You will be a great star one day, like George C.

Scott." I was thankful for those words of encouragement, but I thought I really could have done the part if I had the time and Joe had the patience.

I left the theater and I started to run. I ran block after block, not knowing what was making me run. I kept going until I stopped at a newsstand and grabbed a *New York Times*. Minutes later I was sitting in the apartment that I shared with Jill, paging through the want ads, as if I were going to find my next acting job in there. You could say I was experiencing a kind of trauma.

My next gig came about because the actor William Devane quit his role in a play by Don Petersen called *Does a Tiger Wear a Necktie?* He left to do another show, and they offered me the part. In a way, there was nothing special about *Tiger*. I'd sort of been there and done that. The play was rooted in social issues, specifically widespread concerns about drugs at the time. It told a story about a group of kids who are recovering and relapsing junkies at a city rehab center. I played another tough guy, Bickham, a wild-eyed addict with a hair trigger. Unlike Murph, he was a total loner and determined to stay that way. The play described him as "a tall, curly-haired blond boy," but it didn't matter—it was a part that any good, trained actor could have done. Bickham was rowdy but beneath his rowdiness was the soul of a poet. In one scene, he goes up to a chalkboard and writes:

SCREW THE WORLD IN THE LEFT EYE.

In another, he reads from a little composition that he has written about himself:

This world was great by me. Everything was here for the taking. We had pretty girls to knock your eyes out. You could buy an egg-cream and stand on the corner and watch 'em walk by in their summer dresses.

When I read that I thought, Yeah, I could play this guy.

Bickham's moment of truth comes later in the play, when he is telling a doctor the tragic story of his upbringing, how he pimped and pushed and mugged his way through the streets, and how he never learned love from his parents. At the peak of their argument, the doctor tells Bickham he must either fix his broken home life or create a new one—"but *face* it."

"I have faced it!" Bickham shouts as he points at his arm. "Here's where I got my love! Right through the main line, Jim. My father was a needle, and my old lady was *heroin*!"

I loved that line. It was extraordinary. Of course it had to resonate with me, because I had felt at times like I didn't have parents—which was odd, because I had a mother who I loved and who I felt love from. It was profound stuff, that kind of trauma that a lot of kids don't talk about or don't realize is responsible for their actions. As for seeing people die from drugs, I knew that game well.

When I read for the director, Michael Schultz, and I got to that line, I broke down. I fell to pieces when I had to say those words. It could hardly come out of me. Everybody was quiet. I had to stop the audition and I said, "I can't go on." And they hired me for it.

I never broke down after that. No matter how many times I performed that scene in the play, I never cried again. It never got to where it got the first time I read it. I saw that director fifty years later, and I said to him, "Michael, only you and I know what that audition was. I never gave you that onstage." He smiled and said, "No, you never did." I said, "I really let you down, didn't I?" I felt that in the play, I'd never given him quite what he had seen in that audition.

I was doing the role, and yet I resisted it coming because I didn't prepare properly. I didn't want to go there every night. I was able to perform it without really feeling it; I had developed a technique to make myself appear as if I did. There's something that happens in the repetition of performance that finally starts to work for you, not against you. But I wasn't paying attention to the repetitions, because we didn't know if the play was going to last, and as it turned out, it didn't—it closed after about a month. During that time, I had the great Sidney Poitier come and see me in that play. Poitier was on the top of the world, and when he visited me in my dressing room, he was practically glowing. He was really kind, and still I could feel him wanting to convey something to me. He could sense that I needed someone to talk to about my future and what it could be like. He wasn't critical, he was very encouraging, and he spoke to me about it in a very subtle way. It was all subtext and so kind and generous.

Tiger was my Broadway debut, and it played at the Belasco Theater, which felt like a dream come true. A few blocks away in one direction was the old Rivoli Theatre where I had worked as an usher. In another direction was the High School of Performing Arts, where I hadn't quite graduated. All around me were buildings and offices where I had worked as a messenger and done other lowly jobs. I was back on my home turf.

When I got a Tony Award nomination for *Tiger*, I brought

Marty Bregman with me to the ceremony. I was up against some really good competition. I thought my odds of winning were from zero to zero, and I hadn't prepared a speech. But as the awards show got under way, I leaned over to Marty and I said, "I've got a speech."

He seemed caught off guard by this. "What do you mean you've got a speech?" he said.

I said, "I know what I'm going to say."

"You know what you're going to say?" The Tonys show was taking place in front of us, so Marty had to speak softly, but I could tell he was skeptical. "What are you going to say?" I may have been a rookie client of his, but he was a respected professional in the industry, and how I came across was important to him.

I said, "Marty, don't get excited. I ain't gonna win a Tony. But let me tell you what I would say if I did." I recited the speech I would say for him: "Hey, thank you for this. It's a great honor. I'm reminded of my grandmother, in the South Bronx where I grew up. Every day, she'd look at me, and she'd say in Italian, 'Sonny, *anche un cretino può vincere un Tony.*' Which translated into English means, 'Remember, even a schmuck can win a Tony.'"

Marty said, "You are not doing that."

Sure enough, when they announced the winner, they called my name. Rest assured, I went with a more traditional speech. I was such a faker up there.

)X(◆)X(

I STILL DIDN'T CONSIDER MYSELF PARTICULARLY SUCCESSFUL, BUT I suppose I was starting to get a little name in what they call show business. I was playing around on a rented piano, trying to compose my own music, which I thought I had a penchant for at the time. For a while there, I thought I was the reincarnation of Beethoven, or Satie, who I love. I wanted to be Beethoven but everything that came out sounded like Satie to my oblique musical ear. In the middle of my artistic undertaking, I was interrupted by a call from that actor from *The Wicked Cooks*, the guy with the lisp, when I had tried to understudy Marty Sheen. I didn't know how he got my phone number. It had been a couple of years now since my brief time in that play, and he always used to condescend to me like I was way down, under the ground. But as he spoke to me now, he said, "Hey, Al! How are ya?" With a kind of lilt, like we were old pals. And I said to him, "Oh, hi." He started to make small talk but there was something unnatural about it. I thought to myself, What is this guy calling for? Oh. I see. This guy wants something from me. He thinks I'm going to get him a job because now I'm kind of in the vicinity of famous. He thinks I'm becoming some kind of big shot.

People who knew me from back in the South Bronx never did that to me when I became famous. But flatterers were people that I felt I had to watch out for, because they will do you in. I didn't know what I was going to do to get out of this conversation. I decided to let him know that I was no longer in the business. So I said, "I've moved on. I'm a composer now."

He said, "What?"

I said, "Yeah, acting just didn't give me what I wanted."

And he said, "Oh, gee, Al. I thought maybe you'd have something—"

I said, "Nah."

He said, "That's kind of too bad. It looked like you had a real future."

I said, "I know, but sometimes you've gotta go where life takes you." And I hung up and went back to the piano.

Perhaps fame was going to be more trouble than it was worth. I hated to think what would happen if I ended up attaining any more of it. It terrified me . . . sorta.

4

The New World

My relationship with the director who would change my life began oddly. Francis Ford Coppola had seen me onstage, when I did *Does a Tiger Wear a Necktie?* on Broadway, but I didn't meet him at the time. He was a young up-and-comer who had already directed a couple of films. Out of the blue, he sent me an original script that he had written, a wonderful love story about a young college professor with a wife and children who has a love affair with one of his students. It was mythical and a bit surreal but beautifully written. Francis wanted to meet with me about playing the role of the professor. That meant I had to get on a plane and go to San Francisco, which is something I would have difficulty doing. I didn't like to fly. I thought, Is there any other way to get there? I can't tell this guy to come all the way to New York, can I? I bit the bullet and I went.

It was my first time in San Francisco, and I was just happy to be out there at the invitation of someone as talented as Francis. He was like a college professor himself, an intellectual with a bushy beard, a toothy smile, and a scarf always wrapped around his neck, Fellini style. For the next five days and nights, he took me to dinner and we talked about his film project over bottles of wine. I thought Francis had been touched by genius. He had this excitement in him. He was a leader, a doer, and a risk-taker.

He brought me to his company, American Zoetrope, in a big building—basically an above-ground bunker where he worked surrounded by a mixed crowd. If my memory is correct, I think I saw George Lucas and Steven Spielberg there. Martin Scorsese and Brian De Palma were also part of the group. I had no idea who they were at the time, but I knew they weren't actors. They were a band of young radicals who came from the sixties and were about to bring moviemaking into the seventies. They were alive to bigger changes in the film culture.

But I was an unknown, and the movie that Francis wanted to do with me got turned down everywhere, never to be made. And I went back home and didn't think I'd ever hear from him again. Months went by, and then one day in the middle of the afternoon, I got a phone call. On the other end of the line, I heard a name and a voice from the past: Francis Coppola.

First he told me he was going to be directing *The Godfather*. I thought he might be fantasizing. What was he talking about? How did they give him *The Godfather*? I had read Mario Puzo's novel, which had become a big hit; it was a huge deal for anyone to be involved with it. But when you're a young actor you don't even put your eyes on those things. Just getting any part in a film is a miracle. Opportunities like those don't exist for you. It just seemed so outrageous.

And then I thought, Hey—maybe this is possible. I had spent

time with Francis. I saw that he carried himself with confidence, and that gave me faith in him. But this wasn't a thing that was done at the time. Wouldn't the studio, Paramount, go to older directors who had reputations, not this talented young avant-garde intellectual? It didn't fit with my perception of Hollywood.

Then Francis said he wanted me to play Michael Corleone. I thought, Now he's gone too far. I started doubting whether he was on the phone at all. Maybe I was the one going through a nervous breakdown. For a director to offer you a role, over the phone, not through an agent or anything, and this role of all roles—that was a hundred-million-to-one shot. I didn't even think of it as a shot, because I didn't believe it. Who was I, to have this fall into my lap? When I finally hung up the phone with Francis, I was kind of in a daze.

When I think of it, I didn't have an interest in show business, and I don't even know why. I knew acting would be my profession, but somehow the whole business eluded me and my lifestyle. I didn't live in Los Angeles, where it was centered. I was in New York, and on the island of Manhattan things were happening for me. I was a theater person. I had my Tony Award and my Obie Award, the Actors Studio and my gang of fellow actors. Hollywood was a distant town, and film was a different world from theater. I would say to Charlie, "How do actors do it? You do a scene in a film that you just did and they say, go do it again." And you do it covered in wires and facing a camera with a lot of people around breathing and getting in your eye range. Oh, and I'm forgetting the smoke—they smoke up the room, which I guess is for the camera. The difference between movie acting and stage acting was like being on that high wire. In movie acting, the wire is on the floor—you can always come back and try something again. Stage acting is up thirty feet in the air. And if you don't make it, you fall. That's the difference in the adrenaline that it takes to be a theater actor.

That's how I felt then. I've changed, but man, you had to be there. I used to love to see the faces of nonactors who were cast in a film to play their real-life professions, like when they'd hire a real doorman or a priest who knows Latin and they had to experience what making a movie is like. At the end of a day's work, they would usually wander off in a fog and need to be led back to whatever transportation got them there.

Movies were the Marty Bregman business, and once I got in with Marty Bregman, his business included me. Marty said, "I'm not gonna make you a star, you are a star." I didn't look at myself that way, but he did. It was his business, he made those calls. I was pragmatic about it. All I knew is, there were roles that I could play and roles I couldn't. I felt that very strongly. Most parts, I thought other actors could play better and I still think that way.

My first film role did not come through Marty Bregman but from a great casting director named Marion Dougherty, who had also done *Midnight Cowboy* and had seen me in *The Indian Wants the Bronx*. She offered me a one-day part on *Me, Natalie*, a coming-of-age comedy for Patty Duke, where I would play a guy she meets at a dance party. Patty was the sweetest of people to me. But I was disastrous, and depressed by that whole thing. I got there early in the morning because I was told to be there early in the morning, earlier than anyone does anything in the morning. I had no one to talk to, and I sat around and I waited. And waited. And waited.

And as I waited, I thought, Is this how they make movies? I don't want to do this with my life.

I hadn't slept the night before because the scene was so early, and when they put me in a costume, the clothes itched me. But this is just who I am and always was. I look at a situation and I say, what am I doing here? And it seems to not matter where it is, what situation I'm in. I want to leave. I don't leave, because I really don't want to be rude, so I stay. But I really want to go.

I danced with Patty and said my lines to her—"You have a nice body, you know that? Listen, do you put out?"—and had absolutely no understanding of what the fuck I was talking about or why I was saying it or what it would look like. It went in the film. My first film credit.

I didn't make another movie for almost two years. *The Panic in Needle Park* was something that Marty Bregman had helped to cultivate and saw for me. The screenplay, by John Gregory Dunne and Joan Didion, was a true story about two young heroin addicts, a guy and a girl, who fall in and out with each other during a dope shortage. Marty also represented its director, Jerry Schatzberg, who was better known as a photographer and hadn't done much in film yet, and they both liked me for the role of the guy, whose name was Bobby. I thought it was something I could play. A few people could have done it, but it was a relatively castable role for me. I had made my theater bones playing these types of street characters, so I was grateful to have that choice for a first film. The college professor that Francis offered me, well, that was probably somewhat of a reach, though I did like the role. I think that's what it comes down to.

If I have a feeling for a role, it's worth it for me to try. When I did my final audition to become a member of the Actors Studio, I was grateful that I got to play two different characters that night. One was from *Counsellor at Law* by Elmer Rice, and the other was from *Look, We've Come Through* by Hugh Wheeler. In the first one, I played a furious communist fanatic, a revolutionary, in a scene with an attorney played by Owen Hollander. In the other, I played a gay streetwalker in a scene with Nathan Joseph. Both of the guys I auditioned with were friends at the time. The characters I played in those two scenes were totally different, and I think that helped the judges, which included Elia Kazan, Harold Clurman, and Lee Strasberg. Seeing the range of the characters, who couldn't have been further apart, may have helped give them a reason to take a chance on me.

Actors have to watch out for being typecast: your appearance identifies you, and sometimes actors get stuck playing the same kinds of roles. I don't think I could have lasted like that. One of the reasons I liked going off to do repertory theater was because I'd get to do roles that I normally wouldn't be cast for.

When you're a young actor with almost no film experience given a shot at a lead role like *The Panic in Needle Park*, you say, okay, I'll jump through that hoop. But there are some hoops I couldn't make myself jump through. I thought I had the role, but as they say, the papers weren't signed and the part wasn't mine just yet. In the meantime, someone asked me to do a reading for a play—another actor was missing and they needed me to fill in for one of the leads. It was a role that I didn't know, which meant that this would be a cold reading, with no preparation before I read it for an audience.

We were up on the stage. The actors were getting their scripts, and I was looking down at the pages, trying to find the name of the character I was supposed to be playing. The audience was almost full, but I peeked up and saw a few people who didn't look like they belonged there. To my surprise, one of them was Nick Dunne, the producer of *Panic*, along with his brother, John Gregory Dunne, and Joan Didion, who wrote the script together. They came in with a couple of other people I didn't recognize. I was shocked. You have to understand, I was never asked to audition for *Panic*; I was offered the part. Now, if they were suddenly expecting me to audition to get it, I wouldn't want them giving me a final checkout at a cold reading of a play I was completely unfamiliar with. I thought, That's no way to treat a lady.

I got down from the stage and walked over to Nick and the people he was with. I said, "I'm sorry, man. You're gonna have to leave." It was not casual. They looked surprised. I said, "I can't do this with you here. I feel like you're here to judge me. It makes me uncomfortable." And he and his colleagues got up and left.

I think I made the right move, but that's the chance you have to take sometimes when the wolf is at the door. The whole time I'm thinking to myself, Al, what are you doing? But when you run on impulse, impulse does sometimes bail you out. People say I take risks, and I don't want to sound like I'm boasting here, but when something's up, I don't care. And this felt that important to me. I'm a fearful person like everybody is. I don't do anything about a lot of things I *should* do something about. It's not the worst philosophy to say, "Ah, whatever. Let it go by. So what?" But every once in a while—I'm talking decades—I say no, not this one.

The Panic in Needle Park turned out to be a showcase for me. It's still lauded today, and Jerry Schatzberg did such a magnificent job. I really enjoyed working with Kitty Winn, who played my girlfriend and fellow addict. I didn't get her and she didn't get me, but we got along. Sometimes she'd shoot me such a quizzical look at some of the things I would say. I would say anything, and I never knew what she was thinking. I had no clue who she was. And it was fine. She won the award for Best Actress at the Cannes Film Festival for *The Panic in Needle Park*. After that, she did *The Exorcist* and a couple more movies, and then she quit acting in films. She was a very engaging and gentle person to be around, pleasant and not overbearing at all. But she just didn't like the business, and she couldn't take some of the stuff that was going on. Everybody's a dark secret.

)(◆)(

PARAMOUNT DIDN'T WANT ME TO PLAY MICHAEL CORLEONE. THEY wanted Jack Nicholson. They wanted Robert Redford. They wanted Warren Beatty or Ryan O'Neal. In the book, Puzo had Michael calling himself "the sissy of the Corleone family." He was supposed to be small, dark-haired, handsome in a delicate way, no visible threat to anybody. That didn't sound like the guys that the studio wanted. But that didn't mean it had to be me.

It did mean, however, that I would have to screen-test for the role, which I had never done before, and that I would have to fly out to the West Coast to do it, which I just didn't want to do. I did not care that it was *The Godfather*. I didn't want to go to California. But Marty Bregman said to me, "You're getting on that fucking plane," and he brought me a pint of whiskey so I could drink it on the flight, and I got there.

Paramount had already rejected Francis's entire cast. They rejected Jimmy Caan and Bob Duvall, who were great established actors, well on their way to what they would become. They rejected Brando, for Christ's sake. It was quite clear walking into the studio that they didn't want me either. And I knew I wasn't the only one being considered. Many of the young actors of the day were reading for Michael. That was an unpleasant feeling. But *The Panic in Needle Park* was responsible for pushing me over the edge. *Panic* hadn't been released yet, but fortunately Jerry Schatzberg gave Paramount eight minutes of footage from my performance that helped convince the studio to at least take a chance on me.

The book of *The Godfather* was a huge success, so everyone was talking about it and was excited about the film that was to be made. Before I even did my screen test, Francis took me to a barber in San Francisco, because he wanted Michael to have an authentic 1940s haircut. The barber heard that we were making the film and actually stepped back, took it in, and started shaking. We found out later that he had a heart attack. Word was out that there was a lot riding on this film behind the scenes. Paramount executives were irate with one another and having shouting matches. You could feel the tension everywhere. So I did my Zen this-too-shall-pass thing. I said to myself, Go to the character. What is going on in the scene? Where are you going? Where did you come from? Why are you here?

I sat through a few days' worth of screen tests wearing an early version of Michael's army uniform and a hangdog expression on my face. I always had that look. I guess it was a façade that I carried with me, because it got me through everything. But I must say the scene I was asked to do was not the best one they could have picked. It was Michael, in the opening wedding scene, explaining to his girlfriend, Kay, what his family really did and who all the players were in his father's operation. It was a mundane scene of exposition, just me and Diane Keaton sitting at a drab little table, drinking glasses of water we pretended were wine, while I talked about Sicilian wedding customs. It was impossible for the impact of the role to come through. My interpretation of Michael was like planting a garden; it would take a certain amount of time in the story for the flowers to grow. How am I supposed to bring across my ideas about him in this scene? I couldn't bring him to life in this scene because nobody could.

But here's the secret: Francis wanted me. He wanted me and I knew that. And there's nothing like when a director wants you. It's the best thing an actor could have, really. He also gave me a gift in the form of Diane Keaton. He had a few actresses he was auditioning for the role of Kay, but the fact that he wanted to pair me up with Diane suggested she had an edge in the process. I knew she was doing well in her career and had been appearing on Broadway in shows like *Hair*, and *Play It Again, Sam* with Woody Allen. A few days before the screen test, I met Diane in Lincoln Center at a bar, and we just hit it off. She was easy to talk to and funny, and she thought I was funny too. I felt like I had a friend and an ally right away.

When I knew I had the role for sure, I called my grandmother to tell her. "You know I'm going to be in *The Godfather*? I'm going to play the part of Michael Corleone." She said, "Oh, Sonny, listen! Granddad was born in Corleone, that's where he was from." I didn't know where my grandfather was born, only that he came from Sicily—once my grandfather got to America and no one was chasing after him, he left it at that. Now to learn he came from

Corleone, the very town that gave my character and his family their name? I thought, I must be getting help from somewhere, because how else could such an impossible thing—me getting the role—happen in the first place?

I still had to figure out who Michael was to me. Before filming started, I would take long walks up and down Manhattan, from Ninety-First Street to the Village and back, just thinking about how I was going to play him. Mostly I'd go alone, other times I'd meet Charlie downtown and we'd walk back uptown together. Michael starts out from a young man we've seen before, getting by, a little loopy, a little lumpy. He's there and not there at the same time. It's all building up to when he volunteers to take out Sollozzo and McCluskey, the drug dealer and the crooked cop who conspired to kill Michael's father. All of a sudden, there's a big explosion in him.

This is mapped out in the novel, because a book can give the narrative as much time as it needs. You wait and see how it unfolds. But what was I going to do in the film?

〉〔◆〕〈

BEFORE WE STARTED SHOOTING *THE GODFATHER*, I GOT TOGETHER with little Al Lettieri, a great guy and a great actor who was going to play Sollozzo. He just said to me, "You should meet this guy. It's good for what you're doing." I sort of knew what he meant by that, so I went along with him. One day we took a drive to a suburb just outside the city.

Little Al brought me to a traditional, beautiful, well-kept home. You pass these kinds of homes all the time as you're going from wherever you are to wherever you need to get to, and you don't even think about who lives there. He took me inside and introduced me to the head of the household, a guy who looked like a normal businessman. I might have guessed he was a Wall Street executive, an investment banker or a hedge-fund manager. I shook his hand and said hello, and he was very welcoming. He had a loving family. He had a wife who served us drinks and light snacks on fine porcelain. He had two young sons around my age. I was just some crazy actor who had come into his house, trying to absorb as much as I could. Our conversation remained polite and at the surface level. I never asked Little Al why he had brought me here, but I thought about what he had said before we came, how this visit would be helpful for what I was working on. Little Al knew some guys. Some real guys. And now he was introducing me to one of them.

I was being given a taste of how this thing looked and operated in reality, not how it was shown in the movies. Not that our host was going to get into any of those details with us. I couldn't know those details. As a matter of fact, we ended up drinking and playing games. Many moons later, photos from that night surfaced, showing me in a sweatshirt, laughing away with a drink in my hand while Little Al showed me a gun. A boys' night out.

I was a kid from the South Bronx. I am an Italian. I am a Sicilian too. I knew what it was to always be assumed that you had at least a connection to organized crime. Any name that ended with a vowel was scrutinized for having possible connections to that world. Instead of being compared to Joe DiMaggio, you were associated with Al Capone.

Most of us will never experience crime, let alone perpetrate it.

And yet we're fascinated with these people who are determined not to live within the rules of society, who are finding another way to go. The outlaw is a particularly American kind of character. We grew up pretending to be Jesse James and Billy the Kid. These were folk heroes. They became part of our lore. The history of the Mafia is part of that lore too.

)X◆X(

MY FILMING ON *THE GODFATHER* BEGAN WITH ITS OPENING WED-ding sequence, which took about a week out in Staten Island. From my humble day-to-day life, I found myself plunged into the set of a huge Hollywood film, filled with equipment, hot lights and dolly tracks, cranes and booms, microphones hovering overhead, and a company of actors with hundreds of extras, all working under Francis's direction.

The scale of it was all new to me. But at the same time, I felt comfortable there, and adapting to it was easy. It was a big scene with a lot of people, but I became used to the environment. You had a place you were told to go—say, at the table with the makeup, and they had big rooms for that. And you went and you sat in a corner in a room. You saw people, you nodded hello. No one knew who I was. So I just went in there and enjoyed my time and I was okay.

Then I would start to work. I always felt as though I had a nat-ural connection with a camera. Even in the theater, people would mention that: "You look like you could work with a camera." I didn't know quite what it meant at first. Perhaps it had to do with my growing up with films. Most actors, when they first start onstage, are always told, "Up! Louder! Louder!" Being on camera is more intimate. I usually didn't know where the camera was, though a good cameraman would understand that I was not that experienced and take care of it. On *The Godfather*, I was in the assured hands of the great Gordy Willis.

Diane and I spent those first days laughing with each other, having to perform that opening wedding exposition scene from the screen test that we hated so much. On the basis of just that one scene, we were certain we were in the worst picture ever made, and when we'd finish shooting for the day, we would go back to Manhattan and get drunk. Our careers were over, we thought.

Back in Hollywood, Paramount started to look at the film that Francis had shot, and they were once again questioning whether I was the right actor for the part. The rumor had got out around the set that I was going to be let go from the picture. You could feel that loss of momentum when we shot. There was a discomfort among people, even the crew, when I was working. I was very conscious of that. The word was that I was going to be fired, and, likely, so was the director. Not that Francis wasn't cutting it—I wasn't. But he was the one responsible for me being in the film.

I felt out of place doing this role, and yet I felt I belonged there—strange things to feel at the same time. No one wants to be anywhere they're not wanted. Perhaps it would have been easier for me to just leave and get away from that discomfort. Now what if they'd fired me, would I have felt I lost out on something? Probably, but I had lost out on things before and recovered. I didn't consider it important to have a career. I never thought about careers.

Finally, Francis determined that something had to be done.

Me with my father and mother. I look like I've been kidnapped.

I know that fur had to have been very comfortable.

My father and mother in the center. I don't know those other people.

There's mom.
I guess that's
where I got
my looks.

Me and my dad. They used to call him "Ty" because he looked like Tyrone Power.

Have no fear—no bullets here.

My father's parents: my grandfather, who was my namesake, and my angelic grandmother, who saved my life.

My mother's parents: my loved ones, who raised me and are why I'm still here.

Mom and the gang.
I'm at the bottom next to
the kid in suspenders.

1685 Bryant Avenue.
We'd scale those
fucking roofs, are
you kidding me?

2997 — 39 BX

Me and my beloved cousin—guess who's who?

Granny and me. I'm usually a little happier, but I don't like parties.

Me at my First Holy Communion. My mother and grandmother are at either side, me at the bottom.

Me and my mother, my cousin Mark and his mother, and our grandfather. That was me on my way to being pretty.

That's the school where I won most likely to succeed.

Around age fifteen.
This is the face that
Chekhov saved.

A moment in time, I'll never
forget it. Twenty-two years
old, on stage at the the
Actors Gallery, in *Creditors*
by August Strindberg.

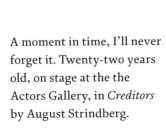

The Indian Wants the Bronx, with John Cazale and Matthew Cowles. The life changer.

My first and only Obie Award, for *Indian*. I don't look as grateful as I should.

My Broadway debut in *Does a Tiger Wear a Necktie?* *The New York Times* wrote, "It goes like a house on fire. Is the blaze Pacino?"

With Kitty Winn in *The Panic in Needle Park*. My first lead movie role, and a great film.

Me and Diane, we go together like two straws and a Coke.

The Corleone men of *The Godfather*. My film family, I love them all.

The scene that saved my role in *The Godfather.*

I know I'm loaded, I hope the gun isn't.

With Francis Ford Coppola and Marlon Brando. Looks like Francis is saying, Guys we gotta get this together, shake hands with him, Al, he's your father.

At the *Godfather* premiere with Jill Clayburgh. That's a clear picture of a drunken boy. She's twenty-five and I still look like her son.

This looks like the end
of a day on *Serpico*.
I can't believe how long
my arms are. What
happened to my legs?

Richard III on Broadway.
At least they got the photo
right. Now, do I look like
I set Shakespeare back
fifty years?

Me and Gene Hackman
in *Scarecrow*.

The Godfather: Part II. John Cazale was my friend and I loved him.

With Lee Strasberg. Put a shirt on, will you? You're showing me up.

Dog Day Afternoon.
I guess that's the way
people look when
they're robbing a bank.

Bobby Deerfield,
with Marthe Keller.
I knew I was
destined to be a
male model.

My friend and mentor
Charlie Laughton.
"You did good, Al."

One night he called me to meet him at the Ginger Man, a restaurant and watering hole for thirsty Lincoln Center types, where actors, dancers, maestros, and stagehands all lined up at the bar. He was having dinner there with his wife, his kids, and a small group, and when I went in and found him at his table, he said, "Listen, I want to talk to you a minute." He didn't invite me to sit down with them. I stood there wondering, what's he doing? He's cutting his steak and looking at me like I'm not part of anything— like I'm just some isolated actor who had come looking for a handout. So I continued to stand there, alone, as he sat there with his family looking up at me. Finally Francis said, "You know how much you mean to me, how much faith I had in you." At this point we had been shooting *The Godfather* for about a week and a half. And Francis said, "Well, you're not cutting it."

I felt that one in the pit of my stomach. It's when it finally hit me that my job was on the line. I said to Francis, "What do we do here?" He said, "I put together rushes of what we've shot already. Why don't you take a look at it yourself? Because I don't think it's working. You're not working."

I went into a screening room the next day. I had already been warned that it was possible I was going out of the picture. And when I looked at the footage, all scenes from very early in the film, I thought to myself, I don't think there's anything spectacular here. I didn't know what to make of it. But the effect was certainly what I wanted. I didn't want to be seen.

My whole plan for Michael was to show that this kid was unaware of things and wasn't coming on with a personality that was particularly full of charisma. My idea was that this guy comes out of nowhere. That was the power of this characterization. That was the only way this could work: the emergence of this person, the discovery of his capacity and his potential. And if you'll notice, he's still not quite Michael when he goes into the hospital to save his father. Even then, he only becomes Michael when he looks at Enzo the baker, who he's instructed to stand with him outside the hospital and pretend that he has a gun, and sees that Enzo's hand is shaking and his isn't. By the end of the film, I hoped that I would have created an enigma. And I think that's what Francis was hoping for also. But neither one of us knew how to explain it to each other.

It was always thought that Francis reorganized the shooting schedule to give the doubters back in Hollywood some incentive to believe in me and keep me in the picture. The jury's out on whether he did that deliberately, and Francis himself has denied that he orchestrated it for my benefit, but he did move up the filming of the Italian restaurant scene, where the untested Michael comes to take his revenge on Sollozzo and McCluskey. That scene was not meant to be filmed until a few days later, but if something hadn't happened to let me show what I was capable of, there might not have been a later for me.

So over the course of an April night I shot that scene. I spent fifteen hours that day in a tiny restaurant under an El, with Little Al Lettieri and the magnificent Sterling Hayden, who played McCluskey. The two of them truly were precious to me. They knew I was going through a difficult time, feeling like I had the world on my shoulders, knowing that any day the axe could fall on me. Here we were in a dead, fetid room that was being filled with smoke and hellish heat—we had no trailers to escape to, no production assistants coming up and asking, "Can we get you some water?" None of that. I was just sitting there, thinking, how do you stand this stuff? The absolute ennui of it could actually kill you.

Sterling and Al Lettieri helped keep up my morale; they set a tone and were role models for me. I looked to them as the people who knew what to do, and how to conduct yourself, and they took me in as a fellow actor. But eventually the script called for me to excuse myself to use the bathroom, find a hidden gun, and blow their brains out.

Then I had to run out of the restaurant and make my escape by jumping onto a moving car. I had no stand-in. I had no stuntman. I had to do it myself. I jumped, and I missed the car. Now I was lying in a gutter on White Plains Road in the Bronx, flat on my back and looking up at the sky. I had twisted my ankle so badly that I couldn't move.

Everyone on the crew had crowded around me. They were trying to lift me up, asking me: Was my ankle broken? Could I walk? I didn't know. I lay there thinking, this is a miracle. Oh God, you're saving me. I don't have to do this picture anymore. I was shocked by the feeling of relief that passed over me. Showing up for work every day, feeling unwanted, feeling like an underling, was an oppressive experience, and this injury could be my release from that prison. At least now they could fire me, recast another actor as Michael, and not lose every dime they'd already put into the picture. But that's not what happened.

They filmed the rest of the car-jumping scene with a stunt guy who appeared out of nowhere, and they shot my ankle up with cortisone until I could stand on my feet again. Then Francis showed the restaurant scene to the studio, and when they looked at it, something was there. Because of that scene I just performed, they kept me in the film. So I didn't get fired from *The Godfather*. I just kept doing what I did, what I had thought about on those lonely walks up and down the length of Manhattan. I did have a plan, a direction that I really believed was the way to go with this character. And I was certain that Francis felt the same way.

><><

IT TOOK EFFORT TO TRANSFORM ME INTO MICHAEL CORLEONE. I had to be presentable, which did not come naturally to me. They forced me to look presentable. I would come in each morning to play Michael, and I would arrive with two or three different faces. One on each side of my head and a third in the middle. Some nights I got very little sleep or none at all. Other nights I had drunk so much and taken so much of everything I could take that my face would become lopsided. Dick Smith, the great makeup man, had to put my face back together. And by the time I got out of his makeup chair, I had become Michael.

I had been introduced to Marlon Brando briefly at a dinner with all the cast members before we started filming. Now, as we were getting ready to do the scene where Michael finds Vito in the hospital, Francis said, "Why don't you and Brando have lunch together?" This was going to be the big talk. I actually didn't want to talk to him. I thought it was not necessary. The discomfort I felt at just the thought of it—You mean I have to have lunch with him? Seriously, it fucking scared me. He was the greatest living actor of our time. I grew up on actors like him—larger-than-life people like Clark Gable and Cary Grant. They were famous when fame meant something, before the bloom went off the rose. But Francis said you have to and so I did.

I had my lunch with Marlon in a modest room in the hospital where we were filming on Fourteenth Street. He was sitting on one hospital bed, I was sitting on the other. He was asking me questions: Where am I from? How long have I been an actor? And he was eating chicken cacciatore with his hands. His hands were full of red sauce. So was his face. And that's all I could think about the whole time. Whatever his words were, my conscious mind was fixated by the stain-covered sight in front of me. He was talking— *gobble, gobble, gobble, gobble*—and I was just mesmerized. What was he going to do with the chicken? I hoped he wasn't going to tell me to throw it in the garbage for him. He disposed of it somehow without getting up. He looked at me in a quizzical way, as if to ask, what are you thinking about? I was wondering, what is he going to do with his hands? Should I get him a napkin? Before I could, he spread both his hands across the white hospital bed and smeared the sheets with red sauce, without even thinking about it, and he kept on talking. And I thought, Is that how movie stars act? You can do anything.

When our lunch was over, Marlon looked at me with those gentle eyes of his and said, "Yeah, kid, you're gonna be all right." I was taught to be polite and grateful, so I probably just said thank you to him. I was too scared to say anything at all. What I should have said was "Can you define 'all right'?"

My costars couldn't have been more supportive, all of them. Almost nobody knew who I was, and when nobody's trying to impress you, you start seeing who people really are. They could tell that I was struggling, and they were so comforting to me. Actors are sensitive people, and they're going to be more attuned to what you're feeling. They live with feelings. Your life is feeling everybody's feelings so that you can play your character. The actors I've seen who are especially talented have high antennae. I felt it particularly strongly from John Cazale, who I had a history with and was my close friend, and Jimmy Caan. The script had assigned them the parts of my older brothers and advisers in the film itself, but they took on those roles naturally in how they interacted with me. They were instinctively protective and were not going to let me fail. There was also Bob Duvall and Richard Castellano, Abe Vigoda, and all the others, who were fully there for me. I really felt liked, which helps in any situation.

What I think audiences received from *The Godfather*, what brought it across and really gave it its impact, was this idea of family. People identified with the Corleones, saw themselves somehow in them, and found themselves connecting to the characters and their dynamics as brothers and sisters, parents and children. The film had Mario Puzo's exciting drama and storytelling, the magic of Coppola's interpretation, and real violence. But in the context of that family, it all became something else. It wasn't just people from the city who related to the Corleones—that sense of familiarity carried the film to every part of the world.

Marlon showed me generosity, too, but I don't think he saved it all for me, because he shared it with the audience. It's what made his performance so memorable and so endearing. We all fantasize about having someone like Don Vito we can turn to. So many people are abused in this life, but if you've got a Godfather, you've got someone you can go to, and they will take care of it. That's why people responded to him in the film. It was more than just the bravado and the boldness; it was the humanity underneath it. That's why he had to play Vito larger than life—his physical size, the shoe polish in his hair, the cotton in his cheeks. His Godfather had to be an icon, and Brando made him as iconic as Citizen Kane or Superman, Julius Caesar or George Washington.

But Francis had a lot on his shoulders, as I would learn when we were working on the funeral sequence for Vito. It was a big scene we shot out on Long Island that involved a large amount of the cast and took a couple of days. The sun was going down and I heard "Wrap! Wrap!" They told me I was done for the day. So naturally I'm happy because I get to go home and have some fun, whatever that means. I was on the way to my trailer saying to myself, Well, I didn't fuck up too much. I had no lines, no obligations, and that was fine.

As I was heading back, I began to hear the sound of someone crying, which you sort of expect in a graveyard. I looked around to see where it was coming from. And there, sitting on a tombstone, was Francis Ford Coppola bawling like a baby. Profusely crying. Nobody was going near him, so I went up to him, and I said, "Francis, what's wrong? What happened?" He wiped his eyes with his sleeve, paused, looked up at me, and said, "They won't give me another shot." He had wanted to film another setup that day, and he had not been allowed it. Even he had to answer to someone else. And he wanted this so badly that to have it denied had actually wounded him.

One never knows if a film is going to be great. You know one thing, if it's a really good script—and Mario and Francis wrote a really good script—there's a chance. An actor comes in and plays his role, but the film is all in what happens after, how an editor cuts it together and how the director figures out the storytelling. But there in that graveyard I thought: If this is the kind of passion that Francis has for it, then something here is working. I knew I was in good hands.

><+><

MAKING THE FILM BROUGHT ME TO SICILY FOR THE FIRST TIME IN my life. I wasn't ready for it. It seemed to me as though it were a gross inconvenience. And then as soon as I arrived, I felt flush with a kind of cosmic energy. Everything came rushing back to me, even things I had never experienced. The paths that led to my being had started here—whatever I was or would become was in some way because of this place. It was eye-opening, consciousness-raising, and totally seminal. As an actor, you're always searching for identity and things you connect to. When I came back from the trip, I found myself telling everyone I could that they must go and see the places where their families come from, to trace their roots back as far as they can. It's a way of checking in with reality, a reminder that you existed and continue to exist.

I didn't know anybody in Sicily, and the people there didn't know me. They didn't know what part I was playing in *The Godfather*, didn't even know I was Sicilian. I was an unknown actor, and being unknown was a pleasure. I never spoke to anyone. I didn't know anything to talk about. But everywhere I went, the locals were curious and so kind to me. They didn't have much, but they were generous and full of grace, and they'd invite a kid from the film, or anybody else really, to come in and *mangia* with them, in their little homes. I'd sit in silence and eat the food that they offered.

When it came time to film the wedding scene, where Michael marries Apollonia in a beautiful ceremony, I stood there in my wool suit, next to Simonetta Stefanelli, who played my bride, and a lot of Italians who didn't speak English. This didn't seem like the most challenging scene to film, but there was Francis with a bullhorn in his hand, shouting out instructions to me. He said, "Al, I want you to do three things. First, go over there and speak to the people in the scene. Then, turn away from them and go to your bride and dance the waltz with her. After that, go off with her to the car and drive away."

There I was, Mr. Method Actor, telling him, "You have to understand, Francis, I don't really speak Italian." He said, "It's okay, Al, just make up something," and I agreed. The camera was at a distance for a medium shot, not a close-up, so they wouldn't see exactly what I said. Then, when he said, "Go over and do the waltz," I turned to him and said, "But I don't know how to waltz." He shook his head and glared at me, and shouted out, "Well, then just dance with her then, and when you're done with that, head over to the car and drive away." I wish you could have seen the look on his face when I said back to him, "I'm sorry, Francis, but I don't know how to drive." How would a kid from the South Bronx know how to drive a car when he'd been taking the subway all his life? I wouldn't get my first driver's license until I was thirty-four. At that point, Francis exploded: "Why did I ever hire you? What can you do?" I said, "I don't know if it would matter, but I can basket weave, so I'll be ahead of the game when they come to cart me away." The extras broke into laughter as they watched this exchange unfold.

I look back at this scene fondly now. He was a director making a film, and I was an actor who couldn't do most of the things he was asking of me. But I danced my way through the wedding, I double-talked Italian to the people there, and I went down the hill, got in the car, and drove that sucker three or four feet. That's why we all love films. Anything is possible.

It got really hot there in July. All of us were wearing wool. We were filming a scene that required a large group of extras to stand in a line, when a lunch break was called and people started to scatter. The assistant director, a top-of-the-line, very experienced guy from Rome who was corralling the extras, started screaming at these Sicilians—"Hey, get back there"—like he was talking to donkeys. Once again, I saw that invisible whip being cracked, like that director from *The Wicked Cooks* had done, and it bothered me. These people had been standing in the heat since early in the morning. One of the men on the line raised his hand, said something in Italian, and pointed to his watch, because it was about two in the afternoon. And the Roman said, in Italian, "You shut up and you get back in line." The extra was a short, thin man with gray hair and a good-looking face. I would imagine he was in his sixties. He had a modesty to him. He just shrugged his shoulders and walked away. He quit the film, which meant he wouldn't get paid.

I loved him. I imagined what it must be like to be him. What courage. These were poor people getting paid a little to help fill in the background of the film. This guy's got no money, and he's walking away because he has his lunchtime to go to. He's going to go somewhere and have some cheese and a little piece of fruit. I had that freedom once too. But I didn't want to trade places with the guy. I was just indulging in the fantasy that he inspired. I watched him, and I thought, That's something I agree with. In spirit. To me, he was a hero.

)X(♦)X(

WHEN I FINISHED MAKING *THE GODFATHER*, I WAS BROKE. NOT THAT I had ever had any money, but now I *owed* money. My manager and agents got their cuts of my salary while I had to live on support from Jill Clayburgh. Me and Jill were at home in our apartment one day when there was a knock on the door. I opened it to find a guy who handed me an envelope containing a notice of service. And I thought, What is this? While I was waiting to be hired for *The Godfather*, MGM had cast me to be in another gangster picture, a Mafia comedy called *The Gang That Couldn't Shoot Straight*, and now they were coming after me. It was like I was some sort of gambler and the bookies were going to get me. I had to hire lawyers to help get me out of that contract. Soon I was fifteen grand in debt to the lawyers too.

I couldn't pay to keep up the fight with MGM, so I asked the head of their studio to meet me at the Pulitzer Fountain outside the Plaza Hotel on Fifty-Ninth Street and Fifth Avenue. It was a hectic location, full of crazies and cool people on their lunch, grown men in hats and suits running to their jobs, women pushing children in strollers. We sat on the edge of the fountain. I was not as strong as Vito or Michael Corleone, and their bargaining skills had not rubbed off on me. I pleaded with him. I said, "You're killing me. I don't have any money, and I have to keep paying for lawyers because you keep suing me." It felt so punitive. "Why do you want to do that to me?" I asked. "I didn't do anything to you. What can we do to figure this out?"

He said, "If you've got a book or a script you'd like to make, could you send it to us first?"

"What else?" I asked.

He said, "That's it."

I said, "Okay, deal." I was flying inside. Men in suits scared me. I never knew what they were talking about—my attitude was always, "Take it, take it." I just didn't have the know-how to negotiate with them, and I had to learn to be smart in this arena.

Before *The Godfather* had its premiere in New York, I had seen it only once, a few months earlier, when Francis had shown me an unfinished cut. At the end of that screening, I gave Francis notes on my performance, and he looked at me with an expression of quasi-disgust. Of course when I'm looking at an unfinished film, I can't help seeing things that I might do differently. But you'd think I would understand that it was not my place to say this to the director of the film, who had just spent the last year of his life dangling from the edge of a cliff by his fingernails to get it made. I was insensitive: he had the grace to show it to me and I came in worried about my performance and not the great film he had made. Sometimes you're a little unconscious as a young actor. You have other things on your mind, and all forms of grace and etiquette go out the window due to your vain impulses and stupid ego. I've seen it in others, I must say. I hope I'm not still that way, but the jury's out on that one.

I went to *The Godfather* premiere at the Loew's State Theatre in

Times Square wearing a bow tie the size of my head. I brought Jill, my grandmother, my aunt, and my cousin Mark, who was like my brother. It was like attending the christening of a ship, so stilted and strangely formal. All that was missing was someone breaking a bottle of champagne across the bow. I only remember standing on a platform with my costars, being asked questions by the press that I couldn't answer. Then we got in our seats, but I didn't watch the movie. I didn't want to see the finished product. As soon as the lights went out, I went out.

You see, I had all kinds of feelings about myself in relation to film. I could never watch myself on-screen while other people were watching me. It was a bit disconcerting and it made me shy, almost embarrassed. As a younger actor, I guess I needed attention and didn't want it at the same time. It's a bit of a paradox, I know, so I tried to avoid putting myself in that situation. Mercifully, I have changed. It's like how I learned to get over my fear of flying—I just stopped caring. There's a speech in *Hamlet* that comes to mind:

> Not a whit, we defy augury; there's a special providence in the fall of a sparrow. If it be now, 'tis not to come; if it be not to come, it will be now; if it be not now, yet it will come: the readiness is all. Since no man knows aught of what he leaves, what is't to leave betimes?

I left the theater and went around the corner to a bar on Forty-Fourth Street with Al Ruddy and a couple of other people who had worked on the film. I spent the whole night drinking, just getting soused. That was the perfect word for it—*soused*—when you can't drink anymore and you keep drinking anyway. It's shocking that

I remember anything else from that night, but what I do remember is that when I got back to the St. Regis Hotel for the after-party, I caught a glimpse of Ali McGraw, and I thought to myself, That simply is the most beautiful person I've ever seen in my life. It is startling that there are people who have that kind of skin. It was mythical.

I almost went my whole life without ever seeing *The Godfather* in its entirety. I don't know why. Maybe I felt that because I was in it, I wouldn't be a good audience for it. Over the years, of course, I'd catch a part of it here or there on TV, and once you're watching it, it's hard to turn it off.

But then I recently watched *The Godfather* at a screening for its fiftieth anniversary at the Dolby Theatre in Hollywood, where a restored print was beautifully projected, with crisp, perfect sound. The whole experience was so uplifting. There's not a scene in the film where there aren't two or three things going on. There's not a dull moment in it, it's constantly telling a story. There was so much that I was struck by. Take the scene where Don Vito gets out of the hospital, after having been shot. Marlon is in his bed, and they have the kids' get-well-soon cards all over him. And Robert Duvall and Jimmy Caan and a few other guys have gathered around the bed. Marlon is going to ask, what happened to Michael, his youngest son and his hope for legitimacy? They tell him Michael killed Sollozzo and had to flee to Sicily. The angle at which the scene is shot is so brilliant. There's a look of such dejection on Brando's face when he turns his head and waves his hand to indicate he's heard enough. Dick Smith did such an amazing job with Marlon's makeup that you can actually see marks on Brando's face; you can see he has been through so much and you can feel the momentous mountain that has been climbed. It was so thought out and meticulous, these details get under your skin. They structured that shot in such a way that tells you everything you need to know. The film is full of moments like that.

But back in 1972, the effect that the film's release had on me was immediate. It happened at light speed. Everything changed. A few weeks after it came out, I was walking on the street and a middle-aged woman came up to me and kissed my hand and called me "Godfather." Another time, I went into a grocery store to get a container of coffee to go while Charlie waited for me outside on the sidewalk. And a woman approached him and asked, "Is that Al Pacino?" He said to her, "Yeah." She said, "Oh, really? He's Al Pacino?" He said to her, "Well, somebody's gotta be."

The film had not been out that long, so I continued to go about my normal daily life as if nothing had changed. One day I was standing at a curb, waiting for the light to change, and this pretty redhead was standing there with me. I looked at her. She looked at me. I said, "Hi." She said, "Hi, Michael." And I just went, *Whoa*. Oh my God. I am not safe. Anonymity, sweet pea, the light of my life, my survival tool—that's gone now. You don't appreciate it till you lose it.

5

Grown-ups Don't Do Things Like This

Fame, as my friend Heathcote Williams said, is the perversion of the natural human instinct for validation and attention. It was so ephemeral and so strange. As an actor I had been trying to shine a light on people I was observing and characters I was playing. Instead, it felt like all the lights were shining on me, and I couldn't see out. I know that we are now living in a different time and fame carries a different connotation, but a half century ago, it just hit me hard. There are few things more boring than a famous person complaining about fame, so I won't belabor it, though I'm tempted.

I saw a picture of myself in the newspaper just once before I did *The Godfather*. It was when I was in *The Indian Wants the Bronx*. I was in Montauk with Marty Bregman and some prominent New York elected official. The next day, I'm reading *The New York Times*, and I stumble on a photo of the three of us—Marty Bregman, this white-haired guy from the government, and me. I was wearing a sort of Russian hat, and I had hurt my knee so I was walking with a cane. I couldn't get perspective on what I was looking at. Was that supposed to be me? I was a stranger to myself. I felt something new, and I was afraid of it. I wanted to stand up there and say to everybody, "Hey, that's not me! I've got a photo—here I am, when I was eleven. *This* is me!" These were still the days when I was working as a building superintendent, only recently past my stint with homelessness.

Fame is a different thing today. People want it, they chase after it. They think it's like winning the lottery. But you pay for it in other ways. To this day, when I speak with acting students, someone will invariably ask me, "How did you get to be so famous?" I just say, "I was in *The Godfather*, man." What do you expect? If you were in it, you'd be famous. My reaction to its success was to distance myself from the film and the performance I gave in it. I put a wedge between it and me. I told myself I had nothing to do with it. There was a good part for me in it, I had some sense of it, and I played it. But I had Coppola, and Coppola is a miracle. He made that movie.

I was leery of the media glare that came with film roles. I saw the future for myself when I did repertory theater. These were plays that could change my life; these playwrights were prophets. They made me a better actor, gave me an education, offered me a deeper understanding of the world, and filled me with joy. Who wouldn't be satisfied with that? I remember feeling I could be perfectly content doing just that. I'd wind up marrying a seamstress and we'd have ten kids. It was a strange fantasy but it gave me some hope. I said as much at the time in an interview with *The New York Times* before *The Godfather* had made me a big star. Years pass and opinions change, which is why it's kind of ridiculous to have an opinion. But the bottom line is, I meant it then, and if I had the opportunity, I'd say that again. Maybe eight kids instead of ten.

But I would not end up having that life with Jill. She was a great actress and getting more work of her own—we were separated a lot, even before *The Godfather* made me this famous person overnight. Our relationship didn't end with desperate arguing and seething disagreement. We liked each other and had been together nearly five years. She went off and did films of her own, and became very popular a few years later with *An Unmarried Woman*, which she did for Paul Mazursky. She and I lived in the same area and were apt to run into each other, so we kept up a relatively consistent contact. We remained friends and the feelings we had were always there.

Meanwhile, *The Godfather* followed me everywhere I went and overshadowed everything I did. I was shy about it, and the world wouldn't let me be shy.

I was absolutely confounded by all the commotion. After *The Godfather*, they would have let me play anything. They offered me the role of Han Solo in *Star Wars*. So there I am, reading *Star Wars*. I gave it to Charlie. I said, "Charlie, I can't make anything out of this." He calls me back. "Neither can I." So I didn't do it.

There are parts I just wouldn't know what to do with in a million years. Get anybody but me. Sometimes I think, at least take a look at the part. Maybe it will click if I work on it—sometimes you can get there. The whole point of acting class, the Actors Studio, and repertory theater was picking things I didn't necessarily feel right for. Sometimes my mind needs expanding. Maybe I'll make a connection in a role, and I won't know until I try.

But there are other times when I just say, wow, I actually *want* to do that. Forget about can or can't—that's different. Sometimes I get a part and have a feeling for it, and there's something, *boom-ba-boom*, in and around me. I really like that. I *want* to do that. But that happens as rarely as I get a toothache.

Back then I had to tell myself to be careful. Don't just do anything because they pay you money. Over time, I turned down Ingmar Bergman. I turned down Bernardo Bertolucci. Fellini. Pontecorvo. Can you imagine saying no to these people? More than anything in my heart, I wanted to work with them. I didn't turn *them* down—I just couldn't be in the movies they were making because I didn't relate to the part.

They offered me the role of Billy the Kid in Sam Peckinpah's *Pat Garrett and Billy the Kid*. I loved Peckinpah. One of the greatest directors ever. Could you imagine doing a movie and getting to act with Bob Dylan? And who wouldn't want to play Billy the Kid? I thought that was something I could do. Then I read the script, and I wanted to do some rewrites, correcting the script with Peckinpah, the way I usually work with directors. I could just see it. I thought, I'm not getting on any horses. They're too big. I'll be down in Mexico with Peckinpah, and I'll probably die of alcohol poisoning because I'd be around it so much. And I passed on it.

But I could only go so long just drinking and having fun. I wouldn't even call it fun, just being unconscious. At a certain point I had to do something else.

⟨⬧⟩

I WAS STANDING IN A FIELD IN BAKERSFIELD, CALIFORNIA. THE temperature was about 120 degrees, or that's what it felt like to me. I'm watching Gene Hackman walk down the side of a sandy white hill the size of a mountain. It was a beautifully photographed shot: a steel-gray sky hanging overhead, unspoiled pastures in front of him, a lone tree on the hilltop. Gene was moving so slowly that the image in front of me hardly seemed to be changing. I could have been looking at a piece of artwork. It took him a few minutes to come down this hill and slip himself through a chicken-wire fence around the field. Despite the heat, he's wearing three coats and all these layers of clothes underneath because his character is a vagabond who likes to stay warm. When the audience watches this scene later, they won't know how hot it was outside when we filmed it. And once Gene was done with this routine, he had to film another take, so he would turn around, go back up the hill, and walk back down again.

I was about thirty-two years old. I thought, Is this the strangest thing I've ever witnessed? This man is in his forties. And he's in these three coats, pretending to go down this big hill, in this heat. And he would do it over and over. Down the hill. Up the hill. Down the hill. He seemed to relish it too. I just could not believe it. This is my profession? This is what actors do? Gene's a grown-up. Grown-ups don't do things like this.

I, of course, didn't want to do *Scarecrow*, my first film role after *The Godfather*. I had gotten comfortable in New York, didn't want to leave the city and my little gang of friends there. But Charlie read the screenplay, by Garry Michael White, about a couple of drifters rambling their way across the country. It was a little bit *Waiting for Godot* and a little bit *Of Mice and Men*, and he thought it was a good text. It was directed by Jerry Schatzberg, who I had worked with on *The Panic in Needle Park*, and that was really good.

And I would costar with Gene Hackman, who had just won the Oscar for *The French Connection*. I don't know if I was consciously choosing something that was very different from *The Godfather*, something simple and small to get me away from the glare of the limelight. But the character I was playing, a fellow wanderer who went by the name of Lion, was a little crazy and silly. He was a poor kid who didn't have anybody, and I loved that fragility in the character.

As the production made its way eastward, it was clear that Gene and I were worlds apart. He was ten years older than me, very funny, a great actor, and a good guy. But that doesn't always mean that you can make harmony together. We weren't fighting at all. There just was an awkwardness between us. I'll never understand why. No one gets along with everybody. Usually with actors and actresses, you keep a politic distance while you're working together, and then you go off in different directions. Every once in a while we find someone in life that we connect with. A lot of guys took me under their wing on *The Godfather* and made me comfortable. I had a lifetime of acting, so I didn't need anybody to tell me how to do it. Honestly, I didn't need guidance. Gene was a bit taciturn, and there was no real communion between us except in the roles we had. We worked. I think Gene might have thought I was immature because I was so crazy wild. And I think he might have been right, really.

I got along really well with Gene Hackman's younger brother, Richard, who had a small role in the film. We were a couple of guys who liked to drink and party. The two of us went carousing around late at night, and I'd show up on set the next morning on two hours' sleep. My face would be so flabby and swollen from all the drinking that it looked like one of those big beach balls they throw around in Central Park.

We'd go nightclubbing all the time. Richard had a conga drum with him, and if we could find a spot with a little stage, in Denver or in Detroit, we would get up there, and he'd play the conga while I played harmonica and a little conga too. We never rehearsed or put the slightest effort into our act. Because I was now famous, these places would let me go on and dance. I actually wasn't bad. My dad was a prize-winning dancer, and I think I was born with his natural flair for it.

One night, somewhere in our cross-country journey, I got so drunk that I could not find my way home. A woman said to me, "Oh, I'll drive you home." And without a second thought, I got into her car with her. But as we drove, even in my daze, I could recognize that she was not taking me back to where I was staying. I said to her, "What is going on here?" And she said straight out, "I'm kidnapping you."

This was not some aggressive flirtation. I was well-known. I had done *The Godfather*. But I am from the South Bronx. When I see some crazy person trying to do something to me, I know how to escape. I said, "No, you're not. I'm getting out." She said, "No, no," and she kept driving. I opened the door as if to jump out of the car. I was a little drunk, but I was ready to leap from a moving car if I had to. This ain't happening to me, man. And she closed the door and took me home. I guess this could have been in Colorado. I don't know their habits out there.

I was doing a scene for the film where I was walking on a trestle, and I fell through it and hurt my knee. It swelled up like a melon, and they sent me to the hospital. Gene Hackman, to his credit, came and visited me there. He told me a little about his life, how he'd come from a broken home and lost his mother young when she died in a house fire. Most of us actors, we've had hellish times, but here we are.

Because my memory of making *Scarecrow* was not a good one, I didn't care for it when I first saw it. It wasn't a commercial success, though it won the grand prize at the Cannes Film Festival, the equivalent of the Palme d'Or. I saw it recently, and I was surprised at how powerful it was, how strongly I felt its impact. But at the time I remember us finishing the shoot seventeen days ahead of schedule. And all I kept thinking was, I don't want to make this film either. I want to go home too. But our sanity is in finishing this film correctly. That's why we're all there in the first place. Don't even do it if you're not going to do it the way it is supposed to be done.

✕✧✕

AFTER *SCARECROW*, I FELT DESPERATE TO BE BACK ONSTAGE. I turned to my friend David Wheeler, who ran the Theatre Company of Boston and who for the longest time had wanted me to play Richard III. So I went to Boston for that adventure, which wound up being one of the more rewarding things to happen to me since *The Indian Wants the Bronx*. Richard III is one of those classic roles that has made the reputations of actors from Edmund Kean to John Barrymore to Laurence Olivier. It would be the first Shakespeare play I did in front of a real audience and the continuation of my journey in learning about the character.

The Actors Studio is where my connection to *Richard III* started. When I was still an unknown, I did everything and anything at the Actors Studio that the commercial world would never give me a part in. I did musicals there; I did Hamlet; I did Richard with Francesca De Sapio as my Lady Anne. This new *Richard* was coming six or seven years after I did it at the Actors Studio, when my life was in a different place. David Wheeler was a consummate director with a wonderful reputation and a man I adored, and our relationship was one of the more important ones I've had in terms of my vocation. During a frigid winter in Boston, we entered into the world of Shakespeare and *Richard III*. It was a very interesting rehearsal period, full of experiments and improvisations. Charlie came up to help me work on the part, and his wife, Penny, was there playing Lady Anne.

It was also a time that I associate with my romance with Tuesday Weld. We liked each other a lot. We'd just sit in bars and drink Brandy Alexanders. I brought her to Boston with me. The theater company asked me, "Hey, Tuesday's here. She's an actress, maybe she could play Elizabeth?" I thought, Uh-oh. I had problems with that. And I did something that I somewhat regret. I already had so much work to do at that stage, and to add someone that you're having a love affair with? It always affects things. I just thought our relationship couldn't hold up under that—living together and doing a play. I thought it would be too overwhelming for me. Whether I was right, I'll never know. I just look back at it and wish I had said, "Yes, let her do it." But I put a halt to it.

Unfortunately, the three weeks of rehearsal were not enough, and I became ill with a high fever. There was Charlie at the foot of my bed, going over the lines with me. Charlie had come to one of the rehearsals and was very enthusiastic about the progress we were making. If we had been doing the play in the sixties, in some derelict theater in Greenwich Village, I guess it might have worked. But the Loeb Drama Center in Cambridge was quite a leap. We had no real set. It was a lot of iron bars on some piece of sculpture that didn't mean anything. I didn't understand it, and I still was trying to figure out where I was going with my performance.

One night I came out for the second act and half the audience was gone. I thought we were finished. I said, "I'm going back to New York." David Wheeler said, "Don't go back to New York. You're here. Do it, Al." He said we needed to give it more time. But where? What goes into a play is everything. If you don't have the right set, the right cast, the right atmosphere, you've got nothing. Even if it's Shakespeare.

David told me I should take a look at the Church of the Covenant. I came upon it one night during a brisk walk on Newbury Street. It's a beautiful old Gothic cathedral with high ceilings and huge stained-glass windows. Its steeple stands out for miles; inside, its ceilings seem to go up to the heavens. You had to pause for a few seconds after you said each line, there was so much echo. It just made everything feel so portentous.

Every night, I would be in the church rectory, dressing to go on. My frame of mind was borderline crazy. My career in New York was taking off, and *The Godfather* was exploding, but I was up here in Boston, doing Richard now for the second time, trying to move on from the experience at the Loeb. I didn't know it, but alcoholism was creeping up on me, and I was struggling in my usual way with my romantic relationship. My general thought was, Where is all of this going? I felt in turmoil, and at the same time, I felt liberated. I brought that wildness to Richard, who is close to that state himself. Without all these things going on, the character might not have been so accessible to me.

I had this intern from Harvard who was assigned to be my assistant and work with me. She was a stocky little Italian girl who, I imagined, could actually have picked me up and thrown me on the stage. We set up a sort of game we'd play, one that had started out with me putting her on but that had turned into a preshow ritual. She would come to me and say, "Al, fifteen minutes to curtain." I'd say, "Who the fuck are you?" And she'd say, "I'm the assistant, don't make a fuss." Don't make a fuss? You think I'm going on there? *You're* going on in this play. She'd come back to say ten minutes. Then five minutes. We would take the charade seriously, always saying the same stuff. Then she would roll up her sleeves and start chasing me around this table. "You've got to go out there." Throwing things at me. I'd shout back at her, "I'm going to kill you!"

Then I had to go out there, hump and all, limping my way to make my entrance, in a state of absolute and utter confusion. My heart would be pumping with adrenaline as I rose from the pulpit, just sneaking my head up, where I would hiss into a little microphone: "Now is the winter of our discontent." You want to talk about Method acting? I did the greatest Richard I've ever done.

When we started performing the play there, I was getting five or six curtain calls a night—each time I would take my bows, stand in the wings, and then return to the stage just to bow again—and not because I was so pretty. It was because the audience had an experience watching that production. It had them. It worked because we had the ambiance of the church; the austerity of that atmosphere brought it to life. And it never worked that well again.

Six years later I came to Broadway to do *Richard III* once more. And of course we weren't in that church anymore. We had no vision, no concept. We were doing it at a proscenium theater with that old schlub of a set that we had at the Loeb. And the play was not taking place. I was trying to repeat myself, but it had been a while since I'd done it, and I was doing everything wrong. The reviews said—and I don't read reviews, but they always get back to you—"Pacino sets Shakespeare back 50 years in this country." I wondered why they didn't say a hundred years.

At the end of a performance one night I came back to my dressing room. I was exhausted. After three hours of playing Richard on that stage, I thought I had earned the right to sit there, bone-eyed and out of it, in my little armchair. And I looked up and there was Jacqueline Kennedy Onassis, who had come backstage with a young woman I believe was her daughter, Caroline, to see me. She was so elegant and beautiful, just radiating class. And as I slumped in my chair, I put out my hand for her to kiss it.

God only knows what I was thinking. Why would I ever do that? Please tell me, what's wrong with me? I must have believed I was dreaming that Jackie Onassis was there. Perhaps I was hallucinating that she was doing the play with me, so she was my queen— and as the queen, after all, she must now kiss the hand of the king. David Wheeler told me afterward that I was like the prizefighter who comes back to the showers and asks, "Who won?" And his trainer says, "You did, schmuck." I did? This happens. You get so self-absorbed when you're an actor. When you're coming back from the stage after performing one of the greatest plays of all time, you're liable to do anything.

After that, I learned: take a little bit of time. Have them say,

"Pacino's in the middle of taking off his clothes," or something. "Could you give him five minutes? I've got to slap him around and wake him up, because he thinks he's someplace else."

>I<◆>I<

JUST AS WE WERE OPENING *RICHARD III* IN BOSTON AT THE CHURCH of the Covenant, I learned I had gotten an Academy Award nomination for my performance in *The Godfather*. It was my first, and for all I knew maybe the only one I'd ever receive. A few weeks earlier I found out I had won an award from the National Board of Review, which had named me Best Supporting Actor. That seemed like a big enough deal, although I could never figure out why they didn't also give Best Actor to Brando. They chose Peter O'Toole instead, and I have nothing but love for Peter O'Toole, but come on—Marlon Brando in *The Godfather*, that was a game changer.

It's always pleasurable to be acknowledged for your work. It doesn't make you mad. Show me someone who says, "I got an Oscar nomination—fuck them, they don't know what they're doing."

I've only recently learned that the perception in the industry was that I snubbed the Oscars—that I didn't attend the ceremony because I was nominated for *The Godfather* as a supporting actor and not as a leading man. That somehow I felt slighted because I thought I deserved to be nominated in the same category as Marlon. Can you imagine that was a rumor that exploded at the time, and I only found out about it recently, all these years later? It explains a lot of the distance I felt when I came out to Hollywood to visit and to work. It was appalling to learn it now, having missed all these opportunities to deny it, not even knowing that this is what people thought of me. I feel I should go up to Forest Lawn Memorial Park, where a lot of the Hollywood old-timers are lying in peace, run around the cemetery, and start yapping aloud to the gravestones, "Hey, man, I wanted to be there! I was just afraid!"

These are the kinds of things that can affect your life in Hollywood. It starts a domino effect. In my particular business, people do have a self-interest in the talent they represent—they could have taken the stance that I was equal to Brando, to pump up the volume a little and elevate that image. If I hired a private investigator to find out where this fictitious rumor started, that could be a possibility, but to this day I don't really know how it happened. Assumptions spread, then those assumptions turn into opinions and those opinions turn into stone and you can't ever penetrate or change them. That's a mouthful, but I do believe that's what's going on most of the time in our world. Fabrications and rumors turn into facts. We're poor little lambs who have lost our way, *baa baa baa*.

Truth be told, I was so concerned with staying out of everything when I was younger. I thought, The less you know about me, the better chance I'll have that you will appreciate what I do when I'm playing a role. So I stayed quiet. But they had me down as some sort of arrogant snob, and that became lore. Like Iago said: "Reputation is an idle and most false imposition, oft got without merit and lost without deserving. You have no reputation at all, unless you repute yourself such a loser."

There was something in the air at that time. Actors were rebelling against the Hollywood thing. It was practically as much of a tradition not to go to the Oscars as it was to go to them. Richard Burton and Elizabeth Taylor didn't go. George C. Scott didn't go.

Marlon turned down his award and sent Sacheen Littlefeather to protest. I said I was working onstage at the time of the ceremony. But I still could have gone—everyone knows they give you time off when you have an Oscar nomination. I was a bit afraid of flying, and I knew I'd have to accompany my flight with half a pint of Scotch. But my excuses were weak, and no one bought them. Truth is, I was overwhelmed by the newness of all this. I was young, younger than even my years, and I was just afraid to go. If you want to be honest—and I don't know if I do—I think I was playing the Garbo card too. I was reclusive and I just wanted to be alone.

)X(+)X(

AT THE TIME IT WAS HAPPENING, THE TRUE STORY OF FRANK SERpico and the Knapp Commission was not on my radar at all. Serpico was one of the first cops to talk about the corruption he saw and chip away at that citadel; you can't really make a dent in it, but he tried. I just wasn't aware of that stuff. Now Marty Bregman wanted me to play Serpico in a movie he was developing about him. If I did it, Bregman would be both my manager and a producer on the film. Of course there's a conflict of interest. There's someone getting paid to produce it while he's getting a percentage from you. But I thought what was good about the arrangement made up for it. Because Marty knew me. He was my partner. He was someone I knew I could talk to. And he would listen.

Peter Maas had written a biography of Serpico, and I was given a film treatment to look at that had been made from his book. Let me tell you, it read like this: He does this. Then he does that. Then he goes here. Then he goes there. Like the book I'm writing now. You read it and you say, well, yes? It's like saying, Hamlet comes home. Then he sees his father. Then he goes to his mother. Yeah, nice. So it didn't interest me. I needed more than that.

But then I met Frank Serpico in Bregman's office. Bregman had set it up. I took one look at Frank and I knew. I said, I can play him. I've got to play him. I saw it in his eyes, and I thought, I want to be that. I'm often offered real people, and I turn them down. I didn't want to be them. Not because they're bad or good. Just because I didn't feel any connection to them.

I spent more time with Frank that summer before we made the film. He came to visit me at a house I was renting in Montauk. We were sitting on my deck, looking at the waves coming in. Finally I said something to him that he'd probably heard a thousand times before. "Frank, why didn't you take those payoffs?" I asked him. "Just take that money and give your share away if you didn't want to keep it?" He said to me, "Al, if I did that"—long pause—"who would I be when I listen to Beethoven?" There was something about that statement that just made me want to play him.

Together Waldo Salt and Norman Wexler wrote a great script, and then we got John Avildsen to direct. He had made some very good movies up to that point, and would later go on to direct *Rocky*. He was fine by me. I was starting to read other actors with him, working as a sort of stage manager at their auditions. And then one day Avildsen didn't show up. He had been fired. That was how Marty Bregman did it. I was sitting there, thinking, what the fuck? I had no idea why he fired this guy, because we hadn't even started rehearsing yet. Avildsen was just starting to talk about how he wanted to make the film. I was so deep in the process of finding the Serpico character for myself, figuring out how I'd play him and growing a beard, that that became my whole world. I was unconscious of anything else involved in the creation of the film. I didn't even know how much money I was making; Marty would give me two hundred dollars a week for taxicabs and that was good enough for me.

Dino De Laurentiis was the big-time producer who owned the rights to Peter Maas's book. He was running the show on this project, and he went berserk when he found out Bregman did this. He would not let Marty go out and find us another director after that. De Laurentiis said that the only way we're going to go on with this film is if you—meaning me, Pacino—get us the new director.

It never can go smoothly, can it? Where do I go to get a director? I've never hired one in my life. I've only starred in three films. I said, "Marty, I don't know how to interview anybody. This is completely crazy." He said, "No, you've got to do it. That's it." So now I had to go to California. I was very unhappy. I went to San Francisco to talk to Peter Yates, who made *Bullitt*. I went to LA to talk to Mark Rydell. I wound up in the Beverly Wilshire Hotel, in what I called the Pompous Room—I didn't know any other name for it. I'm talking to some guy who's sort of quiet like me, who's young and just starting out, but he's hot off an art film of sorts called *Mean Streets*, which I hadn't seen yet, and I'm too busy looking at the tables with red and green felt and the wallpaper with ducks and peacocks on them to understand that I'm speaking to one of our finest filmmakers ever, Martin Scorsese. I was just dizzy and I don't think we hardly said a word to each other. I guess he must have known I didn't know my ass from my elbow when it came to hiring a director.

I came home from the trip empty-handed, but then I met with Sidney Lumet. His career had taken a little bit of a curve at the time. You know how it is in this business: you're hot, you're not. But he was still one of our greatest directors. In 1960, he had directed Jason Robards Jr. in what was the greatest living performance I ever saw, in Eugene O'Neill's *The Iceman Cometh*. It was adapted from the production that José Quintero had directed at Circle in the Square Theatre a few years earlier, and Lumet's film of it ran on public television as part of a series called *The Play of the Week*. This is a three-and-a-half-hour play that they showed every night of the week, and I at nineteen years old watched it in my South Bronx apartment every night it was shown, because what Robards does simply boggles the mind. I saw it again recently, because I was wondering, does it still have that impact? Oh my God, it does. It simply soars. If three and a half hours is too long for you, you can watch it on YouTube in stages. It certainly changed Robards's life, and mine too. And it will change yours as well.

So I went out to Lumet's place in East Hampton to see if he'd be the right director for *Serpico*, and I'm still as dumb as a donut. I don't know what I'm doing. I'm looking around his home. And he starts—kind of, in a way—criticizing me. He said, "Your work in things, I don't know. I have a problem with it sometimes. I do things a little different." As if to say, hey, kid, you're not so great. And I'm thinking, this guy's insulting me. I don't even know him. And he wants the job? He wants to work with *me*? But directors have insulted me throughout my life.

I didn't defend myself, mercifully, because I didn't know how. He was my superior intellectually, and decent in so many ways. I think he might have felt, what is this little schmuck interviewing me for? I know he did. Who wouldn't? I suppose all the other directors did, too, but he was older, and he had a kind of authority and an overwhelming sense of experience. He didn't abuse me. But he wasn't impressed at all with what I had done. And I saw his work, and I thought, What the hell, this guy's great. That's the guy I like. Sure enough, they hired him.

When I was preparing for *Serpico*, I went on a ride with a bunch of cops to see how they did it. My squad was called in to investigate a possible robbery in progress in a tenement building. They all ran up the stairs with their guns drawn, and that was as far as I went. Because they didn't know what they would be in for when they got to the door. I said to myself, That was the first and last time I was going to do that.

I didn't need to, really. I had the real Frank Serpico as my resource, who was very smart and very helpful. I could say to him, "What did you do here? What did you do when this happened to you?" He would tell me, and I'd go to Sidney and say, "Listen to what he did. Maybe we could do a scene like that?"

During the summer we were making the movie, I was taking a taxi to a location where we were going to film, and I was wearing my *Serpico* clothes. We ended up behind a truck that started to belch out huge blasts of exhaust. As its fumes filled the air, I got so pissed off that I told the cab driver to get up close to the truck, and as I rolled down the window, I flashed my *Serpico* badge and shouted, "Pull over to the side of the road, you son of a bitch. You're polluting the air." As if the air wasn't polluted enough already. And then I realized what I was doing. I said to myself, Are you impersonating an officer, Al? No, I was just being a New Yorker. I told the cabbie, "You'd better keep going."

X✦X

I WAS STILL DATING TUESDAY WELD WHEN I STARTED WORKING ON
Serpico. I would get up each morning and go to work on a location.
Then at night I was out drinking with her. I had already been shooting for a couple of weeks, and I knew how much the work was going
to ask of me. That put pressure on the relationship, and it was clear
to me that we couldn't last much longer. We were young enough,
and we hadn't been together long enough, so I guess I thought I
saw the handwriting on the wall, so to speak, that this would be
the time for us to break up. I couldn't be in this film and be with
someone at the same time.

I could see a pattern already starting in me, some innate understanding that work is work, and romance and life come second.
I hear it said a lot about people who are so engaged in what they do
and so focused. They lose important relationships because of their
connection to their work and their need to go in 100 percent. I can
happily say that I'm not like that anymore, but at that time, I was
already beginning to reach that conclusion about myself.

I took refuge in my work on *Serpico*. The best part of filmmaking is the toast before you start shooting. You're a cheery bunch,
all talking about how lucky you are to be doing what you're doing.
For *Serpico*, we held it in the home of Dino De Laurentiis, who had
this great apartment at the tippy top of a building on Central Park
South. It had windows from floor to ceiling. You could see China
from his place. I felt like I had arrived. Peter Maas was there. We
had Waldo Salt and Norman Wexler, Sidney Lumet and Marty
Bregman. Not a woman in sight. There the six of us looked like lit-

tle Lego people standing in the center of all this opulence. Everybody had gathered around for the toast, patting each other on the back and putting each other down with a wink after each little quip. "Will he like me?" "Will he love me?" The kind of stuff I call pebble talk—but necessary. Then I stopped the conversation cold. I said, "Guys, I know this is premature, but I think I came up with the musical score for the film." They said, "Excuse me?" I said, "Yeah. It just came over me. Maybe you guys'll like it." And they said, "Well, can we hear it?"

We were standing around in a circle. I said, "Here's how I hear it. There's no music for the first thirty minutes, just the sounds of the streets and everything else. And then as the story of Serpico gets more and more intense with the graft, the money, and the corruption, the music starts to build, and there's this slight, almost barely audible chorus." And I began to sing:

SER-pi-co
SER-pi-co
SER-pi-co, *Serrrrrr*-pi-co
Serrrrrr-pi-co
Serrrrrr-pi-co

There was dead silence. They were stunned. And I just looked at them, waiting for the laugh. Bregman had to turn to them and say, in the driest speaking voice I'd ever heard him use, "He's joking." I remained in that mood pretty much all the time.

I was given a driver who would pick me up every day, take me to wherever we were filming, and bring me home at night. He was an older guy, and I really liked him, but he hated the job. He hated being a driver, hated being stuck in traffic, and he was always upset. I used to kid him just to see if I could get a rise out of him. On one ride he said to me, "Hey, Al. I gotta pee so bad. You mind, I go in this restaurant, drain the pony?" I said, "Hey, Eddie, I didn't even know you had a pony. I've never seen it. Go ahead, don't mind me." He pulled in front of the restaurant and got out of the car with the key in the ignition and the engine still running. As soon as he did, I jumped in the front seat and took off with the car. But I only drove around the corner so I could spy on him as he came out of the restaurant and watch his silent bafflement as he tried to figure out whether his car and the star of the film had just been stolen. He looked around, and all of a sudden I pulled up and said to him, "Come on, Eddie, let's go! I'm going to drive you now!" He said, "You son of a bitch," and we both laughed. I did a lot of antics like that during that film.

When *Serpico* was finished filming, I went out drinking with Charlie at this swanky bar on Madison Avenue, around the corner from where I was living at the time. Charlie and I were ossified, and I met this woman who was also a little loaded. She was a tall girl with a wild black dress and—it was the particular era—six-inch heels. Charlie went home, and I took her up to my apartment, where I passed out in my bed, fully clothed. So did she, six-inch heels and all. The two of us didn't do anything. I woke up the next morning, and I thought to myself, Who the fuck is that? Where am I? "Oh God," I said out loud. "I'm late. I'm late." "Late to what?" she said. I said to her, "They're having a screening of a movie I just did, and I have to go and give the ol' lazy feedback." She said, "Oh, really?" I said, "Yeah, come with me. I could use some more feedback." I was still drunk.

I went across town to a screening room where they were about to show the first rough cut of *Serpico* and walked in with this girl in her black dress and her six-inch heels. And they were all there: Sidney Lumet, Dino De Laurentiis, and Dede Allen, the great film editor who had worked on *The Hustler* and *Bonnie and Clyde*. Marty Bregman was there, and he was steaming. But Sidney gave me the old shrug, as if to say, "He's an actor and this is what actors do." He had made a lot of films, and he had seen far worse than this. The room went dark and the film played, and afterward I asked this girl how she felt about it. I don't recall her exact words, but I remember her attitude was one of general indifference.

)(✦)(

SERPICO TURNED OUT PRETTY GOOD. IT GOT ME MY SECOND OSCAR nomination, and Marty Bregman had done everything for me and for this film, so I couldn't not go to the ceremony. But I was still terrified. I got on the plane with Marty, and I brought Charlie with me, as well as Diane Keaton, who I was making *The Godfather: Part II* with at the time. Of course I got stoned.

After arriving in Los Angeles, I was brought into a big, beautiful bathroom to make myself presentable and I took a shower. I had just learned what the wet look was, and when I came out of the shower and saw my hair still soaked and sopping, I thought it looked good on me. Bregman saw it and offered his verdict: "You fucking idiot." He sat there with me, frantically blow-drying my hair before the show started. I wasn't often drunk in front of Bregman, and I'm not sure he even knew I had an issue with drinking at the time. But I was in the bag and popping Valium, and I'm laughing while he's shooting hot air at me. I was pathetic. As my hair dried out more and more, it rose higher and higher, like a soufflé. I had friends back in New York who watched the show on TV, who said that my hair was the only part of me they could see. They said, Al, what the fuck was on your head?

We got to the auditorium where the Oscars were being held and people seemed to be startled by me. One of the first people I saw there was Jack Valenti, the head of the Motion Picture Association, who had worked for LBJ. He had a shocked look on his face like, what are you doing here? I thought to myself, Well, I am an actor and I got nominated, that's why I'm here, not to clean up. I can do that later, after I lose. So why is he looking at me like this? That was fifty years ago, and I couldn't understand it. But since I've come to realize how Hollywood had judged me when they thought I was giving them the cold shoulder after I got my first Oscar nomination, I get it now.

When I was seated in the audience, all those feelings came rushing back, of being in a place where I never felt like I quite belonged. You could never tell that there was anything wrong with me. That's the kind of face you put on for it.

I was sitting with Diane to my right, making little jokes about the show, and she was laughing. But then the jokes started to get a little tiresome, and I'm popping Valiums and waiting for something. To my left was Jeff Bridges. I could still tell time at that point. I looked at my watch, and I thought, This is crazy. They haven't gotten anywhere near to the Best Actor award. So I turned to Jeff, who I would come to know in the future as one of the most wonderful human beings and such a great actor. But at the time, I didn't know him at all, and I guess the impending dissipation of my altered state led me to say, "Hi, excuse me," as he looked at me like he was looking down from ten feet high. I said to him, "The hour is almost up. I guess they're not going to get to the Best Actor." He considered me like I was some poor, pathetic wretch. "It's three hours long, man. *Three hours long.*" And I said, "Oh. Thank you." I went numb after that.

I was vaguely aware when it came time to announce my category. I'm blotto. I'm in such a state that I need to go somewhere and sit quietly and have someone give me shock treatments. I thought, This can't happen. I cannot win in this room. I'm nominated against Robert Redford, Jack Nicholson, Marlon Brando, and Jack Lemmon. I had no speech because I was so sure I wasn't going to win. I was more positive about that than anything.

But then this other thought hit. It just started going through me. You know that voice: What if you *do* win? I've lived a life where terrible things like that have happened to me. It's actually possible that they'll announce my name. They're very vengeful, these Academy people. They'll probably give you the award just to fuck with you. Then I started to shake. I was so pumped up with Valium and scared of everything. They announced the names of the nominees. And then I heard—as if a light were shining in the sky and heaven was whispering to me—the presenter say the words: "Jack Lemmon for *Save the Tiger.*"

I just smiled and screamed inside myself with joy. If anybody saw me on television, they probably couldn't tell. They just saw my numb look, but inside the feelings were real. Real relief.

6

The Business We've Chosen

Mario Puzo was someone I could always rely on to tell it to me straight. One night he asked me to meet with him at the Ginger Man. It was to let me have my first look at the script he'd been working on for *The Godfather: Part II*. He passed me a copy across our table so that I could take it home to read in my own time, while I contemplated the heavy proposition of whether I wanted to return to the role of Michael Corleone and all the obligations that came with it. Before I started, there was one thing in particular he wanted me to know.

"It's crap," he said. "I don't think the script is very good. But they gave it to me to give to you. I just want to tell you."

So I said thanks. And I read it. And Mario was right. I thought, I can't do this. It's not there.

As I would later find out, Paramount had gotten Mario started on a *Part II* script before we'd even started filming the original *Godfather*. It was just in case they decided later that they wanted to make a sequel, if by some chance the movie turned out to be a hit. It was just to protect their position. Nothing great is ever produced from that.

And nothing about it sounded like *The Godfather* to me. Francis didn't want to be involved. He had turned it down, though they were still going after him. They wanted me, too, because my character was still alive at the end of the first picture. They kept coming to me with prices, and the prices kept going higher. First $100,000. Then $200,000. Then they got it up to $600,000. That was real money at that time. But I didn't like the script. Mario was a great writer, and he was going to crack it. But they wanted me to commit to something that wasn't there.

A producer on the film called me into his office in New York. He put a big bottle of Scotch on the table, and I thought, Wow, he's going to get me high. We liked each other a lot, and I started talking to him as he poured me a drink. Finally, we got down to business: "Al," he said, "what about doing *Part II*?" I said, "Well, it's always the script, isn't it?" And then he reached into his desk, and he pulled out a tin box. He said to me, "Al, what if I told you there's one million dollars in cash in that box?" I was starting to get the message. I said, "Can I give it a sniff? How about if I lift it up?" I just wanted to know what it felt like in my hands. He was looking at me, smiling, but it could have been any amount or anything at all in that box. It could have been a million bucks or packets of sugar, or it could have been empty. It was all out of my league. It was an abstraction. And it didn't make one bit of difference.

Then they brought Coppola around, giving him the producer role too. Coppola knew me. He must have told them straight out, "Stop raising his salary. He doesn't want money. He just wants a script. He'll do it." So they gave me a script with some changes from the one that Mario had given me, but still not something I could immediately commit to. It was unfinished. Charlie and I both read it and felt it wasn't there yet. Francis was annoyed: "What are you doing? You're holding me up here." I said, "No, I'm not holding you up. I just want a better script."

So Charlie and I went out to San Francisco, got in a room at the Fairmont Hotel, and we worked back and forth. We'd talk to Francis, Francis would write, bring it back, we'd talk again, write, bring it back. I don't have any idea how to write a script. I just knew that furniture was already there, but you need moving men to carry it into the house. That's what Charlie and I were. There were missing links in the story. Francis kept saying, "We can take care of that."

I knew that with Francis, we were working with an exceptional writer and a person who was out to make a great film. And hopefully it was helpful to him to have a colleague on the other side to discuss the pages and the levels it was aiming for and where it was going. It was work, and we labored, six days and six nights, on a script that was already almost there. I was grateful that he allowed this kind of thing to happen, and that he had this gift, to be able to take what we said and make it manifest.

When we left the hotel at the end of the week, Charlie looked up at the room number, 617. "I think we all made history here, Al," he said. And we were gone.

Coppola once explained to me that *The Godfather: Part II* was a kind of metaphor for what happened to second-generation Italian Americans, and I'm sure it's true of other nationalities and ethnic groups as well. A sacrifice was made for them by their parents—the first generation, the immigrant generation—so that they could have their chance at the American way of life, and it's baffling to them. They were born here, born as Americans, and they were left to figure out how to adjust.

Michael didn't have those dimensions of his father, Vito, whose character had been forged by his life in the old country and the rigors of poverty, pulling himself up by his bootstraps. And though Michael was brought into his family's brutal domain by circumstance, he could navigate it fluently. That is the person we see in the first *Godfather* film, learning that he has this gift, if you want to call it that.

Part II is about a different Michael. By the end of *Part II*, Michael is so withdrawn that he's practically mummified. But to get him to that place, I had to reconnect myself with where I had left Michael at the end of the first film, when he became that suddenly intimidating figure who could make other men gladly line up just to kiss his ring. The image that he projects at the end of the first *Godfather* is simply, who is that guy? I don't want to go near him. At least that's what I was trying to do —portray him as enigmatic and dangerous. The danger for me was in the task that lay ahead, getting myself back to where Michael already was at the end of that previous journey, and pushing myself to figure out where I would take him next.

〉◆〈

ONE OF FRANCIS AND MARIO'S BRILLIANT CREATIONS FOR *PART II* was a new rival for Michael, a veteran gangster and former associate of his father's named Hyman Roth, who comes to him in the guise of an ally and a partner. See, it's always the ones you least suspect that you have to watch out for, at least in that line of work. Hyman Roth was a take on Meyer Lansky, meant to be as smart as Michael, if not smarter. Francis had wanted Elia Kazan to play him, but Kazan turned it down, and though I read with some other unusual candidates like Samuel Fuller, the director and screen-writer, no one quite seemed to fit the bill.

Charlie was the one who suggested Lee Strasberg. Back before Charlie was an acting teacher, when he was still an actor himself, he had studied with Lee, and he always looked up to him, in the same way that I looked up to Charlie.

Francis still needed to be convinced, so I took him to a big celebration that they had for the Actors Studio. It was in a ball-room with a group of speakers all sitting up at a dais. And when it was Lee's turn to address the audience, we sat and listened to him, and he spoke with such wit and humor. He had been this esteemed instructor to Marilyn Monroe and Dustin Hoffman, but he could be as funny as Groucho Marx when he wanted to be. So Francis was won over and gave him the role, and I thought how great it was going to be—now Lee and I were going to work together, and I was going to get to know him a little better.

I suppose you could say that it added an Oedipal dimension to the story of *Part II*. I already thought of Lee like a grandfather. To Michael, Hyman Roth was a substitute father, and one he would have to kill for the sake of his own survival.

I seemed to have found and accumulated these kinds of people throughout my life, surrogates for the father I never had. Now I had three in the mix at once: there was Charlie; there was my man-ager, Marty Bregman; and there was Lee Strasberg. Whether they felt a possessiveness over me I can't pinpoint, but I have to imagine it was there. They occupied different lanes. Marty had to do with my professional progress, my success and fame and all the trimmings that came with that. Charlie had more to do with the actuality of my work and the person that it made me. I think Charlie and Marty kept a certain diplomatic distance from each other. Charlie understood Marty and respected him, recognized his power and intelligence. Marty knew that Charlie was important to my development as an actor and good for my soul. I'm sure they each had their own read of the other, and they were diplomatic enough not to air it in front of me.

Lee coming into that formula didn't necessarily complicate things further. Lee was a totally different kind of thing. Lee was always very nourishing to me, and I enjoyed his company. I was interested in him, like I am in all people who have that kind of intellectual reach and unpredictability in their viewpoint. There was a brevity and a directness in how Lee expressed himself. He kept a home on Fire Island, where he would take his family in the summer. And as the story goes, they all went swimming on a hot day, all of them but Lee, who just sat and watched the rest of them. They kept calling out to him: "Come in the water! It's great, it's warm! Why don't you come in the water?" He answered, "I think the water's fine. I just don't want to get involved."

I considered Lee a friend, but when I do the math, he wasn't really. I was a member of the Actors Studio, and I did work there that he occasionally saw, but I wasn't his star pupil or anything like that. He represented a certain artistic ideal and something to me that was familial. He would offer me cryptic advice like, "You're very sensitive, so you have to watch what you eat." But Lee saw me in a precise way.

Sonny Boy

WHEN WE WORKED TOGETHER ON *THE GODFATHER*, FRANCIS AND I were younger and greener, and that forgave a lot of the mistakes we made and the conflicts we occasionally shared. *Part II* was different. Once Francis agreed to direct it as well, I could see how so much of the responsibility for its success fell on his shoulders. We had a difficult time on *Part II*, but I still had such admiration for him, and we wanted to do what we could to work together.

When we started filming in Lake Tahoe, we began with the scenes from the party for the Communion of Michael's son. We were out in the cold one night, all of us sitting around a table with Mike Gazzo, who was so superb as Frank Pentangeli. It's so cold we're putting ice in our mouths so that smoke doesn't come out of our mouths when we talk. They had finished shooting my sides of a party scene, and now they were filming Mike Gazzo. On the take where the camera was on him, Mike shouted, "Ah, *vaffanculo!*" And he knocked over a bottle of wine. Then, hey, everybody's happy, it's a wrap. People in the scene began to leave for the night, and preparations were made to start breaking down the equipment. We're all out there in the freezing cold. And I said, "No, Francis—he didn't do that on my take. We've got to go back and just get Michael's reaction to that." We needed to see Michael as he runs a mental inventory on Frank. This is a guy who works for him. What state is he in? Is he drunk? Is he reliable? It gives a sense of how Michael manages his operations.

Now you could see Francis grit his teeth a little bit as I said this to him, and I was gritting my teeth that I had to bring it up. It meant that everybody had to come back to their places in the scene, all the gear that they started to take apart had to be put back together, and further takes would have to be filmed. It really was not my place to ask for any of this. But Francis knew that it meant I was deep into my role and thinking things through from the character's point of view. If somebody behaves that way at a table, is Michael Corleone going to react to it? Of course. Francis did it, because he knew that's what was needed. That's what working together is.

While we filmed in Tahoe, there was a guy who was put on me as my bodyguard. He was extremely short and very thin like a wire, the type of guy we used to call a wolverine. He was a real guy from the West, whose roots must have gone way back, before the Civil War. He wore a sheriff's badge, though I don't think he had been a sheriff, and he kept a gun at his side that was half his size. He completed the look with a cowboy hat. I had developed my own habit of wearing one for some reason, and when we'd go out to the bars in New York, Charlie would have to nudge me and say, "The hat, Al—you better take it off. We may get in some trouble here." Because it could encourage a small spat. The barroom brawl was always a possibility in the places we frequented, and we did get into some real skirmishes a couple of times, but we always tried to avoid it.

My bodyguard would chain-smoke cigarettes all the time, and he told me that he never slept. I grew to love him. Charlie and I once in a drunken stupor made up a story of how my guy got excited one day and shot another actor on the film who was sort of a pain in the ass with that gun of his, and they had to close down the set for a while. What inspired that story in the first place is that we had gone into one of those bars they had out there, with a lot of what we would call bear-men: half-shaven guys wearing mackinaws and smoking cigarettes that looked like cigars, looking for whatever they called trouble out there. When Charlie and I would drink, we would collapse into these spasms of laughter that got us fishy looks. But when my bodyguard walked into that bar, with that hat, that gun, and that badge, those bear-men became very quiet, almost possum-like. When they saw he was with us, we were safe. He was understandably notorious around that part of the state and he had a fierce face; he could really stare the paint off a wall. He'd shoot you as sure as looking at you, and you knew it.

A few weeks into filming they invited some of us to see some of the rushes, footage that we had shot so far. I got together at a screening room with Francis, Diane Keaton, Robert Duvall, and Gordy Willis, our great cinematographer. It was a scene of Michael and Tom Hagen talking about how they would respond to the failed attempt to have Michael assassinated. And as we watched, I did my usual thing of leaning over to Diane and cracking jokes. I whispered in her ear, "I think they're going to have to add a line in here." She said, "What?" I said, "I'm going to have to ask Bob Duvall in the scene, 'Don't mind being in the dark, Tom, but I needed to talk to you this way.'" She started laughing. Because the footage was so dark you couldn't see anything that was happening.

When the lights came back on in the screening room, everyone was quiet. Without saying a word, Robert Duvall stood up from his seat, went out the door and into the next room, a rec room that had its own kitchen. Through the silence you could hear the sounds of his muffled screaming and banging dishes. I thought he was having a kind of mini fit. I looked at Francis, who was stone-faced, and Gordy Willis was right there next to him. I said, "Francis, what are we going to do? We can't see this thing." And he said, "It's fine." I said, "Really?" He said, "Yes, it's fine." I said, "I don't think so, Francis. You can't have a scene like that." I really was upset.

Diane and I went back to my place and started drinking. I called up Robert Duvall, looking to commiserate, and said, "What are we going to do here, Robert? What the fuck is going on?" Robert answered—and this happened, Diane's my witness—he said, "My fucking makeup man." I said, "Bob, you mean you saw your makeup in that scene? I couldn't see a damn thing." I thought he was experiencing a kind of transference. He was so upset, but he couldn't bring himself to blame Francis or Gordy Willis. He had to blame somebody, so he blamed his makeup man.

The whole situation was too big and too stupid. I thought, How could I fight this? And Diane saw things similarly. I said, "What do I do here? Do I call Paramount?" But I didn't have to. A short time later we got word that we were going to shoot the scene again— something I don't like doing, but it had to be done. The studio must have seen the footage, too, so they didn't need my prodding. I guess it was good to wait.

I used music on the film periodically, maybe for a couple of scenes, to find my way back into Michael. I would go into a dressing room, put on headphones, and turn the sound up really loud while I listened to Stravinsky or Beethoven or Mozart. I would just flood my brain with it, and then I'd emerge and go perform in a scene. It was a process I came up with so I could teach myself where my brain should go—where my entire spirit should go—so I would have a sense memory of it when I filmed the scene. While

the cameras were rolling, I didn't have to hear the music anymore—
I could just go to that place in my head and it was there. I've seen
actors do this with animals, where they study the essence of a
bulldog or a swan, and they try to find an element of that in themselves. This was just an intuition I had about music, so I didn't have
to bang on tables or jump up in the air, and it seemed to serve the
role. It wasn't a technique I used on the first *Godfather* or for any
other parts I played. But it's what I needed for Michael at the time.
I never give away these kinds of secrets, but people like to know
these things.

Diane and I were always fond of each other and enjoyed each
other's company. We had met because of *The Godfather*, but somehow in *Part II* things had changed, and I couldn't get back that
same connection with her. I was still carrying the hurt from breaking up with Tuesday, who I loved, still pining and whining after
her, still wading through that aftermath. I was very much into
alcohol and drugs, getting high and putting myself in a fog. I preferred to be in a state of semiconsciousness. Charlie spent a few
days with me in Tahoe, but when he left I was alone. I was going
through something that was not as severe as depression, but a certain melancholy had settled in me.

More than likely it was also because of the character I was
playing. I thought I was engaging in the role. But I was in a Michael
Corleone trance and doing the part took a lot out of me. I did understand Michael, mercifully, from having played him in the first
Godfather. But on *Part II*, I was dealing with a different version of
this character—on the same spectrum, but with different issues,
different complexities and dimensions. He went to certain places
within himself and getting myself there took some effort. I put

myself into this character, let go of the reins and the control, and thought I would just fly with it. I found it beneficial to see the young Michael at the end of *Part II*, early in his life, younger than he was in *Part I*. You got a sense of his core and the kind of person he was, which enabled him to absorb the life he was in and live through it. His father knew he was capable of it. That's why Michael was picked.

His arc in *Part II* is a shedding of one layer after another, one connection after the next, until he's just sitting there, looking off into the distance, wondering, how'd I get so isolated? How am I so alone? I certainly didn't see contentment or resignation there—just a kind of despair. You could call Michael one of the real tragic heroes.

The thing about acting is, you don't really do it and yet it's real. That's the phenomenon. That's the paradox. We actors have to go through it to find it in ourselves, so we can paint it. In Tahoe I proceeded to cut myself off from Diane and everyone else who mattered to me. And then the film moved to Santo Domingo, and I didn't even have them.

✄✜✄

THE SHOOT IN SANTO DOMINGO, THE CAPITAL OF THE DOMINICAN Republic, which was doubling as Havana at the end of 1958, was not very joyful. In the film, Hyman Roth and the other heads of the organized crime families have gathered to cut Cuba up for themselves, but Michael is not so secure, because he's recently seen a revolutionary blow himself up in the streets, and he's left wondering whether the Cuba they want will still be that Cuba anymore. And soon enough, the government is overthrown and Michael and his associates have to get out—it's every man for himself. Cuba is also where Michael has to confront the terrible fact that his brother Fredo helped to set up the attempted murder of him and his entire family back in Tahoe.

I felt isolated. I'm not sure why, but the set didn't feel right, and the days stretched interminably. Sometimes it would take four days to shoot a scene while they waited hours for the light to be just right. I was young, only thirty-four, but it was trying on me. Meanwhile, I'm carrying the feelings of a man who has found out that his own brother tried to have him killed. It was weighty. As an actor, I'm supposed to be used to this. I play characters all the time who are dealing with heavy circumstances. I have the role, I do the role. I've since learned how to handle the craft a little bit more so the role doesn't take quite so much out of me. But Michael Corleone was a very difficult man to live with, a very difficult place to find in your own soul.

So I felt more and more alone and withdrawn. I couldn't say what it was then, and all these years later I still can't pin it down. The dynamic with Francis on set felt less friendly, but whether I was reacting to him or he to me, who can say—feedback loops can happen, especially when you're in extreme environments.

We shot the scene where Fredo brings Michael to see the decadent nightclub act, and Michael hears his brother slip up and say something to make him understand that Fredo has been in league with Hyman Roth all along. You see Michael almost collapse from the weight of that realization. I had to get that moment when he hears it. But it only happened to me on one of the takes. I did other takes, but I said, "I'm not going to get there again, Francis." And it's in the film, the one time when I got it.

Then there is the moment where the brothers find each other on the floor of the New Year's Eve party, and Michael grabs Fredo and kisses him, whispering to him that he knows he's betrayed him. He kisses his own brother on the mouth, the kiss of death. That was in the script, and so beautifully directed and done. Sometimes you say to yourself, boy, I just hope they caught that on camera, and you're grateful when they do. It reminded me of what John Barrymore said when he had to kill his brother, Lionel, in a movie. He was asked, how could you do that with such commitment? And he answered, "I really hated the scent of his hair cream." Sometimes that's all you can say about explaining your own performance.

But when we weren't shooting I found myself feeling lonely and in search of companionship. John Cazale and I of course were longtime friends, but he had brought his girlfriend with him. I would go in the pool with Lee Strasberg's kids, and we'd swim together and play, but they were very young at the time and really there with their mother and father. I was drinking, but not to the point where it would interfere with my work. I never did that. But a cloud had moved in on me.

My social gene just wasn't developed yet. I was still escaping the fame thing and all that came with it. I wasn't a sad sack all the time. We were in Santo Domingo when I found out I got my Oscar nomination for *Serpico*, and I threw a party to celebrate and invited the whole crew and everybody that was around. So I was happy at that moment.

There was a certain kind of feeling in and around *The God-father: Part II*. Here I was, playing this powerful sort of demigod, and here was Francis, at the height of his powers in filmmaking and show business. Because of *The Godfather*, we now had positions in the world, power and notoriety, and both of us were here in the Dominican Republic, stripped away from the lives and people we knew back home. We agreed on the script, the interpretation of Michael and the way in which the character was evolving.

There was a tension between us at times. Perhaps it was just the element of familiarity and a lack of communication, or maybe it stemmed from those six days and nights with Charlie that we spent working on the script. I saw how much it meant to Francis that I play the part of Michael, even more than it meant to me. He saw me in the role, gave me a great opportunity, and he fought for me. And yet we were worlds apart. I actually reached out to him recently and asked him about that time in our life together during *The Godfather: Part II*. He couldn't recall it and couldn't quite say. But I remember it as a period when we were somewhat distant from each other and I'm very grateful it didn't last long.

Francis and I saw a lot of things the same way, and I admire him greatly. He has a brilliant mind and talent of epic proportions, and I enjoy hearing his take on any subject. He had made this one incredible film and now we were trying to finish a second.

)X◆)X

I HAD SEEN *PART II* A FEW MONTHS EARLIER, JUST BEFORE IT opened, in a screening room with Charlie. I thought Francis did an amazing job. I remember thinking Bob De Niro was really good too; I was very impressed with his Vito, for which he won an Oscar. God knows my portrayal of Michael in that film may be one of the better performances I've given in my life.

I hear a lot of comparisons of *The Godfather* and *The Godfather: Part II*. To me, they are tonally different. They are both high-value films, though *The Godfather* has more popular appeal. Plus, it had Marlon Brando and that could never be duplicated. What could I do in *Part II* to compare with that? What does Michael have to offer an audience on that level? There are definite signposts throughout *Part II* that Michael is not a complete person. However, *Part II* does take the character of Michael to a more complex place and has something more insightful to say about his condition. That's why that flashback scene at the end, the birthday party for Vito that Francis and Mario wrote, has such an impact. It was great fun to film, to be reunited with guys from the first film, like Jimmy Caan and Abe Vigoda, and to try to conjure up a little of the young Michael, before he'd even joined the armed services—to reach back and be that kid who was so idealistic and ready to fight the Axis, so sure of what's good and what's evil and how to defeat it. This was who he was. What happened to that person?

By the end of *Part II*, Michael's trajectory was resolved. His downfall was complete. He had fully turned himself to stone. I couldn't see myself ever playing him again.

7

Maximum Velocity

I was staring at the purple curtain in my posh hotel room in London. I watched as a mouse ran up along the fabric, and then, as if from nowhere, a bat swooped in and attacked it. I didn't know if what I was seeing was real, a hallucination, or a flashback to that showing of *The Lost Weekend* my mother had taken me to when I was five years old. I was spinning out.

I cast my wobbly gaze into the distance, and I could see that Charlie was there with me, sitting at the other end of a long table, each of us with a large bottle of hard liquor by our side. I thought I could see my future: getting so drunk that I'd start to see things that didn't exist. I had the potential to develop what they called the d.t.'s—delirium tremens. Back in my twenties, when I was recovering from surgery in a New York hospital, they gave me morphine, and when I came to, I thought I was floating through the air above Central Park. Now here I was in London, and as I looked out from a sixth-floor luxury suite onto St. James's Park, I wondered if a similar sensation would come over me and carry me right out that window.

I started raving to Charlie about why I didn't want to make this next picture that Marty Bregman had lined up for me. What was I doing with my life? Did I really want to get up there again, holding a gun in my hands and committing crimes? Having starred in all of four movies, maybe I just didn't want to be a film actor anymore.

Charlie was very understanding and supported my decision. He said, "I know, Al. What do we do next?" I was lashing out and tired of it all. I said, "What I'm going to do is not do this film. That's what I'm going to be doing."

I'm not above the occasional outburst of insanity. I am guilty of inconsistency and off-the-wall choices. The haze of the limelight was still new to me, and the anxiety of that attention had infested my environment. My decision-making process was also clouded by my consumption of alcohol and drugs. Now my brain was giving me a warning, and I thought I'd better take heed of it.

Frank Pierson had written a firecracker of a script about a failed bank heist that had turned into a hostage situation out in Brooklyn a couple of summers earlier. Marty Bregman had worked diligently to get many of the real people involved in the heist to sell their rights to the story. Bregman had gotten Pierson to do the screenplay and had Sidney Lumet, our golden boy from *Serpico*, lined up to direct it. Naturally he wanted me to be the star. Naturally I turned it down.

I went back home to New York, having passed on the project, when I got a call from Bregman at a very opportune time. He wisely waited until he knew I wasn't drinking, and he asked me if

I would read *Dog Day Afternoon* again. I thought that was absurd. And he said, "You're not high now, are you?" And I said, "No. I'm here with you. I'm fine." With an unfamiliar gentleness, he said, "Why don't you give it a read for me? Do it for me. I really need you to read it." I said all right, kind of reluctantly. But I respected and trusted him. So I read it, called him back immediately, and said, "Why am I not doing this film?" He said, "That's all I wanted to hear." And we were off.

Lumet gave us three weeks to rehearse *Dog Day Afternoon*—that was time I could use to figure out my character, who was called Sonny Wortzik. Then I shot that first day on the film. For some reason, I went to the rushes afterward to see the footage, which I would hardly do in most things I've been in. But something drove me to look at it. And when I looked, I thought, I'm playing nobody. I don't have a character. I need to be a person here, because I don't see a person. As I left the screening room, I whispered in Marty Bregman's ear, "We have to shoot this over again." Then I fled out of the room. He shouted after me, "What do you mean?" But I was gone.

I had this little apartment in a wonderful neighborhood on the Upper East Side on Sixty-Eighth and Madison. The area was quiet, wholesome, and rich, and the building was very private, which was the way I liked it. It had no doormen and no lobby I had to pass through to deal with other people. The apartment used to belong to the actress Candice Bergen, but now it was mine. The rent was relatively low and it had just three rooms: a tiny bedroom, a living room with a couch and fireplace, and a very small kitchen with a window that reminded me of the one my Grandma used to hang out when she washed it. The space suited me. It kept me sheltered away from the madness of the city, except for a lady I would hear screaming every other night. She was in the throes of something extreme. It could drive a person to move, but I stuck it out.

The night before the reshoot for *Dog Day Afternoon*, I found myself in the apartment alone with half a gallon of white wine. I spent perhaps half the night pacing the floor, drinking the wine, and figuring out which way I'd go with the lead character in the film. I felt as if I were trying to compose a sonata or write a short story. In my solitude I was struggling to find a place I could go, a lane I could be in, that would motivate the character and lead to some spontaneity. I had to come up with something quick.

I came in the next morning playing my character a bit differently. He was antsy, animated and agitated. There were whispers from friends of mine in the cast, "Is Al having a nervous breakdown?" But I knew I wasn't. I would come to know what a nervous breakdown was and this wasn't it. I hadn't changed my approach drastically, but enough for it to be noticed. I had found a certain mindset that allowed the character to blossom and bear fruit without forcing it. I continued that way for the whole six weeks of shooting.

This time I was careful to cast the film where I could with actors I had already worked with, people who knew the real me and not just the image. Penny Allen played one of those unflappable bank tellers, and Charlie Durning was the police sergeant trying to negotiate with the robbers. My character's mother was played by my idol Judith Malina, the cofounder of the Living Theatre, who chain-smoked marijuana on the set and would give me little tokes every now and then. The sweaty bank manager was played by Sully Boyar, a chubby character actor who I had known since I was seventeen. He was a bit eccentric but had a great sense of humor.

One time I asked him, "Hey, Sully, how come you didn't make it and I did?"

He said, "You took a door that was open just a crack and you went through it."

I said, "Why didn't you?"

He answered, "I was taking a bite of a hot dog."

Charlie was the one who suggested that we get John Cazale to play my partner in crime. Even though Sidney Lumet wanted somebody younger, Charlie was exactly right—John was an absolute pillar of that film, and the relationship between our characters was a brilliant inversion of how we related to each other in the *Godfather* movies. Anyone who went in expecting to see a rehash of Michael and Fredo Corleone was in for a surprise.

When the shoot was over, the character I had played just flew out of me. I had been possessed, and then it was gone. Even Sidney commented to me that he saw it go, like a spirit. And then when we came back later to reshoot a couple of things, the spirit didn't come back. We did the reshoots and I got through it. Some of these moments weren't fulfilled to my satisfaction, but I had done enough of the film to get by. I doubt any viewers could tell which portions came from the reshoots, because when I look at the film myself, I can't see the difference. Sometimes we have these images of ourselves and they're just totally askew.

〉〈◆〉〈

THE SEXUALITY OF THE CHARACTER I PLAYED IN *DOG DAY AFTERNOON* is a complex thing. What I interpreted from the screenplay was that he is a man with a wife and kids who also happens to be in an affair with a person who identifies as a woman, and who today we would understand is transgender. But knowing this about him didn't excite me or bother me; it didn't make the role seem any more appealing or risky. Though I may be a kid who started in the South Bronx, I had been living in the Village since my teens. I had friends, roommates, and colleagues who were attracted to different people than I was attracted to, and none of that was ever rebellious or groundbreaking or unusual. It just *was*.

Perhaps at the time of *Dog Day Afternoon* it was an uncommon thing to have a main character in a Hollywood movie who was gay or queer, and who was treated as heroic or worthy of an audience's affection—even if he did rob banks. But you have to understand that none of that enters into my consideration. I am an actor portraying a character in a film. I am playing the part because I think I can bring something to the role. As far as I was concerned, *Dog Day Afternoon* was just cool, a continuation of the work I had been doing my whole life. It was inevitable that an audience would have certain feelings about me because of the choices I made, and the slings and arrows were going to keep coming either way. I try to stay away from things that are controversial, and I find myself in controversies anyway. If people think that I helped to advance a particular issue of representation, that's fine. If there is credit or blame to go around, I don't feel entitled to any of it. All I know is, I play a role to find as much humanity as there is that I can portray.

There was one thing that bothered me. The script originally had it that, in the middle of this whole hostage crisis, Sonny's lover, Leon, played by Chris Sarandon, comes to the bank dressed as Marilyn Monroe, and they kiss outside in front of everybody. I thought, This is absurd. It didn't happen that way. I guess the film-makers wanted to pump up the volume on the situation, but it was bullshit. Not only was it not true, it was overly exaggerated—a comedic send-up of some sort that minimized the situation. We had a big argument about all of that. To a group that included Bregman, Pierson, and Lumet, I said, "We are dealing with human beings, whether they are heterosexual or homosexual. We're just human beings." I thought, Why are we talking about this? Would the cops have let that kind of display take place?

In our film, the police allow Sonny and Leon to have a phone call in which they are effectively telling each other goodbye. This film was based on a true story, after all, and I did the research and found that they made a phone call. They didn't kiss—they didn't even touch. No one was dressed up as Marilyn Monroe. It never went down like that. Because Sidney Lumet was so brilliant and knew that Chris Sarandon and I had lived with our characters for a while—we had rehearsed together and had already been filming for several weeks by that point—he let us work out the dialogue of that phone call through improvisation, which he would then use to write the scene. That is Lumet magic. Sidney brought in micro-phones and recorded us on tape. We did three separate takes of improvisations and then Lumet cut and pasted them together with me and Chris to create the scene. The phone call you see in the film was the result of that improvisation. That was flying with-out a net, but that whole film was flying without a net. As Sidney Lumet told me at one point while we were shooting, after he had spent the day standing up on a ladder and talking to a crowd of five hundred extras, "This thing is out of our hands, Al." Or as Charlie once put it, "You just pull the pin, baby, and let that grenade go."

The most powerful moment in the whole film was a spontaneous invention. In one scene, as I'm going out on the street to talk to the crowd, Lumet's assistant director, Burtt Harris, whispered in my ear, "Say 'Attica.'" I said, "What do you mean?" He says, "Say 'Attica.' Say 'Attica.'" He was talking about an upstate New York prison that just a few months before had been the scene of a riot that was brutally put down by the governor, the prison officers, and the police. So I got out on the street, and I was talking to the crowd. All of a sudden, I say, "Remember Attica?" And the people started going fucking crazy. And I thought to myself, That's what film can be. Go out there, go for it. Something may happen. And that's what Burtt Harris knew. And of course we went with it and there it is. It's Attica. Bravo, Burtt Harris!

)X◆X(

NORMAN ORNELLAS WAS ONE OF MY CLOSEST FRIENDS IN THE acting community. He had been with me for several of my professional milestones, and I felt I knew him very well. But I only met his father for the first time in a hospital when Norman was dying of cancer. Norman was thirty-five years old, much too young to be on the verge of death. Norman was a wonderful actor from the Actors Studio; he had done a stint in prison, and he had a wildness and had that kind of rough edge. But he was very smart and very gifted, and I loved him. He had been in *Serpico* and acted onstage with me in *Richard III* and *The Resistible Rise of Arturo Ui*, and he had just made his Broadway debut a few months earlier in a play that Joe Papp had directed. After Norman got his diagnosis, he started on treatments; he had been doing them for a couple of weeks when we sat down for lunch at the Ginger Man, where he told me what was happening. In the conversation, he said to me, "You know, Al, three months, thirty years. There is no difference." He seemed to have some profound knowledge. That's how you look at time when you're losing it, and it's going by at a speed you can't control. I didn't quite get it then, but I sure as hell would come to understand what he meant.

Norman's father was a Portuguese man who had raised his family in Hawaii, and he was very close with his son. Once we crossed paths in the hospital hallway. By that time, Norman had lost a lot of weight and was coming closer to death. His father looked at me and said, in no uncertain terms, "Can you bring back Norman?" He was making an out-and-out plea for me to help his son.

Maybe it seemed like an outrageous request from his poor father, but it was no more preposterous than some of the things I had tried to do to help Norman as he grew sicker and sicker. I got pretty desperate in my own search for answers, turning to psychic mediums and people who performed séances, quack doctors who promised ridiculous cure-alls—pretty much any method that claimed it could rid him of his cancer. Whatever it is, you think to yourself, Why not at least give it a try? Ultimately, you come to realize that it's all out of our control.

Norman's father would never have asked me that question if I was an unknown. I might have the connections to a good doctor, to a better hospital, to someone who could help, no small things, just because I'd been elevated to stardom. What this career afforded me, the outsize reality that I occupied—I saw it in the eyes of this beautiful man who was reaching out to a celebrity because he thought I could help his dying son.

While I was reflecting on this, Norman's father spoke further. He said, "I would trade places with him. Is there any way you could help me with that?" I knew he meant it. Did I ever love someone enough to want to switch places with them? Could I do something like that? I had known love for my grandparents and for my mother. I felt love for my cousin and for my friends. I never had that with my dad, though I flashed on my grandfather, after my mother had passed, when he sat in that chair, just stomping his foot. He wasn't even my grandfather anymore—a feeling had taken over him that I never saw in my whole life. Now I realized as I looked at Norman's father, that was a parent's love—a father's love—for his child. There was a depth to that kind of love, and I was seeing it right in front of my face. I would come to know it myself later in life.

We had been talking about starting a theater together, me, Norman, and John Cazale. Joe Papp was involved, and we were discussing with him the idea of starting a national theater for America, which would be subsidized by the government, like they have in England, and we'd involve other actors like Meryl Streep, who John was dating at the time. But it turned out it's very hard to have a national theater in New York, because the film business is on the West Coast. You can have a national theater in London, because all the actors live there. But in America all the actors aren't in one city—they are split between New York and LA, three thousand miles away from where we wanted to do it in New York.

I was living in a dream world, too, because I was becoming a star. I thought, I can't get locked into doing just theater when I know I have another life ahead of me.

John Cazale never visited Norman in the hospital, and it surprised me. I don't know if John knew yet that he had cancer himself. John was a sensitive person, and he understood how actors are prophets and seers. I think he didn't want that prophecy of what could happen to him. I knew John didn't want to have kids, and maybe that was why.

When John got his own cancer diagnosis and began telling other people about it, I would sometimes go with him to his doctor's office when he went for his treatments. He was a great artist and confidant, and I wanted to work with him all the time. He said to me once, as a joke, "I'm always with *you*. I've got to work with other people, don't I? I've got to go out there and do more things." I was laughing. I loved it.

When he started to get really sick, I saw how Bob De Niro and his other costars on *The Deer Hunter* put up their own salaries to cover the insurance in case John was somehow unable to complete the film. That was a deep and very heavy gesture. But what I thought was incredible was how Meryl Streep was there for John, every day until the end. She is one of the greatest actresses that we've ever seen, and the spirit and dedication she had for John, it touched me so deeply. She took him through it, and I just loved her so much for that. I still do to this day.

Within about three years of each other, John and Norman were gone. Like Cliffy, Bruce, and Petey. It was a good thing I understood how to be alone, but it was becoming a bad habit.

)X◆)X

DOG DAY AFTERNOON WAS A SUCCESS, AND I WAS ON A ROLL, extending the unlikely run of films that I had with *The Godfather*, *Serpico*, and *The Godfather: Part II*. Another critical success. Another box-office hit. Another Oscar nomination that I didn't turn up for. (Everyone told me I didn't have a chance against Jack Nicholson in *One Flew Over the Cuckoo's Nest*, and believe me, I was psychologically incapable of going, whether or not Jack was a sure thing.)

My fame was not just bigger after *Dog Day*, but more intense. That will happen sometimes to certain people, for reasons that have to do with circumstance and timing, the doors opening and closing. The time just happened to be right for someone like me. Now all this attention was isolating me and affecting me deeply.

You're very much on your own in dealing with it. There's not many people around you who can tell you, here's how you cope with it, here's how you reckon with it—this new intensity of a changed life, one that leads to desperate solitude and a strange way of being set apart from the world. When I sought advice from Lee Strasberg, he told me, "Darling, you simply have to adjust." It remains, as far as I can see, an unanswerable question. And the way I dealt with it was I took drugs and drank. I wasn't living the high life. My manner of coping was more low-key and private. I did try going to the theater again. I went back to the Actors Studio and attempted a few things. But I was dealing with tremendous anxiety. Nerves. And I had a lot of trouble with drinking. And all of it, all of it, with me alone in a small apartment.

I started to wonder, Do I deserve this great gift of celebrity that's been given to me? Where is the acceptance in all of this? How do you live with the feeling that you don't fit in with other people when you already feel like you don't fit in with yourself? That's a tough one to sort out. The movie stars of old reckoned with their fame by playing among their own kind—they got handed a lifestyle that was backed up by the powerful movie studios of their time. I didn't live through that—you have to understand it's very different now, and I have heard other celebrities express their difficulties with it. At a certain point, dealing with fame is a self-centered problem and one should probably keep their mouth shut about it. Here I am talking about it now, so I'm starting to feel I should keep my mouth shut too. Hello.

Charlie had finally stopped drinking because he knew he was an alcoholic. He and I were going all the time. I think Bregman looked at us and thought, That's just what they do. As I've said, I was rarely drunk in front of Bregman. He didn't even know I had an issue with it. *I* didn't know I had an issue with it. But Charlie knew, and he knew I didn't know. I thought I was fine. I didn't drink when I worked—that was my big thing. Work was always first. It was what gave me identity and solace, made me feel I was closer to who I am.

But, God, drinking was a way of life for me. That's finally what Charlie said to me. He said, "Al, you're just drinking. You don't even know. You think everybody drinks." I was shocked when somebody at my table didn't want to have a drink. They seemed freaky. Now, many years later, I get that look from other people, as if to say, what's the matter with this guy? And I think to myself: What the fuck happened to me? When did I stop having fun? Frank

Sinatra gave me that look one time, the first time I hung out with him. It was a look that said, you don't drink? I thought, He sees it, too, and he doesn't understand it. It was the way I used to look at people when they didn't participate in my world of drinking and alcohol.

But Charlie knew that drinking was going to get me in trouble, big-time. He was the one ending up in doorways—I had so-called control. I liked my Heineken beer and I had a low tolerance, so it took very little to get me high. I didn't have to get to a point where I was abusing my body. And then I started waking up, having forgotten the things I did the night before. I was having blackouts and that scared me. After a couple of panic attacks, I knew I needed help.

I went to Alcoholics Anonymous for a bit. I got a little taste of it, but for me, it wasn't anonymous. I also just didn't relate personally to that environment, but I understand its value, and the service it provides to people who need it is indescribable I just felt I was out of place there, so I moved on.

Getting more into one-on-one therapy helped. It helped me to keep going, and it helped me to quit drinking. I almost feel it's mandatory in my position. C'mon, buddy, you've got to get your head shrunk. Because your head gets so big, you need to shrink it. You need to go to some guy who's going to tell you what you already know about yourself and pay attention to you for an hour straight. Which we all like. We all need a little attention.

The first time I ever considered therapy was back in Boston, during my run in *Richard III*. I was staying at our director David Wheeler's house for a few days, and he came into my room one morning to share some good news with me. "Hey, Al!" he said. "You just won the National Board of Review!" It was my first major film award for *The Godfather*. I said to him, in the softest voice I could summon up, "I was going to ask you, David, do you have the name of a psychiatrist? Because I need one." That was my answer to him. Not that I was unhappy about winning such a prestigious award, but there were just other things on my mind.

I saw a psychiatrist in Boston first, and then I went and got myself a guy in New York. I fell in love with the process, and I got to a point where I was in therapy five days a week at certain times. I highly recommend therapy if you're at all leaning in that direction. Maybe you don't need it five times a week, but give it a whirl. There's an old story: A woman goes to a therapist for years. It's her last appointment, because she feels she's come to a great place in her life and is ready to move on. She wants to congratulate her therapist and say goodbye. So she tells him, "You've done so much good for me. I love my husband so much. Every day with my kids is just a joy. My work is going off the charts. I'm seeing a whole new side of life. You've been so wonderful. I never hear you speak. You just take it all in. Please tell me, how did you do it?" The doctor looks at her and says, "*No habla inglés.*" That's an interpretation of therapy too; you need to talk and get it out. When I was living with Jill, before I ever went to therapy, I used to just sit in the bathtub alone and talk about things. I cleared my mind to myself.

It's an unusual relationship that you forge when you find a good doctor, someone you feel has that kind of commitment to you. And then they take some colossal amount of time off, and you don't see them for the whole summer. I had one of those episodes when I couldn't find my doctor. I might have been spared about twenty years of tsuris if I could have avoided it. It's a good idea that when your psychiatrist goes away, you know where they are and you can call them when you're in trouble. They need rest too. I can deal with, "Hey, my daughter's graduating college, I'll be out for a few days." But going up a fucking river somewhere, to not be available for, like, six weeks? Come on, my life was capable of going right off the rails in far less time than that.

I used to have recurring dreams in which I go to my psychiatrist's office but can't find him anywhere. He's in the building, but he's unavailable. I'm at the door, but there's not even a buzzer I can press to let him know I'm there and no way to let me in. That was my dream. Now I have that feeling about my agent.

)X(♦)X(

I STARTED GETTING WEANED OFF THE ALCOHOL, AND SLOWLY I GOT out of it. The first film I did afterward was *Bobby Deerfield*, which remains to me one of my more revealing performances. I was trying to get inside someone who was isolated and terrified of death but who challenges it every day. Bobby's life choice is to drive Formula 1 race cars faster than anybody, a profession where every mistake could be fatal. He is chased by adoring fans but disillusioned with his fame, and he has already given up on his family and his old life when an accident in a race kills a driver and paralyzes another. The whole thing leaves him in a sort of walking, talking coma.

While he's visiting the surviving driver in a hospital, Bobby meets a woman there who's been diagnosed with a fatal disease. She's trying to feel life in some way, to experience it and give herself over to it. She's not impressed by his career or aware of his celebrity, and though her fate will be tragic, and because of her youth, she's trying to overcome whatever happens to a young person when they're told they're not going to live for very long. Bobby makes contact with that, and it changes him.

As much as I didn't want to make the film, Charlie kept telling me to get over to Europe and do it. But my usual line was "No way I'm leaving my little apartment." I know the film had been developed originally for Paul Newman, and when he bowed out I think the studios wanted Robert Redford. But I would be coming into it with all my strange residue—my pain and depression from this period, which I thought could be interesting. I thought it was possible I could express what I felt the character of Bobby Deerfield was going through and pour a lot of what I was dealing with into him.

It's a very private film as well, I think, for Sydney Pollack, who was a great director. It was an exercise for him in dealing with issues in his life that he believed were reflected in the film.

Certainly, there was nothing like driving that race car. You haven't lived till you've seen one of those cars turn the corner at 170 miles an hour. It doesn't seem possible, and yet it happens. I got to meet a couple of the great drivers of the day, Clay Regazzoni and Jackie Stewart, and learn from them at Le Mans. It's very hard to get behind the wheel and do what they do, and hard to capture it on film.

Now, did I have the courage to take the car up to 120 miles an hour? No way. They have fifteen gears in that thing. I'm lucky I went twenty miles an hour. I was so scared I'd go off a cliff. But I got to know the guys and study what they do. They had a team of expert drivers they would use to film all the difficult racing scenes, and those would be inserted into the movie. Thank God for inserts.

There were a couple of people that the studios and Sydney Pollack wanted for the love interest in the film. I met a few actresses who seemed fine to me. But then they went with Marthe Keller, a great actress who had also been in *Marathon Man* and *Black Sunday*. Marthe was Swiss and very sophisticated, a woman who had studied at the great theaters in Berlin and spoke English with a slight accent. She was totally foreign to me. But I fell in love with her. And somehow she fell in love with me.

Not right away. I wasn't interested in her. Nor she in me. She never gave me any signs. I always thought she was a little disappointed that Redford didn't do the film. I could understand that perfectly. But I was wounded when I met her, and it's possible that some part of her was attracted to the Bobby Deerfield in me. I had never met anyone like her. And she had certainly never met anyone like me. She was this tall, elegant, refined European woman. And I was this guy from the South Bronx, self-taught and perhaps, by her standards, a little bit unrefined. And sometimes that is what makes a relationship.

The wild, eccentric genius Charlie Bluhdorn, who ran Paramount Pictures, was a friend of mine because of the success of *The Godfather*. I ran into him at one of the more sophisticated New York parties that I'd get invited to with Marthe—the kind of party where you may end up shaking hands with everyone from Andy Warhol to Henry Kissinger. Well, Charlie Bluhdorn saw Marthe and me together at this party, took one look at us, and coined the phrase that described us to a tee: the Odd Couple.

From *Bobby Deerfield* onward I was done with drinking. I was totally off it and every encounter I had after was slightly tinged with a degree of distance and shyness. This seemed to be the countenance I possessed after I cut off the booze, which had been my medication. After that, it was like I was always on tilt. I feel fortunate that I overcame that, and Marthe helped a great deal to get me through that time. There was a lot of love there. Our relationship has lasted through the years, and has taken many different forms, mainly as friends, but I'm greatly appreciative of her.

As for *Bobby Deerfield*, it is just not a great film. It's okay. It's got a good performance in it from Marthe and a relatively good one from me, but I think Pollack missed some opportunities. It just breezed along on a romantic current and never risked making any big waves. *Bobby Deerfield* was largely promoted with my name and my face, and it was the first film I had made that was really just rejected, by critics and by audiences at large, setting me up for another ten straight years of these kinds of reactions.

I don't know what the reviews said about *Bobby Deerfield*, but I'm sure they said things that were negative. You can always tell that when you do a film. After it came out, I got a note from a friend who said how upset she was about the vitriol against me. I hadn't read any of it, of course, but now I knew. She meant well, but I would have preferred not hearing that. So I myself took a negative view of the film.

When it opened in New York, the studios held this big party at Tavern on the Green. I didn't even show up to it. That got me in a lot of trouble. Somehow I knew that if I went, I was not going to like it. This was not my thing, especially when I thought the film didn't work. The studios actually got me my own sports car as a gift, an Alfa Romeo. But it had a manual transmission, and I didn't know how to drive it. Then *Bobby Deerfield* was such a failure that they took the car back.

So I went and bought a new car. Charlie and I ended up in a BMW dealership, where I was contemplating this beautiful porcelain-white sedan, top of the line, maybe $30,000 at the time. I didn't think the car suited me, but I figured, let's try it on for size, and drove it off the lot with Charlie. We cruised along the city streets and cut across Central Park to make our way back to my apartment on East Sixty-Eighth Street to have some coffee. As luck would have it, I found a parking spot right in front of the building; that just never happens. As Charlie and I got out and started to head into the building and up the steps of the stoop, I looked back at the car and just had a sense that something felt off about it.

After an hour or two had passed, we decided to drive some-where else, probably to drop Charlie off downtown at his place. We took the elevator down and headed out to the street. Just as I opened the big iron doors at the front of the building, I could see that the car was gone. It was stolen. Here I am, saying that car isn't me, then—*poof*—it disappears. No, I don't think the universe works that way, and I'm sure we weren't the first people this had happened to. This was before car alarms and other tracking de-vices. The thieves had a scam going where they just had to wait for people who drove off in new cars from the dealership, then they'd follow the owner home and know they'd have just enough time to get into the car and take off with it. There I was, standing in front of this empty parking spot, no more porcelain-white BMW to drive, so Charlie and I laughed it off and took a walk. I knew the car was insured and it would get figured out. There were other things I was more worried about losing—my mind, for one.

I didn't look at *Bobby Deerfield* for another twenty-five or thirty years. But then someone told me to watch it again. I thought, It's spotty and unsure of what it's saying, but something does come through. Sydney Pollack was coming through. Marthe Keller, a great actress and artist, was coming through.

I think part of the reason I was afraid to revisit it was because I thought it would remind me of what I was personally going through at the time. But when I saw it years later I recognized someone who was exorcising himself using the medium of his work. I did put a lot of my own turmoil into the character where I thought it would be appropriate. I was grateful that I could put that to use, but I could have used a little more objectivity, which might have helped to draw in a larger audience and make it more appealing.

Making films without drinking wasn't solely what brought me back into the world, but it was a step. Right after, I started going out to colleges, in Los Angeles, in the Bronx, and around the country. I did not take any payment for these appearances; I did it as a contribution to these schools, and I would have paid them, because it was therapeutic and very valuable for me to get out there and start speaking. I would read to the students there, performing poetry or roles from plays that I did. I was no longer self-isolating. We would have question-and-answer sessions afterward, where I would engage with the audience. One time, in one of these sessions, a young woman in the audience said to me, "Why do you not like your audience?" I was taken aback. I said, "What? No, my audience is why I'm here. They go to my movies. They see my plays.

Why wouldn't I like them?" But what I was projecting by not doing interviews or participating at certain events was being interpreted as me not liking my audience.

I told the woman who asked that question that I had trouble accepting the media attention. I had not understood that the media is really serving the public—they're giving the audience what it wants to see, and the audience wants to hear more about the various people who perform for them. Being shy, I didn't like all that attention from the media, and I certainly didn't like the paparazzi interfering with my life, though I've since learned that the media and the paparazzi, well, they've got to eat too. I didn't know how to deal with it at the time. But now I was starting to connect with the world again, and it felt good. It almost felt like survival.

By going out to the colleges, I was reviving something in me that was theatrical and connecting to audiences. I think that's what lead me to my next project, David Rabe's great play *The Basic Training of Pavlo Hummel*. Joe Papp had put it on at the Public with different actors and I had done it in Boston years before, so I revived it on Broadway. *Pavlo* is about a soldier who gets killed in Vietnam; it's a big show with a cast of about twenty-five or thirty people and we all worked together as a team. We were brilliantly directed by David Wheeler, and I won my second Tony Award that summer.

I think it still would be running if I hadn't left it, but I had my cross-the-ocean relationship with Marthe and that's a difficult course to navigate. We stopped the play for two weeks in the middle of August so I could go see her in Munich where she was working, which is not a good idea to do when something is running at that level of success, but I found myself driven by my love affair. I did come back to *Pavlo* for a few more weeks after that, but at a certain point I needed to work again in movies, so we ended the play and that part of my life was over. But I seemed ready to trot again.

8

Every Day Above Ground Is a Good Day

I stood in the emergency room of a Santa Monica hospital looking like someone who had already died. I was waiting to be treated by a doctor. My eyes were limp and gray, my skin soaked with sweat. My clothes were ragged and stained with blood. I had been told to keep my arms in the air, because the machine gun I had been using had become fused to my hand. A nurse beckoned to me and said, "Follow me. We should go this way." As we were walking down the hospital hallway, she turned and looked me over more closely. She said, "Hey—are you Al Pacino?"

I said, "Yeah."

She said, "Oh, I thought you were some scumbag."

Only hours before, I was on the smoke-filled set of a mansion where the crazed, coked-out Tony Montana was making his final stand. I had just fired off thirty rounds from my "little friend" in a gunfight with the small army that had come to take me down. With bullets flying everywhere, the scene called for me to get shot in my upper body, sending me backward. Squibs inside my costume exploded with red dye, and I went flying to the ground. In my character's drug-induced state, I grabbed the red-hot barrel of the machine gun I had been firing that was lying next to me. And suddenly my hand wouldn't move—it was stuck to the barrel.

I would have to take two weeks off from making *Scarface* while I recovered from the burn and the skin on my hand grew back. During my recuperation, Brian De Palma would film that shootout scene from every imaginable angle, over and over, adding more bullets, more bodies, more carnage, inviting other directors to sit in and help make the sequence longer and more outrageous. Even Steven Spielberg came by for a day to oversee a few explosions. Meanwhile, where was I? Home in bed.

)X(+)X(

PAUL MUNI SEEMED LIKE HE COULD DO ANYTHING ON-SCREEN WHEN he played Tony Camonte in the original *Scarface* that came out in 1932. When I watched Muni in that film, the one written by Ben Hecht and directed by Howard Hawks, I was no longer a kid sitting by my mother's side in an old movie palace in the South Bronx. I was a grown man and a successful actor.I was inspired by Muni. I wanted to imitate him. I wanted to *be* him. I said to myself, I think I can do *Scarface*. I think we can remake this.

It would take a few more years for us to make our version of *Scarface*, which came out in 1983. It had the writing of Oliver Stone, the direction of Brian De Palma, and the vision of Marty Bregman. It was in your face, a provocation, just like the original. And it was our way of coping with an idea that was already everywhere in the 1980s, before we said it in the film: "First you get the money, then you get the power, then you get the woman." That was as American as the flag. Depending on how you look at it, you could say *Scarface* was the most successful movie I ever did. But not right away, not even close. In fact, it was part of a group of films that made me quit the movie business for almost four years. I got wrecked for it, and after that, I was out, down for the count.

Bregman had been my rock-solid supporter, but in 1978 we had a falling-out over a film project and I took it too far. We broke up. We went our separate ways for a couple of years. And in the meantime, I started running into problems.

During this time, I was working on . . . *And Justice for All*. It's by no means a bad film; it had some good stuff in it and it works. It's still enjoyable and entertaining today. I even got an Oscar nomination for it. It was directed by Norman Jewison, an iconic director who had made some really good films. But he and I did not hit it off.

The climactic scene in the film, which probably got me my Oscar nomination, is when my character, a Baltimore defense attorney, has to defend a judge he knows is guilty of rape and sexual assault. Instead, he goes in front of the jury and the whole court to tell them that his own client should go right to fucking jail, in a great big barn burner of a speech. That outburst became part of the culture in a way that the movie itself did not. To this day, people still say *"You're* out of order! The whole trial's out of order!" without knowing that this is where it came from.

We had spent weeks making the movie in Baltimore and several days on that scene alone. When the courtroom sequence was completed, the production was going to move to Los Angeles. After a few days of shooting that court scene, Jewison decided he was done with it, and now it was time for us to go to LA and finish the rest of the film.

I said, "I don't think this is done."

He said, "What?"

"I just don't think it's done, Norman. We're missing something."

He got really mad at me. In his mind, the scene was finished.

We continued to argue in his office and I said to him, gingerly, "Look, you're yelling at me and it doesn't matter. It doesn't change what we need. We need to stay and do some work. It's not done."

He said, "It is, and that's it."

So we went back to LA to shoot the rest of the film, and I went to my agent at the time, Stan Kamen, who ran the motion picture department at William Morris. Stan was elegant and soft-spoken, a diplomat who knew how to say things to people. I said to Stan, "This is not right. We left it in Baltimore and it's not finished." So Stan reached out to Jewison and told him, "Al has his own feelings about things and sometimes he's wrong. Sometimes he's right." He persuaded Jewison to put together a private showing of the scene for the three of us and let the chips fall where they may.

We got together in a screening room on a studio lot. Norman, Stan, and I sat together in the audience, watching the scene. When it was over, Stan looked at Norman and said, "I think Al has made a point. I think it doesn't quite work, Norman." Jewison knew. We had to go back to Baltimore and finish the scene.

I noticed this happening on films more and more, though: when there were delays that were caused by creative disputes—I don't mean some movie star holding out for a bigger trailer, I mean a genuine disagreement about how something is to be executed—

stars were taking the brunt of the blame. I've felt it throughout my career. The star gets labeled as being difficult.

Now what is difficult? Someone is saying, I'm interested in making this film. I'm interested in how we build the world of the film and how it comes through. The people shelling out the dough say we're driving them crazy when we do this stuff, but this is our sanity. We do it for the sake of film. If you're fighting for the betterment of the film, then you're not being difficult. You're not on a film for perks. The size of a trailer, fourteen assistants, lunch breaks every five minutes, demands that bear no relationship to the work you're doing—that's being difficult.

Here's an interesting irony—if I hadn't been in Los Angeles at that time because Jewison needed to go back there just at that moment, I might have missed out on something extraordinary. I was in West Hollywood with a group of friends from . . . *And Justice for All*, just walking along Sunset Boulevard, when we passed by the Tiffany Theater, a revival house that showed old movies. And there on the marquee, in all capital letters, was the word "SCARFACE." I recognized the title right away—I knew it was a classic gangster picture and one that was loved by Bertolt Brecht, who drew on films like it to write his play *The Resistible Rise of Arturo Ui*. Back when it was made, Muni's *Scarface* was a favorite film of a lot of people, including my grandfather; I had grown up hearing him talk about George Raft casually flipping his half-dollar coin in every scene, making that a trademark of on-screen mobsters. I had never seen it before, and I led our little group into the theater to check it out.

It was an amazing piece of filmmaking by one of the greatest directors who ever lived, Howard Hawks. The original *Scarface* is a wild commentary on the excesses and failings of the Great Depression era. It was full of violence that it seemed to excuse by declaring itself, in its own title cards, "an indictment of gang rule in America and of the callous indifference of the government to this constantly increasing menace to our safety and liberty." And at its heart was Paul Muni, who seemed like nobody could touch him. He was like Brando in *The Wild One*, a figure totally unrestricted by boundaries or conventions. He made me feel something. He was free.

)X◆X(

BUT THE NEXT FILM I MADE AFTER . . . *AND JUSTICE FOR ALL* WAS *Cruising*, and I didn't find that freedom there. Billy Friedkin, who wrote it and directed it, talked about it being a dark vision. I had done the undercover-cop thing, and he had made *The French Connection* and *The Exorcist*, so I went with it. I thought the script, about an unknown killer who is menacing men in the gay clubs of Manhattan, was good when I read it. I thought it was exploring something and expressing something that had real insight and posed a couple of questions to the world. I was at a place in my life, too, where I was still a little unconscious but interested in pushing the envelope in a way that I hoped would shed light on certain subjects, open the door to more understanding of an ever-changing landscape, and reveal the evolution of our acceptance—I was hoping for a kind of enlightenment, for both the audience and for me.

But *Cruising* became very controversial during its production. We had a lot of trouble during the filming of it in the summer of

1979, with protesters showing up to our shooting locations almost every day. They believed that it would present gay people unfairly and stereotypically. I got bomb threats and had to have bodyguards protect me. I already don't function well in controversies, especially when you're the so-called movie star, and you're assumed to have all the power, but you really don't. I've always thought that the best thing to do is to be quiet in those situations, because once you start yapping, it gets worse. You have to take the punches. It's the nature of the beast.

However, it was an exploitative film. I didn't see it as that when I was doing it. When I said yes to it, I thought it was going to be a murder-mystery thriller with some edge to it. But I was not as sensitive as I could have been about the stigmatization of the gay community and how this material depicted them. And I knew when I saw the film that it was exploitative. Since I never did publicity at the time, let's face it, I remained quiet. I got a call from one of the producers who said, "Al, say *something* about the film, will you?" I said, "I don't feel anything about it." He started badgering me: "Just say it was interesting. It was mysterious. It had some powerful scenes." I agreed to something because, after all, they had paid me a lot of money, and I wasn't going to just abandon them. But I wanted to go somewhere far away from the madness. I'd had enough.

I never accepted the paycheck for *Cruising*. I took the money, and it was a lot, and I put it in an irrevocable trust fund, meaning once I gave it, there was no taking it back. I gave it to charities, and with the interest, it was able to last a couple of decades. I don't know if it eased my conscience, but at least the money did some good. It was always donated anonymously, because I didn't want to make it a PR stunt—I just wanted one positive thing to come out of that whole experience.

Two years later, I made the comedy *Author! Author!* I couldn't say no to Israel Horovitz, who wrote its screenplay and had written *The Indian Wants the Bronx*. *Indian* gave me a way of life—a career, if you want to call it that. Let's face it, it did. *Author! Author!* was a comedy that was trying to explore how people raise children in broken families, how they deal with divorce and the drama and trauma that go with it for them and their kids. And I loved being with those kids on the film.

But the film's director, Arthur Hiller, and I were not what you would call in sync. (You may be sensing a pattern.) I was late to arrive for a scene in the middle of winter in Gloucester, Massachusetts, of all places. It was freezing cold and constantly snowing on and off, and I was back in my motel room, waiting for them to call me to the set. So it was a miscommunication, nothing more. But I was late and it gave Hiller a chance to vent what had been brewing in him for six weeks. He went berserk, trashing me to the crew and damning me in front of everybody. So I got in my car and I left. I had one of the bigwigs of the film with me, and he had those kinds of eyes that eat fleas. He told me, "You've got to go back. Or you will pay for it." That really got to me. I knew I was being threatened. I thought to myself, *You're going after the wrong guy there, fella.* But then I reconsidered: No, Pacino, keep your head. If you walk away, that means costing you money. That means calling in lawyers. That means going to court. That means publicity. I didn't want to play games with these people, so I said I'd go back. I was just trying to get through this film.

Author! Author! was received with venomous disdain. The handwriting was on the wall. I could feel myself slipping into obscurity. What would that be like, obscurity? And why was I welcoming it?

><(•)><

OF COURSE, THERE'S THE GENERAL BELIEF THAT I'M A COCAINE addict or was one. It may surprise you to know I've never touched the stuff. However, I've always had abundant energy—I'm always up, and Tony Montana allowed me to pour that into the character. There was also a certain liberation that he offered me. He saw an advertising slogan on the side of a blimp that said THE WORLD IS YOURS and he truly believed it. That's what inspired me about him and what I took from him.

Our *Scarface* was not set in the suffering of the Great Depression, the world of the Bowery Boys and the plays of Clifford Odets, when everything was scarce and no one seemed to have two nickels to rub together. Our *Scarface* was about the greed of our present day, the time we made it in, the Reagan era, when everything was abundant and still somehow just out of reach. We were mocking the whole idea of trickle-down economics and the grab-everything-you-can philosophy of the moment. Oliver Stone would later boil it down to just three words—"Greed is good"—in his film *Wall Street.* Look around today. We knew that this world was coming. We wanted to call out the avarice we witnessed and still make it entertaining.

The time that Marty Bregman and I had spent apart had ultimately been healthy for us. He had wanted to make films on his own, away from me. And when I came to him about *Scarface* he roared back into action, as if no time had passed. He immediately set about making a deal with Universal for the rights to remake the film and began assembling the talent. Bregman brought in our old pal Sidney Lumet to direct and David Rabe tried a version of a script that was more closely modeled on the original film, but it didn't work. So Bregman got Oliver Stone, now an Academy Award winner for *Midnight Express*, to write it.

Lumet wisely supplied the idea to modernize our *Scarface* by setting it during the Mariel boatlift and making Tony Montana one of the thousands of Cuban refugees who came to America as a mocking gift from Fidel Castro. But Bregman wanted to keep away from anything that resembled *Serpico* or *Dog Day Afternoon*, while Lumet wanted to make the film grounded and realistic and invest it with themes of social consciousness. Bregman said we've seen that before. Pretty soon the two were at odds and Bregman had Lumet axed. The Don had struck again. In came De Palma, who wanted the film to have an operatic style, colorful and wildly entertaining, which was how Bregman envisioned it too.

Oliver was energized by the political nature of our story—he is just not a writer if he's not being political—and the commentary that it allowed him to make. I loved Oliver and I continue to love him; I saw him as a madman whose madness would come and go. I brought him up to my country house in New York to talk about his *Scarface* screenplay. He would tell me stories he had picked up from the real-life criminals and drug dealers he had met as he scoured the underbelly to research the script. He had heard about one gangster who had gotten high on his own supply, and as he was being shot up in a gunfight, he would mime the act of throwing the bullets back. I thought that image was spectacular—the ferocity and insanity of it; the level of cocaine that this person must have been on to allow him to do that. Another anonymous coke dealer supplied a quote that became the epigraph for the *Scarface* screenplay: "Every day above ground is a good day."

But who wouldn't want to play someone like Tony Montana, who, when he's facing down a rival who would chop him up with a chain saw, turns to the man threatening him and says, "Why don't you try sticking your head up your ass? See if it fits."

With Tony Montana, what you see is what you get, and fuck you. His two-dimensionality is the beauty of him for me. If we wanted to get inside Tony, I didn't have to dig deep inside me. It was right there, in the writing. You saw it on the page. The way I played him, the character never has any inner conflict until the moment he kills his best friend, Manny, after finding his sister in his arms. That is the only time you ever saw him puzzled, in self-examination, confused for a bit about what he did. That's when he goes to that third dimension, but only for a short while—as far as anyone can go on that much cocaine. You know there's nothing but death after that.

I spent the summer preparing for *Scarface* at the Outrigger, a big condominium complex on Malibu Beach, getting deeper into the role of Tony and figuring out as much as I could about him. I'm not certain, but I can almost swear to it that a porno film was being made next door to me. I would from time to time hear wild noises and see my neighbors come and go in skimpy costumes that offered clues about their cinematic pursuits. But in my room, with its view of the Pacific Ocean, I was meeting with my costume person, my makeup person, and my hair person to talk about my character. *What about the scar? How did he get it? Where does it go?* I came up with an idea. I said, I want a scar that goes through his eyebrow and into his face. It says it right away. There it is, *chaos*. That's Tony Montana. All you have to do is look at him.

I was put on a special diet and an exercise program, including daily rounds of racquetball, to get that lean, mean, sinewy look. I trained closely with a guy who was an expert at knife combat, and I worked on my accent with a dialect coach, Bob Easton, and my co-star, Steve "Rocky" Bauer, a Cuban native who was playing Manny. Accents are interesting in how they help create a character. You're not ever going to get an authentic accent unless you grew up with it. De Palma described the movie as an opera because it was bigger than life and everything about it was exaggerated, so I put that to use for the accent.

I was inspired by the plight of the underclass that Tony Montana came from, the marginalized people that he belonged to, because I felt I was part of it, too, because of my background and upbringing. That gave me the opportunity to uncork the underclass in myself.

In my own way, I was expressing what I'd learned in my forty-one or so years up to that point, applied to the world of the film. Performers are like painters—crazy, wild painters who paint characters. That's what I was in *Scarface*.

We encountered some production problems early on when we started filming in Miami that fall. There was a conservative contingent there that was bothered by how we might portray Cuban people in our movie—would we be exploiting them, would we be derogatory, would we be pro-Castro?—and they would occasionally try to make trouble for us at our locations. Usually when you dig deep enough into those things you find out some politicians are trying to make points or somebody's wheel didn't get greased. But soon enough the biggest villain on the set would be me.

I came to work one day to do the scene where Tony Montana causes a stir at a very elegant restaurant. As he's being thrown out of somewhere he should probably never have been allowed into in the first place, he realizes he has the attention of everyone else in the room, and he announces, with his usual bravado, "Say good night to the bad guy." It was crucial to the scene that I and my fellow cronies wear tuxedos, to emphasize how very out of place we were among the highest of high society. Underneath it all, we were still wild animals.

When I walked into my dressing room, I saw all my other familiar clothes—Hawaiian shirts, white suits—but no tuxedo. I said, "What am I wearing today?" And I was told I was going to wear my usual Tony Montana look because the scene had now been moved to the nightclub that catered to Tony and the other gang members, the same spot they always go to. I thought, This doesn't belong there. It has to happen at a restaurant with the ritzies, with the privileged class. If it happens at the nightclub, it has no resonance. It has no contrast. I asked the A.D., why are we doing this? And of course the bottom line was the bottom line. They wanted to take a location out of the budget. Brian was going too far with the costs of the film, and by cutting out a location, they felt they could save a few bucks.

So I decided to make a stand. I had Bregman and Brian in my dressing room, both of whom were, understandably, concerned about the money. And with all due respect to them, I said, "You cannot do this. This is not what Oliver wrote. It's even in his stage directions—he said it has to be formal clothes. This is not how the scene was meant to be done. It will lose its meaning." I think I spoke for close to forty-five minutes. By the time I finished, they both looked at me and said, "We're all in trouble now." I said, "I'm always in trouble, guys. Whether I do this or I don't, I'm in trouble. But what are we supposed to do?" They were smart. They agreed that the scene had to be done at the restaurant. But we would lose this day of shooting at a cost of $200,000. And so it became a mark on my reputation. Boom: he's difficult. *Can you believe what he did? He wouldn't shoot.* Even if what I was doing was right for the film and faithful to what was in the script, the studio never forgives you for something like that.

)(◆)(

I WAS VERY GRATEFUL FOR THE WONDERFUL RELATIONSHIP I HAD at the time with Kathleen Quinlan. I had first met Kathleen at a party at Lee Strasberg's home on Central Park West, where on Sunday nights Lee would get people together and lecture about music, theater, and the arts. Bob De Niro was there with me, and at a certain point, I happened to catch a glimpse of Kathleen. She turned and looked at me. I looked back at her, and that was it. The thunderbolt had hit me.

Bob and I were standing in the long hallway of Lee's apartment, looking at the photographs and portraits of great actors, artists, directors, and writers from centuries of theater history that were hanging on the walls. I said to Bob, "Something just happened to me." Bob, who is always very accommodating, said, "What do you mean? What's the matter?" I said, "This woman has gone right through me." He said, "Oh, okay," and he smiled. I think he saw, in a way, that I was going through some sort of spasm.

I was a grown person acting like I'd seen something for the first time in my life.

It turned out Kathleen had a boyfriend, and any woman with a boyfriend or husband is off-limits. I just will not go there. I guess it's somewhere in my ancestral roots, who can explain it? I might have forgotten about her, but I was doing these readings from time to time with a group of other actors, where we'd get together and read stage plays or screenplays that interested us. I went to one of these readings for Shakespeare's *Othello* in a basement-level apartment, and there was Kathleen, reading the role of Desdemona. At one point during the reading I looked up at that basement window and saw her boyfriend crouched down and peering into the reading from the sidewalk. I just had this sense that he was hovering protectively to check up on her, as if he were afraid someone there was going to swoop in and snatch up his beautiful girlfriend.

As fortune would have it, they eventually broke up. I found out on *Scarface*, because my boy Rocky Bauer heard it from his then wife, Melanie Griffith. He said, "I know someone who likes you— this girl Kathleen." Unfortunately, I had another girlfriend at the time, a long-distance relationship that was gradually coming unraveled.

Kathleen and I started seeing each other casually. She was from another world, Mill Valley, a beautiful town outside San Francisco, and while she was a great actress, she was also into kayaking and gymnastics. Perhaps having only one foot in her vocation of acting gave her an interesting color. She would be offered roles that were really big and important, and she would turn them down and other stars would take them. Kathleen wanted to go in a different direction. What a gift she has. I was quite taken with her in *I Never Promised You a Rose Garden*; if you've seen it, you know what I mean.

After a couple of months of dating, Kathleen and I had dinner at the Beverly Wilshire Hotel, where I stayed during *Scarface* to be closer to the set. She was talking to me at that dinner, telling me a story about her life, revealing herself much more and telling me things that really made me see her. She was speaking about her life and her feelings, in a way that made me understand what I felt intuitively the first time I saw her. And then it happened: the thunderbolt came back. It took me a couple of months to figure that one out. From that point on, we were together for a couple of years and there was a lot of love in that partnership.

Kathleen was my comfort during *Scarface*. It was a joy to come home every night to someone I loved, who would tell me about her day, what she'd worked on, who she'd spoken to, what annoyances she'd encountered. It would help me get my mind off my own work, the place that *Scarface* put me into, days spent being pounded by that crazy character, the smoke and the blood and the three-hundred-pound machine gun. We stayed together after I finished *Scarface*. We even took a great trip to Europe where we made our way around in a van, almost like hitchhikers. It was a glorious time and it felt so simple—so unfettered, no fanfare. She was a good traveler and she took care of a lot of things that I was and still am incapable of doing. We were living together, too, which was emancipating in a manner of speaking. Our life together was workable and easy.

My time with Kathleen was the closest I've ever come to getting married. But I've always shied away from marriage. I guess I didn't see how it would help anything. I just wanted to avoid what I thought, at the time, was the inevitable, an entrance to the pain train.

I thank God that Kathleen is still my friend to this day and I love her. But it wasn't easy to say no to marriage with a woman I loved. She knew what she wanted and she got it, only it was with someone else. It hurt when she left and I carried the hurt with me for years.

><•><

MY WORK ON *SCARFACE* WAS DONE IN BETWEEN RUNS OF DAVID Mamet's great play *American Buffalo*. I spent a couple of years sporadically doing the play off Broadway at Circle in the Square, where we opened it in 1981. We had been performing it in the round, but we were preparing to take the play on a run that would bring us to San Francisco, Washington, D.C., Boston, and London, where they had proscenium theaters. That meant we had to get a proscenium theater to practice in, and it's not always easy to find that in New York. But in 1983, right before *Scarface* came out, we were offered a great opportunity at the Booth Theatre, a beautiful Broadway house.

I didn't read reviews at that time, but when we were performing the play downtown, the feedback was generally positive, and when we went to Broadway, it seemed they weren't as enthusiastic. Somehow there was a sense we were using Broadway as a stepping-stone on our way to a larger tour, and I was just doing the play to make money. That was one of many false assumptions made about the play. But for the record, I was being paid Equity minimum so that I would only have to do six performances a week, instead of the eight performances a week that are usually required.

They also seemed to come down hard on my costar in the play, my dear, beloved friend Jimmy Hayden, who was giving a performance that was very special. Jimmy was a great actor and a real good-looking kid. He was in his twenties, and he had no family of his own, but I loved him like we were related. He also happened to be a drug addict. But he had the gift. He had the looks and he had the talent. He had it all. I have known people like that my whole life, who just have that greatness and that wildness about them. They are vulnerable.

American Buffalo was a living, breathing showcase for Jimmy— anybody who walked in was going to notice him. During the Broadway run, we lost Jimmy to drugs; once again that's how it went. It of course broke our hearts, and till this day it troubles me. When you're that close to someone and realize the loss, it pains you and there's nothing you can do or say about it. Jimmy was going to go far, and at that time, everyone thought so.

We did still manage to take the play to London, without Jimmy, replacing him with Bruce MacVittie, a wonderful actor and friend. A few weeks into the London run, we were performing the play. We're in the middle of the first act, talking about this robbery we're going to do, and down the aisle came this woman. She was a little tipsy, and as she walked right to the edge of the proscenium, she looked up at us on the stage and held out a cigarette. In a strong Cockney accent, she said to me, "Got a light?" Still in character, never breaking stride, we said to her, "We're working here! We're trying to figure out a heist. You're interrupting, lady." I thought, Is this the sophisticated London theater I've been hearing about all my life? But by that time, the security at the theater had gently grabbed her by the arm and walked her up the aisle.

Sometimes an audience doesn't know exactly what it's seeing right away, and they need time to take it in and absorb it. It's a lesson I learned from *American Buffalo*, and also from *Scarface*. At its opening, *Scarface* was a flop—not commercially, but critically. Artistically. Spiritually.

There was a premiere for the film in New York that people walked out of. I went right from a performance of *American Buffalo* on Broadway into the *Scarface* after-party at Sardi's. Whoever had chosen the guest list had clearly miscalculated, because sitting there were all these sophisticated, upper-echelon people, and they were all in full-on zombie mode. When I walked in, Liza Minnelli came up to me. She hadn't even seen the film yet—she was just there for the party—and she said, "These people just saw your movie. What the fuck did you do to them?" I said, "I'm just an actor, Liza. You should ask science." I slunk to the back of Sardi's with Charlie, and from this massive crowd of cold, unsympathetic faces came Eddie Murphy with that big smile of his. He walked right over to me and said, "Al, that was fantastic!" and he gave me a hug. I think he was the only one in that whole room who understood and appreciated that film.

Those of us who had worked on *Scarface* were devastated for days. Oliver Stone had seen the film on his own, among civilians, in a Times Square theater and excitedly reported back on the audience's response: "You know what it is, Al?" he told me. "It's anarchy. They were dancing in the aisles." He seemed to expect the polarized reaction, but Brian De Palma took it hard, as did Marty Bregman. My head was spinning. I kept asking myself, Why is it getting this response? For weeks on end, I had some of the biggest directors in the world—even Lumet—haranguing me about how bad it was. Milos Forman said to me, "You made *Dog Day After-noon* and you go and make a movie like this? How do you do that?" Warren Beatty was more sympathetic. He told me, "You know, we had a slow start with *Bonnie and Clyde*. Give it some time, Al." He was right.

When you feel confident about something, that criticism is sometimes easier to take. These things can happen when you make films. Some of them turn out to be controversial and get condemned by a faction of the public, and I can't for the life of me understand why certain ones get to go on and enjoy a second life. Me, I had never read a newspaper headline in big, black, bold letters that said PACINO FAILS MISERABLY AS SCARFACE, until I got that from a lady who was excited to see me backstage at a performance of *American Buffalo*. She wanted my autograph, and that's what she grabbed for me to sign. Now, if that kind of headline doesn't do twinkle-toes with your brain, I don't know what else will. But this woman couldn't have cared less about that review. She could see the future.

Rocky Bauer and I were both nominated for Golden Globes, but *Scarface* got no attention from the Academy Awards. I cannot overstate the unbelievable job Brian De Palma did on *Scarface*, mapping the film and charging it with such dynamism and reach. He took it to the limit. Why he wasn't honored for it will forever make me wonder. When the Oscar nominations were announced, I was doing *American Buffalo* in San Francisco at the Curran Theatre, where we had police officers on horseback to help manage the crowds that waited after every show. On that day, when there were no nominations for my performance or anyone else's contributions to *Scarface*, a group of fans came after the matinee performance and made their way past the police to give me a homemade Oscar they had constructed to make up for this perceived oversight. It looked just like a real Oscar, only bigger. It felt like the right kind of award, a trophy from the people, and I have kept it to this day.

I don't know why it was surprising to anyone involved in *Scarface* that it wasn't received well by the establishment when it first came out. The whole film was a blatant indictment of the 1980s and it went against the status quo—the "Just Say No" campaign of Nancy Reagan and the establishment of the time. It certainly didn't fit into the Hollywood mold either.

In time, *Scarface* would be embraced by the hip-hop generation, who related to the mythology of Tony Montana and gave it credibility. You can't forget Tony Montana was heading to the sun like Icarus, flying higher and higher until he exploded. Rap artists and their fans embraced the movie. They understood it and went with the metaphor. They recognized the film as a parable, a story about how you view the world when you're taught that life is cheap and dispensable. They were the catalyst and the springboard for the movie's eventual success, because once they bought it, the world started buying it.

People from all walks of life started finding the film. Some came from low incomes and others were elites—college kids, prison inmates, and professional athletes. The movie became counterculture. The legend of Tony Montana spread worldwide. Tony Montana lets people break out of themselves and their situations—break out of your rut, break out of life as you're told to live it. There's something about the journey that is sweet. That's why the people who actually come from the world that it depicts, who have really walked that turf, related to it and survived it. They knew the joke from the drama.

When *Scarface* had its thirty-fifth anniversary in 2018, we held a big reunion event at the Beacon Theatre in Manhattan. It was the last time I saw Marty Bregman, who was ninety-two years old and using a wheelchair; he died just a few weeks later. We had a sold-out audience, thousands of people, most of whom had seen it before but never on a big screen. I also invited a few of my friends who I knew were not fans of the movie. I love these people, and I admire and respect them, and they're still my friends. I told them, "I would like you to see it with an audience." I didn't make a big thing of it. I said, "Just take a look. Do it for me."

When the film came up on that big, beautiful screen, it was like it was being blasted out to the stratosphere. The magnitude and the magnificence of it became clarion clear. Even people like De Palma felt the film more. My friends who hadn't previously cared for *Scarface* didn't come out saying it's the best picture they ever saw, mind you. But they saw that there was a richness to it. They accepted the spirit of the thing, which I knew they would when they saw it with an audience. They were allowed to understand where the laughs were, where the nuance was, and where the drama was too. *Oh, that's what that means.* The audience was, in a way, their subtitles, providing them with the inner language of the film.

To this day it's still the biggest film I ever did. The residuals still support me. I can live on it. I mean, I could, if I lived like a normal person. But it does contribute, let's put it that way.

I think if they were to release *Scarface* tomorrow, it would get the same reaction, stir up the same controversy. It's just too damn unwieldy. That's all there is to it.

9

It's Over

I was out. My movie career was through. What I had put to-gether, role by role, was gone, squandered in the span of a few years. Each consecutive failure felt like a heavier weight pushing down on my chest. I began to question the very essence of what I was doing and why I was doing it. I felt trapped, creatively drained, distant from any connection to why I became an actor in the first place.

And so I quit. No notice given, no statement made. I simply stopped accepting film parts. I didn't care. I said, this is fine. I've still got a lot of things to be grateful for. I've got New York. I've got my friends. I can read plays all day long, and I still have a choice of what I do. But when it came to films, I was finished.

I made a couple of mistakes when I quit. One was that I thought I could come back anytime I wanted. But people are ready to move on without you far faster than you realize. When you're counted out, you're out, and even more so if you look like you don't really care about getting back in.

)X(◆)X(

RIGHT BEFORE I BOWED OUT, I WAS WORKING ON THE FILM *Revolution* in England. Every day in Norfolk I woke up on a farm. I was a hundred miles away from London and far away from anywhere that felt like home. The place wasn't posh, just a cottage with a bit of wear and tear in the British countryside. Creaky floorboards greeted my every step. A king's ransom in secondhand furniture. But that can have its charm too. I loved waking up to the sunlight and the sounds of barnyard animals. Horses, cows. Fucking geese. But horses and cows.

I had come here to escape. The reaction to *Scarface* hadn't particularly warmed my heart, and then Kathleen and I had our breakup, which was extremely tough for both of us. I needed something to get me away from all of that—some film projects were around, and this one offered me a sabbatical of sorts. I was already in the mindset that I knew I wasn't long for this business.

I don't know what went wrong with *Revolution*. Sometimes it's just the usual culprits. I must admit, I liked the director, Hugh Hudson, the British filmmaker who had just won the Oscar for *Chariots of Fire*. He had quite the persuasive tongue when he talked to me about the project. The film *Revolution* would tell the story of a rugged man who has been banged around by life, and who arrives with his young son in New York on the day that America has declared its independence from Great Britain. Hudson promised a re-creation of colonial life that was vivid and unsentimental, and I had lengthy discussions about the script with Charlie, who encouraged me to do it.

Hugh was the kind of artist who did what he wanted to do. He was still in the throes of an I-can-do-anything euphoria, and he asked a great deal of his crew, transforming a humble Norfolk town square into the Wall Street of 1776 or building an entire army encampment in the British countryside. The costs were an enormous financial strain on Goldcrest Films, the British studio that was paying for it, and Hugh worked me hard as well, sending me to chase after horse-drawn carts, push heavy machinery, and carry the young actor who played my son over my shoulders for hours.

When they finally put together a rough cut of the film and showed it to me, I said, "Hugh, it's just not ready. There's greatness in it, but if it's released like this, it will not go well." He seemed to understand that some changes were needed, and we talked about adding more voice-over narration, but that was about all he was allowed time for. Warner Bros. wanted it out in December so it would qualify for the Oscars. The studio put together a publicity campaign that was capitalizing on my fame at the time. They sold *Revolution* with my face. When you looked at the posters, all you saw was my head with that vacant, shell-shocked look. I saw it and thought, This is just not the film. Sadly, it turned out to be a disaster.

Aside from driving me out of the film business, *Revolution* put a dent in a great director's career. Hugh Hudson was a talented artist, but he had alienated others with his dogmatism, and when the film bombed, the industry pointed a finger at him. He had a tough time with his career afterward. Its failure stayed with both of us for a long time, and it took Goldcrest Films off the charts.

For a twenty-year period after *Revolution* was released, Hugh Hudson and I continued to get together, finding more ways to work on the film, putting in things we thought were missing, cutting it down where we could. We raised our own cash, and I got friends to write some of the voice-over narration. After Hugh passed away, there was a special screening of the new cut of the film, called *Revolution: Revisited*, for a couple hundred people at the Aero Theatre in Santa Monica. When you saw it on a screen of that size and in a theater with those acoustics, you saw a great director attempting something magical. These new changes made *Revolution: Revisited* a more tolerable film and gave it a certain resonance that didn't land with audiences forty years ago, and that was due to the additional narration and cutting. The new version sure did look good on that big, beautiful screen at the Aero.

These are the walls you run into in our business sometimes. This is the wire you walk on up there. It's risky doing this thing—when you take chances, you can fall. And then you have to decide to get up or not.

It seemed like every time I brought something to the public, to the commercial world, I was scrutinized and put down for it. I felt lost in that arena. So I tried to stay within my comfort zone, focus on work that I had started developing at the Actors Studio and found enjoyable. I still needed to experiment, so I started to film that work—making films of things that I liked, that I had strong feelings about. It was a way to ground myself and get back to the essentials of acting. But the only way for me to make these films without being blasted off the face of the earth was to do it privately.

There were people who would tell me, "Don't spend your own money to make your own films. That's rule number 1. Don't get high on your own supply." Certain people are cautious like that. They're just built that way. But Marty Bregman gave me some of the best advice I ever heard: "You don't go uptown to do this—you go downtown." You don't take your toughest and most difficult ideas that you're still trying to figure out for yourself, the itch that you're still trying to scratch, and put them in a movie that you're getting paid millions of dollars for. You take it away from those expectations and judgments—you put it a bag marked LEGACY, and you hope that someday someone picks it up, opens it, and sees what's inside. You do it with your own money, and you end up broke. A friend of mine said to me, "What are you doing, Al? You're becoming an off-off-Broadway movie star. That's an oxymoron." But it didn't matter. If I was a painter, this could be one of my many sketches, a kind of practice where I would get to learn some of the fundamentals of filmmaking that I hadn't picked up as an actor. I'm too old to go to film school, and I'm not going to college—I don't need those credits. I'm just playing with ideas, and I'm not putting it on the main stage. As a matter of fact, I'm not putting it on any stage. It's an outlet for myself.

Sometimes you just have to do things away from commercial pressures and the demands of box-office opening weekends, which I just had no understanding of. But I ask myself sometimes, as I grow old, how many illusions do I have? Charlie and I used to say that when you're put in the grave, your illusions come out of whatever box you're in, they hover over your tombstone and evaporate into the sky. They're the last to go.

〉〈◆〉〈

WHEN I STEPPED AWAY FROM WORKING COMMERCIALLY, I WENT back to the plays and ideas that had interested me long before my sojourn into Hollywood. *The Local Stigmatic*, a one-act play by Heathcote Williams, had fascinated me as a young man. Now, in my middle age, it brought me back to those bohemian days, to the very ethos of the world that had inspired me as a teenager making my first travels into the Village. I hadn't realized just how much it had inspired me then, in my time at the Living Theatre and other performance spaces, and I wanted to rediscover that and get it out of my system.

Williams was just twenty-one years old when he wrote it. The savagery of the dialogue, the turbulent way he put his words together, was something I never got over: "Fame is the first disgrace, because God knows who you are. God knows who YOU are?" The action of the play is very simple: two nihilistic gamblers who bet on dog races go into a bar where they meet a celebrity, an actor they recognize. After a lot of small talk and funny lines, they start to walk the actor home, and the energy starts to change and become dangerous. One of the gamblers gives a monologue in which he claims that the actor saw him on the street but pretended not to recognize him. The men throw him to the ground and start kicking him, and though they don't kill him, they mark him with a cut on his face. The mark is symbolic—it's their way of saying, we were here, we exist.

The Local Stigmatic is a story about identity and envy. It's about those of us who have a need to be seen, and how it can make people envious. Heathcote was talking about what that evokes in certain kinds of people who feel outside the margins. He was only a kid when he wrote it, but he understood that somehow and articulated it so well in the play. These can be hard ideas for audiences to embrace.

I saw *The Local Stigmatic* performed before I ever acted in a film. I read it before I did my first Broadway show. When I acted in it onstage, after I won my first Tony, we were unable to bring across the point of the play. The audience had such a bad reaction. I guess if enough people signed a petition they would have thrown us out of New York. But the great Jon Voight saw the play and gave us a thousand dollars to run another week. He had just become a movie star, and in my eyes he became a deep, deep friend. So I knew that I had to make a film of *The Local Stigmatic* myself. Everything it was talking about was coming true.

Heathcote, who I befriended, was a vibrant, ferocious intellectual, an Oxford graduate who was a beautiful poet and painter and a total political anarchist. He was my British Cliffy. He loved to stage magic acts. He lived in a treehouse and dated the model Jean Shrimpton. I walked the streets of London with him while he carried two shopping bags, and God only knows what was in them. Together, in some offbeat restaurant as we parked our asses down for tea, we ran into Rudolf Nureyev, perhaps the greatest ballet dancer of all time, who told us how much he had enjoyed *Scarface*. That was a lift—I needed that one. That got me through my whole stay in England.

Years later Heathcote helped me on the movie *The Devil's Advocate*. For my role as the Devil, he wrote me dialogue, like this line where I'm talking about lawyers and hedge funders: "Every one of 'em getting ready to fist-fuck God's ex-planet, lick their fingers clean as they reach out toward their pristine, cybernetic keyboards to total up their billable hours." I put that forth to Hollywood and guess what? They ate it up. Then Heathcote wanted screen credit—just a mention, not as one of the main writers, of course, but that was an impossibility for them to do. So I paid Heathcote out of my own pocket, which was not impossible and totally worth it.

We shot *The Local Stigmatic* for a few weeks in Atlanta, with David Wheeler as our director, and a principal cast of myself, Paul Guilfoyle, Joe Maher, and Michael Higgins. When it was finished, we showed the film around to people we admired. We had a great dinner gathering of artists and literati in London. People like Tom Stoppard and David Hare, who all sat at a long table. Harold Pinter had seen the film twice at this point; he sat at the head of the table, and when he wanted to speak to everyone, he rang a little bell and the group fell silent. "Every once in a while," he said, "we see something different. We come into contact with art in film." I just sat there stunned. Heathcote was in the room, fiddling with a coin and not looking up at anyone, playing the role of the shy genius. He'd been described as a protégé of Pinter's, but to actually be in the same room as his literary idol, I guess it all was just too much for him.

I ran the film once for Elaine May, the great actress and filmmaker, who told me, "I liked it very much. But don't you ever show this to the public. You don't know your fame. You don't understand it, and you don't understand how it registers. You must recognize it." And she was right. You're too well-known for this sort of thing. You have to be careful, because you're going to startle people. Don't put this in a theater.

I showed it to Jonas Mekas, the independent-film impresario of downtown Manhattan, who ran *The Local Stigmatic* at his Anthology Film Archives and told me, somewhat optimistically, that I was going to win an Oscar for it. I kept calling Andrew Sarris, the film critic for *The Village Voice*, to come and see it. And he said, "Stop bothering me, Al. I've seen it three times already. I've told you what I think. Just show the thing already." I was trying to get the confidence to screen it for wider audiences. I never did.

I've come to realize that when I do my own things, nobody goes. Those avant-garde influences that I was brought up with never left my brain. When I'm left on my own, that's just what seems to come out. It's a drawback. People come in with expectations, and they leave angry. *The Local Stigmatic* is such a specific distillation of me and my take on this subject. It's 150 proof, which can be a little strong for some people.

)X(♦)X(

BEFORE I WORKED ON MY OWN FILM, I COULDN'T HAVE CARED LESS about how movies actually got made. I was just an actor. As a friend of mine used to say about himself, "I'm just trying to break out of show business." Fortunately, some wonderful partners and collaborators heard my cries for help and joined me on my delirious crusade. I gained such a fondness and respect for editors, witnessing the transformative power when a film falters, is rearranged, and suddenly comes alive.

And I was editing *The Local Stigmatic* forever. We were working with physical 16-millimeter film on flatbed consoles, threaded into Steenbecks. We were always waiting for prints to be copied or loaded onto the machine. As I sat around at the Brill Building and wandered into other editing suites, I met great film artists like Skip Lievsay, Martin Scorsese's longtime sound man, and the composers Howard Shore and Elmer Bernstein, Oscar winners who were seemingly responsible for writing half of all the scores in Hollywood.

And then one day, on another visit to another editing bay, I heard it. I heard the laugh that I heard back on the set of *The Godfather*, when we had to convince ourselves that we weren't on the verge of throwing away our careers. I saw the smile that reassured me through all those interminable screen tests that I was safe and someone was there to protect me, and the eyes that had seen me and known me. There was Diane Keaton, working on a film of her own.

I have always liked women, but from the time I was very young, I have been shy around them. I don't woo them. I don't pursue them. Women either respond to you or they don't, and if they don't make the first move toward me, I am a bit reluctant to try again. But with Diane this time things were different. We always had a connection. She understood my read on things, and it felt comforting to have someone who got me. So I went after her. We hung out together, and after a couple of months we decided to get together. We found a tempo and a temperature that was right.

Diane was working very consistently at the time, making movies that were highly commercial. When she starred in *Baby Boom*, it was a big hit for her. Having a partner who was more successful than me didn't faze me or intimidate me. I wasn't particularly motivated to get back into the game or change my approach to my own work. I just wished Diane joy in her work, which she had. She'd go off and make a film for a few weeks; I'd stay home and do a reading of a play. I knew what an artist she was, and I admired all the different ways she applied her talents as an actor, a singer, a writer, and a photographer. She used to tease me affectionately and call me "a lazy eye-tie,"—a corny old insult for Italians—which would just make me laugh. But she was extremely supportive of *The Local Stigmatic*, thought it was good for me, and knew why I needed to do it.

Diane got to know a few of my close relatives, and she was so taken with my grandmother who raised me that she started to make a documentary about her. My grandmother was born in New York, but her family was from Naples. With her blond hair and bright blue eyes, when she spoke Italian it surprised you. She was eccentric, maybe the most out-there person I've ever known, and she was the one who raised little Al. Which could possibly explain why, on one of our visits to her, Granny took out a manila envelope and pressed it into my hands. "Take this," she said to me. I opened it up and inside was seven hundred dollars. I had been helping to support her financially for years, so I couldn't quite understand the gesture or what it was for. "I don't need the money," I told her. But Granny insisted: "Take it," she said. "Buy yourself some new clothes, please." She could never believe the way I dressed. Even after the first time she saw me in *The Indian Wants the Bronx*, she said—and I quote her—"Can't you wear different clothes?" This time, I couldn't get Granny to take the envelope back from me no matter what I did, so I just quietly left it for her on top of her console television. Diane was delighted by this, and by Granny's unpredictable takes on just about everything. That's the thing about family: you're used to them, and though you may take them for granted, other people become mirrors to them. You learn to find them fascinating all over again.

I brought Diane to my father's latest wedding in Los Angeles. He was a very smart and resourceful man who had set up his own bar, restaurant, and nightclub in West Covina, which he called—what else?—Pacino's. When somebody would say to me, "He's trying to trade on your name," I would say, "Hey, schmuck—that's the name I got from *him*. It was his first and he can do what he wants with it." The wedding was a true melting pot. I mean, talk about diversity—you never saw so many people and so many kids of all kinds, all my half brothers and half sisters from my father's previous marriages. The man liked to settle down. He was married five times in all. Me, not even once. I guess we balanced each other out that way.

Diane had a house in California, which I enjoyed. I'd go in and out as my sleepy, weepy self, and I was doing fine. Perhaps that's what I was meant to be, a backward glance to what my life was before I was known, when I would spend it reading and thinking, walking and talking. In New York, I could stroll through Central Park as I did regularly, and I found as time went on, people looked at me less and less. That took some getting used to, but there was something about it that gave me peace.

I was out walking in Central Park one day, as free as the elements, when some fella came up to me, who I thought was maybe going to ask me for directions.

"Hey, Al!" he said, in a friendly and familiar way. "Where you been?"

I tried to look at him and see if this was someone I knew, but I didn't recognize his face.

Ol' friendly Al.

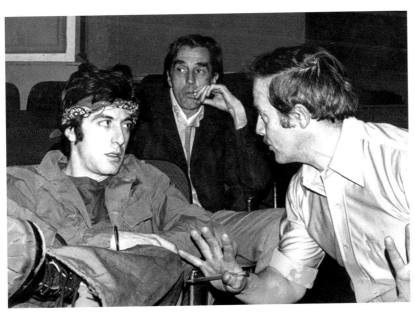

Rehearsing *The Basic Training of Pavlo Hummel* with David Wheeler.
Charlie Laughton always had my back.

American Buffalo. No need to pray, it's not going to change the reviews.

. . . And Justice for All. I want off this film!

A more contemplative
Tony Montana. I see
a ray of hope.

I guess there
was chemistry
there with
Michelle Pfeiffer.
Good casting.

Scarface. Hey, I look like I mean it.

With Liz Taylor. I love this girl! Just the sweetest.

Revolution, with Dexter Fletcher. A father and son's survival.

Sea of Love, with Ellen Barkin. I'm about to be turned down. Can you guess why?

In Rome for *The Godfather: Part III*. We could laugh. Everybody else had to work.

At the premiere for *Sea of Love* with Diane Keaton. At least she got dressed for it.

Dick Tracy. Somebody had to teach Madonna how to dance.

With Suzanne Bertish in *Salomé* at Circle in the Square. I liked wearing the costumes, especially lipstick.

Glengarry Glen Ross. Where's Jack Lemmon? He usually shows up.

Dancing the tango with Gabrielle Anwar. Don't kid yourself—she's leading me.

Scent of a Woman.
I guess I just liked
wearing uniforms.
The medals were
over the top.

Finally, I can quit this business.

Looking for Richard. Did you get that shot? I can't do it again,
we have to move on.

With Bob De Niro in *Heat*. Just the table between us.

As Roy Cohn in *Angels in America*, Tony Kushner's masterpiece.

Donnie Brasco
with Johnny Depp,
my adult Cliffy.

With Marty Bregman in 2003. There's no Pacino without the man in the suit.

Me with Jack Kevorkian, who I played in *You Don't Know Jack*. A man I loved, and the most pro-life person I ever met.

The Merchant of Venice at Shakespeare in the Park with Lily Rabe. It's hard to imagine, but Lily is the daughter of one of the biggest loves in my life.

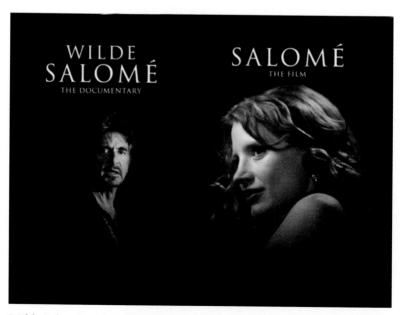

Wilde Salomé, with Jessica Chastain. She was only getting started here.

With David Mamet. He's always trying to get in front of me.

Helen Mirren and me in *Phil Spector*. People want to know why I fired my hairdresser. Well, open your eyes, man.

When I look
at this picture,
I actually
scare myself.

Once Upon a Time in Hollywood, with my two friends Leo and Brad. I believe they think I'm someone else.

On the red carpet for *The Irishman*, with Bob De Niro and Marty Scorsese. We're being interviewed, why are we singing?

House of Gucci.
You know I'm gaga
for Gaga!

All is well. I'm with my kids.

Look who's ready for his close-up.

"On the *screen*," he said. "I haven't seen you in a movie in a long time. We need you up there. We *need* you, man."

That man wasn't the only person who brought this to my attention. One day, while Marthe Keller was visiting me in New York, she mentioned it, too, on another walk in Central Park. It was always Central Park, what a place. She said, "You have to get back to working again. It's who you are." She said it with a little more finesse and wisdom than I'm expressing now, and I heard her, but I didn't feel it yet. I was too happy.

I guess it had been a while since I'd made a film that most people could see. I appreciated what these people were saying. I was sort of tickled by the idea that my absence was not just being noticed by some people but actually impacting their lives, because I was feeling okay, I really was. I felt free to engage, to dabble, to travel, to absorb these things that were happening to me, that had been on hold for what felt like twenty years. When I look back on this period now, I'm touched and I feel like I miss it. It was a departure from something I wasn't really feeling good about. Being with Diane had a lot to do with my sense of peace and comfort. I had found that kind of comfort that makes you feel and think with the world. I enjoyed the ability to continue this experimental journey, free from the pressures of having to fulfill anyone's expectations but my own, if I wanted to. But I wouldn't have a choice in the matter for much longer.

)X(◆)X(

SOMEHOW I HAD MANAGED TO GO BROKE. I LOOKED UP AND I HAD no money. I could say I got taken advantage of. I could blame my accountants. I could blame Marty Bregman, who had put me into some sort of tax shelter that went south. I could blame myself, but then I'd have to take responsibility for my own actions. In any case, I looked in the cupboard and it was bare. I had about ninety grand in the bank and that was it. I had a lifestyle to boot. I had my home in the country, which I didn't want to give up. I was spending and not earning; I was putting out but I wasn't bringing in. I think there's a word for that.

I can't even explain why I didn't care about the money. I was never a materialistic person. I don't know where I got that from. I appreciate the finer things in life as much as the next guy, and I won't refuse a good meal or a first-class seat if someone offers it to me, but to actually go out and seek that for myself? That's another story.

I enjoyed my life with Diane, and I enjoyed not being on the scene. But she could sense that I was having money trouble. I had to tell her what was going on. I said, "I got hit with something." She took me into New York to see my lawyer.

My entertainment lawyer was a sweet guy named Arthur Klein. He sat me and Diane down in his office, which was decorated traditionally, with family photos and baseball memorabilia. Arthur began to explain that I was insolvent, due to mismanagement of my assets. He didn't play a part in it, I know that. But the words just washed right over me.

Diane, however, was furious. She got up from her seat, and she started to question him: "How could this happen?" He was hemming and hawing, well, you know, this and that.

She just exploded. She went up to Arthur and was now face-to-face with him. She backed him into a corner of his office, pointed at me, and said, "Do you know who he is?"

He said, "Well, you know."

She was practically grabbing him by the lapels: "No, tell me who he is." He started to speak, but Diane jumped in again: "Yeah, you're going to tell me, 'Oh, he's an artist.' No. *He. Is. An idiot.*"

I just stood there. What could I say?

Diane went on: "He's an ignoramus. When it comes to this, you've got to take care of him."

She meant when it came to my finances—what I'd come from, my upbringing, my early life, right through until then. And she was right. I didn't understand how money worked, any more than I understood how a career worked. It was a language I just didn't speak.

So what was I going to do now? It didn't matter to me if I had to put it all back together again. I had support. I had my friends. I had Charlie. I always knew that I had the power to go back to work because I had been getting offers for the four years that I stayed away from films. The thing that had stayed with me and propelled me was a beeline I could trace all the way back to that night I stepped onto the stage of the Actors Gallery to perform in Strindberg's *Creditors*. That moment when I said to myself, I can do anything now. And I don't have to be rich or successful or famous. I know I have this. It's the appetite to do this. It will serve me regardless. When you have an appetite, you'll find a way. I'll wait, and I'll find my people.

Diane was even more encouraging. She said to me, "What are you going to do, mope around all day? You're going to go back to the Village and live in a room and do your little art pieces? Is that what you think you're going to do? Come on, Al, you're not in the sixties anymore. Who do you think you are? There's no going back. You've been rich too long."

〉〈◆〉〈

WITH DIANE'S PROMPTING, I BEGAN TO REENGAGE WITH THE FILM industry. I got myself an agent who couldn't do much for me, but he did at least try. He brought me out to Los Angeles to meet with one of the heads of the studios there. We drove past one of those magnificent security gates and onto the lot and were brought into his offices. You could already tell what a great effort it was for this guy to deign to meet with me; he was running late and kept us waiting in an outer chamber—not even his inner room—for forty-five minutes before he made an appearance. I had been nominated for five Oscars at this point, but my agent was acting like I was looking for a handout. I wanted to ask him, did you happen to bring your hat so you could pass it around?

Once we got past the introductions and pleasantries, I started to tell the studio head about some ideas I had. But I could feel the condescension and disdain emanating from the cloud above me on which he sat. I said that I wanted to do a film based on the play *K2*, a moving and wonderful story about two mountain climbers. I thought it had the makings of a great adventure picture.

That got me a vague look in response.

I said to him, "I was thinking maybe I could star with Dennis Quaid."

"No, no, stop there," he answered. He was very firm and direct. "His plate is full."

I then started to pitch an idea about Edmund Kean, the legendary British actor of the early 1800s, his insane life and everything that had happened to him. I thought it could make an interesting, funny, and tragic film. I explained there were biographies of Kean and plays based on his exploits, and I'd be happy to get them to the exec so he could better understand how wild Edmund Kean's talent and life were. The exec remained silent and was looking at me like I was some sort of recovering leper who was about to turn contagious in front of his eyes. You know how some people have a way of saying things without saying a word. But to be totally honest, I knew this wasn't going to go well the moment I walked into his office. That was the first and last time I ever took a meeting like that. I never found the language to express myself in that environment of businesspeople and those who engage in that sphere. That's all alien to me.

I returned to New York empty-handed. Out of nowhere, Diane made a discovery for me. She's an industrious person, and she had found a screenplay that she practically threw at me. "Read that thing. This is your film."

So I started to read it. The script, by Richard Price, told the story of a veteran police detective who has drunk too much over the years, feels he's undervalued, and has lost any passion he once had for the job he's been doing forever. Already I could feel a connection to this guy. He investigates a murder, which then turns into a series of murders, and as he does, he finds himself falling for a woman who could be his lead suspect. It was called *Sea of Love*.

When I had finished reading it, I looked up at Diane and said, "I guess I could do this."

She said, "You *better*."

There was one problem, which was that another actor was attached to *Sea of Love*—he had expressed an interest in starring in it, but was now dragging his heels about making the film. Before I could really think about what to do next, my muscle memory kicked in and I found myself calling Marty Bregman.

Marty and I hadn't made a movie together since *Scarface*, which was now several years behind us, but he was aware of my money problems. He knew what I was going back to work for: moolah. The financial advice he'd given me was partly why I needed it. But as always we fell back into our familiar rhythms when we started to talk shop. I said, "Hey, man, do you want to do *Sea of Love*?" Once he'd taken the time to read it, Bregman agreed: "Yes, this is good for you." I said, "But it's in someone else's hands." And he said simply, "I will handle it."

And like magic, Marty Bregman took over the project and *Sea of Love* was ours. That's what you call a facilitator. As always there were still a few loose ends to sort out. The studio had hired a director they picked up from television and who they felt was the next new hot thing. He came to my house in the country and told me, "I heard you're a troublemaker." He was not trying to be charming; he thought he was laying down the law before we got started. He was a schmuck. "You know I like to work a certain way," he said. I said, "Any way you work is fine by me. I don't care." Once he started to loosen up a bit further, he said he would use me in the film. But I had barely learned this guy's name before the Don got rid of him. He was gone.

I said to Bregman, "What'd you do? You fired the guy?" He said, "Yeah, I got this guy Harold Becker." Becker had made some other great thrillers, like *The Onion Field*. He was really a good, smart director, as I would find out. We became pals. I needed the support because I hadn't made a movie like this in four years.

We spent that summer shooting *Sea of Love* in Toronto. Though I had played romantic leads in other movies, this film became renowned for a long, slow sex scene where Ellen Barkin holds me against a wall and gives me a bit of a pat-down before our two characters start going at it. The scene was brilliantly choreographed by Becker.

I'm not usually one to perform graphic lovemaking scenes, and I don't think many other actors like to do them either. It can become sort of borderline porn. I realize it is futile for me to complain that we're no longer in an age of movies like *A Place in the Sun*, where Elizabeth Taylor and Montgomery Clift could have an entire audience swooning in their seats without ever showing their naked bodies.

Sea of Love is a really good Hollywood film, a commercial film, and a showcase of Harold Becker's expertise. It is all suspended by a very thin wire of believability. There are a couple of faux pas in the storytelling—a few little inconsistencies, but I'm not going to tell you where to find them. It was a great boost for actors like Richard Jenkins and John Goodman, who were not as widely known at the time. Ellen Barkin blew the screen apart, sensually and artistically: what a performance. I was lucky to be a part of it.

The film made $100 million out of nowhere. For the first time in a long time, I was part of a hit film. I didn't make much money because I didn't have an appropriate back end, meaning I didn't have one at all. They knew I had been out of commission for four years, so they didn't have to cut that sweet a deal. Those people know when you're down. But I went from having no money to being back in the chips. I was flush with opportunities to act in movies again and even make a couple more films that I produced and directed myself. As I found out in Hollywood, sometimes not wanting something is the best way of getting it.

10

Just When I Thought I Was Out

I may not have been a Victoria's Secret model, but I knew how to pose for a camera. The photographer from *People* magazine was treating me like a very delicate baby, as the shutter clicked and the flashbulbs popped. "Give me playful, Mr. Pacino." *Click.* "Give me pensive, Mr. Pacino." *Pop!* "Be naughty." "Be coy." "Okay, now let's shoot you upside down." I gave them every position and every expression they asked for. I rolled around on the floor like a wrestler without an opponent. I was all too happy to comply. It was a sign of just how rapidly the world turns that, several years before, when *People* magazine was new and *Bobby Deerfield* was opening, they asked me to be on their cover and I said no. Instead, they just dug up some paparazzi picture of me and Marthe Keller and splashed it on the front of their magazine with a tawdry cover line that said CO-STAR IS HER LOVER OFFSCREEN TOO. Now, fifteen years later, not only were they going to put me on their cover in a classy photo shoot, but they were going to give me a big, distinctive title to go with it. It certainly wasn't "Sexiest Man Alive," but something nice and highfalutin like that. Talk about survival of the fittest: I had survived the old days, and these were the new days. I was ready for it.

In 1990, I was still riding the momentum of *Sea of Love*. They were making a big fuss over me at the photo shoot because *The Godfather: Part III* was about to be released. More than fifteen years after the second and seemingly final installment in the film saga that pulled me out of obscurity and threw me into the arena with the lions, a third chapter was coming. Francis Ford Coppola was back. I was back. Michael Corleone would return.

Then the editors from *People* magazine saw *The Godfather: Part III*, and, wouldn't you know it, I got taken off the cover of the magazine. I didn't get any story at all. It was canceled, dead on arrival. The photo shoot was spiked. I had been getting the red-carpet treatment, and in the blink of an eye, it was gone. All that time I spent in front of a camera, writhing like an insect like the guy in the Kafka story, for nothing.

Nonetheless, having almost been counted out in the eyes of Hollywood, I was about to experience the proverbial comeback. You know how it goes—everyone loves to see you tumble off your perch, but if there's anything they love more, it's a comeback story. Perhaps it's my dumb ego, but I didn't regard it as a comeback, though it was dramatized that way. I simply went back to work.

The comeback that got started with *Sea of Love* was nearly de-railed with *The Godfather: Part III*. The audience had issues with it, but in the span of my four next films, I would find myself a changed man. I had matured. At the end of that run, I was ready to stop re-treating from my past, let down my guard just a little, and accept the accolades and recognition I had been avoiding in my early successes.

Sonny Boy

WARREN BEATTY KNEW EXACTLY HOW TO TALK TO ME. WHEN HE was making a movie based on the Dick Tracy comic strip and he needed someone to play the bad guy, a vainglorious gangster named Alphonse "Big Boy" Caprice, he cajoled me. He's a good friend and a great artist, just about the smartest person I've ever known, and at the same time he has a way of getting what he wants. He started by asking me for my opinion on something. Who do you think would be right for the role? Did I know anyone who could play this part? I offered up names here and there. Then he uttered the fatal words: "What about you, Al?" I thought that's what he wanted in the first place, so I said yes.

Dick Tracy was wonderful, and working with Warren was total bliss because he'll just let you run wild. He'll give you as many takes as you want when he's at the helm, and his sense of things is so spot-on. He will always make you look better—you know you can't go wrong. *Dick Tracy* was a beautiful film, given vitality by the production design of Dick Sylbert and the cinematography of Vittorio Storaro. I felt a renewed appetite to engage my imagination and create a character that had a real identity. I had my own idea of this guy. They called him Big Boy because he had elephantiasis. Parts of him were swollen to an outrageous degree. Oversize hands. A jutting chin. A bulbous nose. The makeup artist John Caglione Jr. and I played with all these designs that we'd show to Warren. I got really grotesque at one point and Warren got me to dial it back a little.

The film was my brief stint in comedy. Big Boy was very funny, constantly misquoting lines that he attributes to great leaders in world history. "A man without a plan is not a man—Nietzsche." He has Glenne Headly tied to a set of giant clockwork gears that are on the verge of crushing her to death, and he declares, quite seriously and emphatically, "Can't you see I love you?" Some of these were ad libs and others were lines I had worked up with my friends Fred Kimball and Joe Hindy. I had the time of my life in that role. I danced on a table and I actually manhandled Madonna—only a little, just love taps.

This was still the dawn of the era of comic-book and comic-strip characters getting turned into movies, and this one eluded the young crowd. It was entertaining, and it made money, but it didn't quite live up to its alleged box-office potential. It had wit and sophistication. I didn't even take billing for the role, I was just having a good time with it. And it got me an Oscar nomination— my first in more than a decade. But as I may have mentioned, it was not the only movie I made that year.

)X◆X(

WHEN I WAS ASKED TO REPRISE THE ROLE OF MICHAEL CORLEONE for the first time in *The Godfather: Part II*, I struggled with the decision and second-guessed myself constantly. Not so for *Part III*. The choice could not have been easier. I was broke. Francis was broke. We both needed the bread. And I thought it would be an interesting challenge to try to find Michael some twenty years after the story of the previous film and almost as much time since I had last played him. To their credit, Coppola and Mario Puzo wrote what I thought was a very good script. It had Michael traveling to the Vatican, to investigate the murder of Robert Duvall's character, Tom Hagen.

At the film's conclusion, Michael would get assassinated on the stairs of a church. He rolls down the steps and comes to rest on the ground at the bottom. Kay, his ex-wife, rushes to his side. She looks into his face and asks him, "Michael, are you dying? Are you going to die?" And Michael looks up at her and he says, "No." And then he dies. Phenomenal ending. A brilliant callback to the first *Godfather*, as Michael ends his life with one last lie to Kay.

The problems started soon after. There was an issue with Robert Duvall, and he didn't want to do the film. These things happen. On *Part II*, Richard Castellano, who played Clemenza, didn't come back. I had conversations with Richard practically begging him to do it because he was so great in the part of Clemenza, and he just refused. Why exactly was never answered. I never knew why Duvall didn't want to do it again either. In any case, his absence from *Part III* was a big miss. With so much of the film depending on his character, none of us knew what to do without him. Francis and Mario had to reconstruct the story, but they were brilliant writers and changed the whole script around. Even the ending that I loved so much had to go—instead, Michael would die of old age, in solitude, after his daughter, Mary, is killed in the attempt to assassinate him.

Winona Ryder was supposed to have played Mary, but when she arrived in Rome she was exhausted and falling apart. Sofia Coppola ended up doing the part. She was young, just nineteen; she was not an experienced actress, though we have since found out she's a very talented director. But the rest of the cast was trying to navigate this at the same time we were absorbing a whole new script for the film. You had the great actor Andy Garcia playing Vincent, the bastard son of Sonny. He was this tough, gorgeous guy who could get a woman by snapping his fingers. Now he's trying to go after the boss's daughter. And to top it all off, she's his first cousin. You think Michael Corleone is going to just let that happen?

But the big criticism of *Part III* had to do with Michael's pursuit of redemption. I don't think the audience wanted to have Michael spend the film seeking forgiveness for his sins. They wanted Michael to continue to be Michael. They wanted the Godfather. That's what we love about him, right? The guy we saw at the end of *Part II* was encased in stone. I saw *Part III* as his effort to break free of that encasement, searching for a way out of his almost traumatized state of numbness.

That one line of his which has sort of become lore and that people still remember from *Part III*, when he says, "Just when I thought I was out, they pull me back in," sums up Michael's need to get out of that state, those chains that bound him.

Eli Wallach and I would hold great card games; we'd play outside at night on the steps of the grand old Sicilian buildings where we were shooting. George Hamilton, who was written into the film as a character to take the place of Tom Hagen, and who also happens to be one of the great humans I have come to know, took me to London on a break in filming. I was laid out in a hotel for four days getting over the flu, except for a couple of nights that I went out and partied with George. We hit the roulette tables at some rich casinos and danced the night away. I was like a college undergrad who had been let out of a dormitory.

When we returned to Rome, I was on the back lot of Cinecittà studios, taking a break because they hadn't gotten to my scenes yet. I was there alone, and I felt a depression moving in on me. Melancholia, I liked to call it. I felt as though I were wandering in the role of Michael and had somewhat lost the appetite I was used to having when I was acting in a film. That may have been the source of my depression. I was looking for a way to revive my appetite, my spirit.

I thought back to *Richard III*, in Boston all those years ago, how it had been so helpful to me when I was trying to unload the weight of the first *Godfather*. I felt there was something I wanted to say about Shakespeare and what his work means to actors, and I thought I understood *Richard III*, in particular, in such a way that I could explore my feelings through it. I wanted to ask very simple things like, Who is Shakespeare? What is the language of Shakespeare? Why aren't more Americans going to see Shakespeare? And why are a lot of American actors turning away from it—actors who are quite capable of doing it? Great British actors would say to me that they thought Shakespeare was even more appropriate for actors in America than in Britain, that somehow Americans were more in sync with the Elizabethan era when those plays were written.

The idea wouldn't leave me. So I would ponder it and ponder it. And then I just said to myself, The only way to understand what this is, is to do it. Make a film of *Richard III* and constantly interrupt it with vignettes of people talking about it—actors, famous writers, people on the streets—while we rehearsed and performed the play. It was a great big collage with me at the center of it. I don't fancy myself a director or a writer. But there was a need for me to express all this, and even thinking about it was starting to pick me up. Color was coming back to my cheeks. If I remember correctly, I saw my own shoelaces tie themselves. I thought about it all through the nineties. Finally, I decided that the only way I'm going to understand it is to go out and start filming it. But it would have to wait.

XⴲX

I HAD BEEN OFFERED THE ROLE OF RICKY ROMA, THE PREEMINENT real estate salesman of David Mamet's *Glengarry Glen Ross*, when it first came to Broadway in the mid-1980s. Joe Mantegna had done the stage production so well he won a Tony Award for his performance. So I was fortunate that they came back to me years later for the film version, which was directed by Jamie Foley, who was also deeply involved in the casting. When you are part of a group that includes Jack Lemmon, Alec Baldwin, Alan Arkin, Ed Harris, Kevin Spacey, and Jonathan Pryce, you know you are going to be taken care of. And they gave us three weeks of rehearsal ahead of filming, which felt like a gift, and by the time we started shooting the movie out in Queens we were really flying.

Recently, I showed *Glengarry* to my son Anton and his reaction was entirely about the language of the film. He asked me, "How does he get that many things in?" Meaning, how does he pack so much information, so much energy, and so much vehemence into so few words? That's the secret to Mamet, I think. Just say the words that he's written and you'll be fine.

Sonny Boy

)（◆）（

MARTY BREST, MY DIRECTOR ON *SCENT OF A WOMAN*, USED TO call me *"el diablo negro"* while we were working on the film. When I'd show up on set and he saw me coming in, he'd shout out, "Hey! It's *el diablo negro!*" In the moments before I came in, I'd be pacing in front of Kaufman Astoria Studios. It was winter, and I was dressed in a long coat with the collar turned up as I strode back and forth, up and down along the chilly sidewalks outside. I was engaging in a kind of personal sign language with myself, moving my fingers and hands, my arms and legs, in repeated patterns. Today it would probably be described as OCD. It was a pattern of behavior I'd been following for years, for whole periods of my life, that would charge up my brain and extract energy from my body.

Actors, we're a strange bunch, and we have these idiosyncratic rituals to help us with the jitters. It's the same way with athletes: a baseball player has his superstitions; he'll tap his bat to his cleat or touch the roof of his clubhouse a certain number of times before he faces down a 95-mile-an-hour fastball. Actors rely on them, too, especially when we're facing roles that are demanding. I've since learned other techniques to help me release that pressure from within myself. But if you had spotted me in one of those strange, semiconscious patrols, you would not have said, "Look, there goes Al Pacino!" You'd have said, "Who is that troubled man staggering around like that? Does he need help? What is he doing?" What I was doing was trying to get myself together so I could stand at the plate and take on that fastball.

Marty Brest had told me about *Scent of a Woman*. Marty is a good person and a great director who had already made *Beverly Hills Cop* and *Midnight Run* by that time. I read Bo Goldman's new script for the American adaptation. I even read it aloud at one point. It was a good script. I did my homework. I did my preparation. And then I got to work.

I wasn't intimidated. I wasn't bored. I wasn't being petulant. But you know that thing inside you that says, I don't want to do this? That's pretty much my calling. I never want to do it. I don't know why that is. I liked *The Panic in Needle Park*. I was young. I was bouncy. I didn't know what I was doing, but it was like I was a kid again in the South Bronx, jumping around on the streets. I liked the people I was playing with. I liked *Dog Day Afternoon* because a lot of my friends were in it, although I was drinking more too. I liked *Scarface* and *Dick Tracy*. And I enjoyed some of the not-so-great films I'd later make, deceiving myself that I would find a way to elevate them from awful to mediocre. I guess I thought there had to be a pony in all that horseshit.

And there was a lot I had to put myself through to play Lieutenant Colonel Frank Slade, the protagonist of *Scent of a Woman*. He was a spouter. He was a real pisspot. An alcoholic and a complete tyrant. He was just nuts. And he was going to kill himself. The whole purpose of his trip to New York, for which he hires the kid played by the wonderful Chris O'Donnell to be his assistant, is so he can say farewell to people. But it's not sentimental or self-pitying. There is a cold, clear determination about what Slade intends to do, the weight of that depression, the way I imagine you have to die spiritually, inside yourself, before you kill yourself. Marty Brest was really the one who captured that—he was so good at keeping me in check and moderating my performance, and he is a gem of a guy. I did go overboard sometimes in that part. I was too big for it at times. I would get too out of control. I could do it better now.

When I was preparing for the role, I would sometimes get handed these gifts as an actor, and I knew that I had to make use of them. This was one: A military officer was teaching me how to disassemble and reassemble a .45 while blind, the way a person without sight would do it. Try it sometime. I kept doing it, over and over, and on those rare occasions when I'd do it well, when I'd finally get all those pieces to fit together just right, he'd go, "*Hoooooo-ah.*" And I looked at him and said, "What's that?" He said, "Oh, when the troops do something that works, we give it a little *hoooooo-ah.*" It was like a bit of punctuation. I said to myself, That's going into the picture. It was like Attica all over again. These are the opportunities that can come in doing the actor's craft.

I got taught how to do the tango by Jerry Mitchell and Paul Pellicoro. I told them I just wanted to learn how to do *this* tango. I'm not going to learn the history of tango. Just map out the tango that I need to know for this sequence and I'll do it. Map it out for me, and I'll follow your steps. Because otherwise I'd still be there, thirty-five years later, trying to learn how to do the tango. God knows it took us four days to shoot the actual scene in the movie.

Of course I studied blind people, read books, and worked with organizations to learn about what happens when people lose their sight, how they work with aides and engage with the world. But all actors do things like that, that's the easy stuff.

The best lesson I got about how to approach my performance might have come from a three-year-old girl. I said to her, "Show

Daddy how you play blind. Do a blind person for me." And you could see right away that she formed a concept in her mind of what that character would be, and she acted it out. She just went with what was in her mental picture and got out of the way of her own inhibition to do something that nobody else would think of. I thought, I could never do that. So I'd better find somebody who will teach me how. Because what she did was the real thing. It's the genius of children that actors are trying to get to in themselves, but of course a child gets it without explanation. She was miraculous when she did it. And that was my daughter Julie.

Julie Marie Pacino, my first child, was born in October 1989. Though I had to adjust quickly to the duties of fatherhood, I really loved being a father. When Julie was very young, she went to the Little Red Schoolhouse in the West Village, and when she finished her day I would take her to an Italian restaurant around the corner from the school. We'd sit outside and have some food, and she'd tell me what she did that day. When people would walk by and start talking to me, she would just disappear under the table. I'd be sitting there, looking at them, saying, "Can I help you? Oh yeah, yeah, I did that." And they're looking at Julie. I'd say, "She's okay. Don't worry about her." So we'd talk a little more. I'd say, "Thank you very much. Bye-bye." And Julie would come out from under the table. It was her way of saying, "Why aren't they talking to me? It's rude. I don't like that, Dad." It's like when Charlie and I would be at a bar together and a guy would start talking to me because I'm the famous movie star, and Charlie would say, "I'm here, too, you know." Julie didn't say that in so many words, but that's what she meant.

Sonny Boy

I GOT TWO OSCAR NOMINATIONS IN THE SAME YEAR: FOR *GLENGARRY Glen Ross*, my seventh, and for *Scent of a Woman*, my eighth. I was honored and grateful for that. But then the conversation around me changed. I had never won one, and people began to talk about me as if it were my turn. How many times could they reject me?

As I thought about it, I decided, yes, I'm going to take this seriously. It's time I take some sort of responsibility and receive the moment with some grace too.

I hired a great publicist named Pat Kingsley. I never had one before. I didn't even really know what they were. She said to me, "Al, go on Barbara Walters and they'll give you an Oscar." I said, "I don't think I can do that. The last time I was on one of those shows, I collapsed." I didn't do many TV interviews, especially after an incident in the 1980s when I was persuaded to do a morning talk show for *Scarface*. But the guy came on with a look of disdain, white as a ghost, asking me how I could have made a movie like *Scarface*. You try responding to that question. I kept my cool at the time, but now I began to worry, how could I handle Barbara Walters? I started to meet with her in public settings around New York. We got together at a café. I met her in the back of a soda-pop luncheonette. She was very charming, and I liked her a lot, but of course she was trying to get me to be on her show. Eventually I agreed to do it.

Initially, I was horrified at the results of the interview. I was there but not there. I was like somebody who was hiding behind the curtains and doing an interview at the same time. I thought, How can you be on a talk show and not say anything? But when I looked at it again more recently, I realized it's not so bad. Okay, so I looked kind of shy. And she was very classy, and we got up and danced a tango. And a lot of people watched, and I looked handsome, I must say. They saw that I was a human, and I said things that were human. So that's pretty good.

When I went to the Oscars for *Serpico*, I felt out of place. When I went back twenty years later, I was in exactly the same state. I was still out of place. I hadn't developed that part of yourself that comes to life and allows you to accept where you are. Someone recently told me that Jack Kerouac was really embarrassed by his fame. Now that's a complicated idea, but I've been thinking it could apply to me. I liked hearing the story about Kerouac because if someone like him could feel that way, it adds a little credibility to my state.

I sat there glassy-eyed and numb as they listed me and my fellow nominees for Best Actor. But just as they announced my name as the winner, I had a feeling that this time they would finally do it. I threw back my head and let out a sigh. This was my first time in eight tries that I'd finally won—having already lost for the seventh time earlier that night—so when I got up onstage, I started my speech with a line that a friend had suggested to me. I said, "Well, you broke my streak." That got a laugh, but there was truth in it too. It was a truly powerful moment to see that entire audience stand up and applaud me, and the gratitude I felt was real.

I made sure to thank my colleagues on the film, including Marty Brest, Bo Goldman, and Chris O'Donnell, as well as longtime acting mentors like Lee Strasberg and Charlie Laughton. I talked about my involvement in SoBro, an organization that's dedicated to the improvement of life in the South Bronx, and a girl there who told me I encouraged her, just because we both came from the same neighborhood. Me giving encouragement to other people—how about that? And then I didn't know where to go. I just left the stage with my Oscar and there was Barbra Streisand in the wings. She gave me a little A-OK hand gesture and said, "I voted for you, Al." And I said, "Thanks, Barbra."

Some people win an Oscar and spend the rest of the night partying away, hopping from one celebration to the next. Of course I felt like doing that, too, but I wasn't allowed. Marty Bregman had a private jet waiting for me, because the next morning I had to be in New York to shoot *Carlito's Way*. (Every once in a while, Bregman would be a killjoy. He had the knack for it.) So I had to leave straight from the Oscars ceremony to catch my plane.

I got right into the car, and headed to the airport, where I was put on a plane to New York. None of the afterglow that I expected. But I was on this big plane by myself, just me and my Oscar, and I could handle the solitude. It was just like the old days, pulling that red wagon full of *Show Business* newspapers along Seventh Avenue in the rain, swigging Chianti and belting out, "I feel fine / with my bottle of wine."

But in that moment on the plane, a feeling came over me. It was tantamount to what I experienced when I just got into the Actors Studio as a kid. I was standing on a subway platform, where I got onto the arriving train and turned around to watch the doors close. I saw my reflection in the subway car window and I thought, I'm an actor. I'm a member of the Actors Studio. Sitting by myself on that plane, a feeling of resolve came to me. It was a profound gift and it's hard to describe it in words because you're feeling so much. I guess this is what it means to feel good about yourself—you sort of don't know why, but you do. It felt like how I would imagine it feels to be one of those hang gliders I would see jumping off the cliffs in Montauk—after you've been up in the air for so long, there's a comfort in finally touching down, and thankfully it doesn't last too long. When you've just won an Oscar, everywhere you go, people know that you've accomplished something special, and they treat you that way, for about a week. I guess that's why we have these holidays like Mother's Day or Father's Day. We need to be patted on the back, something worthwhile in all that we go through. When you think of what life has to offer, probably people wiser than me designated these pockets of applause for all of us. "Hey, job well done." "Ahh, Happy Birthday," as you get your cheeks pinched, "you've been around a long time and you can still walk, look at you." Or, on Father's Day, "Thanks, you're a great Dad." I believe I have that posted on a miniature Oscar that one of my kids gave me. These kinds of gestures help get us through a night—or a lifetime.

11

Forty Dollars a Day (and All the Donuts You Can Eat)

W hat happens when you win an Oscar after twenty-five years in the business? Not much, to be honest. I'm not really aware of how it changes your status. The attention I was getting was mainly on the street, where congratulations were coming to me regularly. There is a financial impact—you do get paid more for the films you make. But the offers and opportunities to make movies were already there and kept coming in. So I could just continue doing what I was doing before: playing roles I connected with. In the next few years, I managed to be in movies like *Heat*, *Donnie Brasco*, *The Devil's Advocate*, *Any Given Sunday*, and *The Insider*, which were recognized with a lot of attention and more Oscar nominations, and gave me the opportunity to work with more great directors.

The first film in this run was *Carlito's Way*, which was a Marty Bregman special. I was back on familiar turf, filming in New York and reunited with Marty, my trusted producer, and Brian De Palma, a great director; it was also my first time working with Sean Penn and Penelope Ann Miller, who were fantastic. Between me, Marty, and Brian, it was a little *Scarface* reunion, but we weren't trying to repeat what we did in that film, and Carlito Brigante couldn't have been further away from Scarface as a character. He doesn't get high. He doesn't fly off the handle. He keeps his cool. He is eventually undone by a fatal flaw in his personality, when he shows a bit of mercy to a rival he probably shouldn't have.

In total, I made five films with Marty Bregman: *Serpico*, *Dog Day Afternoon*, *Scarface*, *Sea of Love*, and *Carlito's Way*. All of them were hits, but *Carlito* was the last movie we would make together. There was no breakup this time, no falling-out; we just went our separate ways. He had goals he wanted to pursue, and I had mine. Marty used to say about me, "You want a successful film? Put Pacino on the poster with a gun." He also used to say, "Al Pacino is the smartest guy I know—ten minutes later." Bregman knew me. He knew the kind of actor I was and that I wanted to be. Of course I played other kinds of parts, too, and though you saw me hold guns in some of the roles that made me famous, they were all different characters in films that told very different kinds of stories.

By this time I really felt that I would only do a gangster film if the character was something I hadn't done before. That was true about *Donnie Brasco*, which I made a couple of years later. My guy, Lefty Ruggiero, was a made man in the Mafia, and that's no small thing. But Lefty was on a lower rung in his organization, with no expectation that he'd rise any higher. Carlito Brigante was also a gangster, a guy of the streets, but Carlito was a romantic and an outsider. With Lefty, there was something almost sad about him that I thought I had never played before.

I hadn't seen *Donnie Brasco* in about twenty years, and then I saw it recently and I was surprised at how touching it was. Mike

Newell, our director, knew that he wanted to say something about a relationship between these two men, Donnie and Lefty, how they became friends and then turned against each other. It was an era when buddy films were on the way out, but I think Mike was wise to focus on that dynamic, because in the end, it made the film.

We filmed *Donnie Brasco* during some freezing cold weeks in New York, with a great gang of guys that included Mike Madsen, Jimmy Russo, and Bruno Kirby, who would all fall out whenever we'd hear Mike Newell, who is British, call it "the *Maff*-ia." But what made it all a pleasure was Johnny Depp, who was so funny and became a fast friend. He would look at me at times and say, "Al, you know you are nuts, right? I mean, did you know that you're certifiable?" I said, "Yeah? You're not so bad yourself." If we were in public school and the same age, they wouldn't have allowed us to be in the same class together. An adult Cliffy at last. We made each other laugh like two toddlers often do. We had very similar reads on things. That happens sometimes with people, and when it does, you never want to part from them.

The year prior to that, I had made *Heat*, my first film with Michael Mann. This time I played a cop, a Los Angeles police lieutenant named Vincent Hanna. Hanna had problems as a human being, problems in his life. He was volatile and edgy and apt to go crazy. He was also chipping cocaine, and I sort of based my entire character on that. We shot a scene where I went into a club, and you actually saw my character taking a hit of coke before he enters. For some reason Michael kept that scene out of the film. It did explain a lot of my character's behavior, and without that explanation, I can see how it made aspects of my performance seem extravagant. If the audience had seen a moment or two when Hanna took a hit, I think they would have been better prepared to see what I did. But even without it, the intensity of his life—how Hanna worked in his profession, the way he dealt with things— allowed him this freedom to apply that kind of energy. It was almost a technique that he used as a detective, and it worked for him.

Heat was a special film for me because it was the first one where Bob De Niro and I would finally get to act together on-screen (unlike *The Godfather: Part II*, which we both appeared in but didn't have any scenes with each other). This was an exciting opportunity to solidify the long history we'd shared together, some of which wasn't entirely in our control.

I can still remember meeting Bob many years ago, when Jill Clayburgh and I were living together in the Village. We were walking across Fourteenth Street when we ran into a couple of people she knew. One of them was a young man with an unusual intensity about him. There was a certain distance about him—he didn't look you squarely in the eye—but he had a charisma that just radiated off him. And that was Bob. Jill introduced me to him and told me he was a great actor. I knew that he had that gift—I could see that, just in passing. He seemed to know some of the stage work I had been doing. We shook hands, wished each other well, and continued on our ways.

In the time since, Bob has become a very dear friend to me. He has always been really stand-up with me. I've never asked him for something he didn't deliver on. And Jill was right, he is a great actor. Bob and I connected through film—it was film that ignited him, that gave him a medium and a means of expression, and we both related to the art in film. And we came together over our struggles with success and fame, which we were often going through at the same time—especially in our younger days, when it was all new.

Then there are all the ways in which we have been compared to each other, placed alongside each other and made out to be competitors, all because we are actors who came on the scene at around the same time whose last names both end with a vowel. While there are things we have in common, we are as different from each other as any two people can be.

And there was competition between us. There had to be. Especially when the offers coming in were similar; roles that would go to either one of us, and that either of us could have played. There, and only there, is the stain of competition.

It happened with another actor, because when I started working in films I went through it with Dustin Hoffman. I didn't dare compare myself to him; I loved him in *The Graduate* and as Ratso Rizzo in *Midnight Cowboy*. I always thought that Dustin was a brilliant actor, but I didn't feel we were on similar wavelengths.

I only recall meeting Dustin once, on the streets of New York, before I became famous. He was out with his wife and a big, big dog, and I said hello to him as people were coming up to him for autographs. I mentioned that I was a fellow member of the Actors Studio, and he was very nice to me. As he continued to sign autographs, he told me, "Don't worry—this is going to be happening to you soon." I didn't know if I was too happy about that, but it was gracious of him to say.

Pauline Kael, the renowned movie critic, used to say that I was influenced by Dustin Hoffman. Actually, what she said about me in *Serpico* was that I was "often indistinguishable" from Dustin Hoffman. There must have been something in the air, because the comparisons were flying left and right. It got to the point where the great theater producer and impresario, Alexander H. Cohen, a guy I liked very much, suggested that Dustin and I get together at Madison Square Garden and fight each other in a boxing match, and he really meant it. But I said to Cohen, "Let me just tell you straight out: Dustin will beat me. He works out. He'll knock me out." I thought Alexander would be better off asking Meryl Streep to fight me instead. But then I got a little worried. Shit, what if she wins? Luckily, the fight never got off the ground.

There was a time in the seventies when Dustin Hoffman, Bob De Niro, and myself were thought of as a group, as actors who were somehow interchangeable with one another. A guy like Jack Nicholson was separate from that. Robert Redford was separate. But while all of us were people who were perceived as being able to get movies made and get them to open at the box office, Bob, Dustin, and I were considered these three New York actors who had made it—even though Dustin had grown up in LA, we had cultivated ourselves and come into our own in New York. It was a tag that certain actors got.

Over the years Bob and I would try to look for ways to work together on a film if we could, but we never could seem to find the right project. When Bob got cast in Bernardo Bertolucci's *1900*, he called me about making it with him. Bob was being encouraging. He said, "Come on, come on, we'll do these roles together." But you know how that turned out. I reverted to type. I said, "Bob, I can't.

I don't connect to the part. I don't understand the story. I don't know how to do it."

When Michael Mann approached Bob and me with the screenplay of *Heat*, he said that we could have our choice of which of the two leads we wanted to play: Hanna, the cop, or McCauley, the thief. It just worked out that Bob wanted the thief and I wanted the cop.

As we prepared to start shooting the film, most of the time I was thinking, How will I do this? How will I play this role? Then we had a reading of the script, where I was with Bob, Val Kilmer, Jon Voight, and a lot of other great actors around the table. Bob was playing a real powerhouse of a character, but I could see that he was giving a performance that was more contained and low-key, intense and lonely. It was beautiful. I knew that I would go in the other direction.

Michael Mann chose me and Bob because he didn't want two guys who were the same—he wanted a contrast. He was ratcheting up the tension for a scene midway through the film, where we sit down together in a restaurant and talk for the first time.

When it came time to shoot the restaurant scene, Bob didn't want to rehearse it. And I thought: He was right. We got there, and we just started. We didn't think about it or talk it over or anything—there it was. It was so wise of Bob to do it that way.

)(◆)(

IN THE TIME SINCE I FIRST IMAGINED IT ON *GODFATHER III, LOOKING for Richard* had started to become a reality. I was able to do it the way I always dreamed. I did it with my own finances, so I didn't have to answer to anyone or conform to the various rules people have when they put money into your film and want that money back. An art film is a gamble, and you can't expect to make back your investment or get upset when that doesn't happen. They aren't made to be commercial, they serve a different kind of audience.

To be as honest as I can, part of me wanted to make this film to exorcise something, like the feelings of how I was treated when I did *Richard III* on Broadway, and the critics said I set Shakespeare back fifty years in this country. And part of me did it out of admiration for artists like Orson Welles, who was the real genius of the film medium. He did it all in his career, and his whole life was spent piecemealing films, trying all the time to raise money to make them, never getting the attention he should have gotten for them. I would never dare compare myself to Welles, but I was inspired by him, and I'd like to think I had a true Welles experience when I made *Looking for Richard*. Going through all that one goes through when writing, directing, and starring in a film—while making a couple of commercial films in the midst of it—took some fine dancing: the wheeling and dealing of casting actors who would drop in and out at different times. We shot all over the world.

I worked on *Looking for Richard* while I was in the middle of making *Carlito's Way*, and I continued to work on it during the making of *Heat*. Michael Mann, with his special generosity and uncanny intelligence, gave me part of his *Heat* crew to use on *Looking for Richard*—without even blinking an eye, just like that. What a gesture. I'll never forget it. I was picking locations. I was casting actors. I was pouring everything I could into it. I was shooting one film by day, then shooting the other that same night. Then I'd go back the next day and do it all over again. I would be sitting by the pool at my rental house in LA, going over the construction of the scenes in *Looking for Richard*, planning battles, organizing things in my mind. Sometimes I would just wait to get to the location and figure out where things went once I got there. In the course of all this, I came to the conclusion that directors are crazier than actors, and I think I can rest my case on that one.

I was so invigorated by it all. There's an energy that you get when you're doing something where you don't have to sit around and wait to be called to go do your takes. When you watch *Looking for Richard*, you're actually seeing me figure out how to direct a scene while I'm in the midst of acting it. The cameras are rolling, the scene under way, and I'm acting in it, I'm directing it, I'm dropping out of frame to get the cameraman to move in on a shot, while I'm orchestrating the movement of other actors with hand signals and gestures like a third-base coach. There's a tornado of acting and directing going on, and I'm loving being the calm in the eye of this storm that was being created.

One day, in the course of filming *Looking for Richard*, I brought my cast and crew to the Cloisters and to the Cathedral of St. John the Divine, where I met Philippe Petit, the extraordinary tightrope artist, who had arms like cables, he was so fucking strong. He had walked on a high wire from a building across the street to the roof of the cathedral, 150 feet in the air, and he had done it all without a net. Remember that. I had wanted to bring my actors in *Looking for Richard* up to the church's roof, but then I saw all this pigeon excrement up there, which I heard was extremely poisonous. Someone on the set mentioned it too.

When I related this to Philippe, he said, "So what? So it's poison. If an actor dies, he dies for his art."

I said, "Die for your art? Literally, I wouldn't go there. But metaphorically, yes."

We eventually found a filming location for the murder of Richard's brother Clarence that didn't have pigeon excrement everywhere. It wasn't the glorious piece of architecture that St. John the Divine is—it didn't make me feel like I was in the realm of Michelangelo, an environment where you feel you can do anything. I thought that's where Shakespeare belongs. But we found another setting uptown on the East Side that was actually an improvement. Now we could kill Clarence. The people in charge of the church were kind enough to let me film there for free. Doing those medieval scenes in the city was so memorable. New York had given me so much already and was now giving me even more. I'd never forget that.

The making of *Looking for Richard* was great for me. I was never happier. I had fulfilled a personal vision. And when it was done, after four years of full immersion, we had to sell it. Oh, there's the rub. My God, what I was in for. I was in a new world. Was I prepared for the ins and outs of that? No fucking way. I had depended on agents, managers, and producers to do the business. And this was an art film—I knew it was going to be a hard sell. Marty Bregman, where are you? Help me!

A couple of people did want to buy it from me and at least pay me back the money I put into it. So I sold it, which meant also selling my control. The movie went to Tom Rothman at Fox Searchlight Pictures, the indie division of Twentieth Century Fox, which had done some really cool films. And as soon as he bought it, he was promoted to be the head of Twentieth Century Fox and he flew away, unreachable, and no longer responsible for my film. That was a real loss—he had no alternative but to go, and I honored that move, of course. Who did they put in his place? He'll remain nameless. If he reads this book, he'll know who he was. I took one look at him, and I actually knew him. He was a stage manager in a play I did once. He still didn't know what he was doing.

I had a few phone calls with Searchlight, and I happened to meet one of their head guys, an executive, on an airplane and discussed the film with him. I was told *Looking for Richard* couldn't be nominated for an Oscar because it was neither a straight documentary nor a traditional fiction film, so there was no category for it. I want to tell you something that Sidney Lumet told me loud and clear: If you shot it and it's on film, it is a film. If it goes from point A to point B, it is a film. If it has something to say, it is a film. I know there is a difference between documentary and fiction. Well, this was a little of both. So sue me. Shoot bullets through me. You can't do anything different in this town. I learned a little, forgot a little, and moved on. No use in crying over spilt Shakespeare.

It was in the marketing where it all fell apart. Even though it was my idea, and I had directed and written and produced it, I still was unable to buckle down and go out there and sell it. When I was younger, I used to sell soap that had been packaged by blind people. I would go door-to-door in the Bronx, and here and there I would make a sale. It was the poor selling to the poorer. I do remember a time when a woman opened the door and I gave her my pitch about the soap. I could tell she had inviting eyes. I didn't take advantage at that time, and I always sort of kicked myself for not doing so. But sales was a difficult job, and I didn't last very long at it.

We had to hold one of those market research screenings for the film. Now it wasn't just my friends looking at it; these were total strangers who were picked out as possible people who might enjoy this crazy stuff I did. I didn't know what they expected to see. Suppose they booed, suppose they just left, in reaction to this thing that I've invested so much of my time and my soul into. All I could think was, My film is really bad.

As I sat there, my hope was that, miraculously, somehow, as the film was moving from the editing room to the theater where we were showing it, some changes would be made that would actually make it good. The audience would rise from its seats and cheer. Then I had a better idea: I'll stop the people from coming at all. Then I thought, No, I can't do that, but you know what I can do? I can tell them, "Thank you for coming, but this isn't really serious. I was just trying things out. I'm just an actor, seeing if I can get somewhere, and this is just not for you. So stay if you wish, but no problem if you don't." At least these spasms of thought made me giggle a little.

I showed the film at my agent's screening room, a relatively large space where I used to show movies by Pasolini and Visconti, films I thought were so good and worthy, to get people in there to look at things that they wouldn't normally see.

One of the people who came into one of these screenings of *Looking for Richard* was a woman in her forties. She was, I believe, a teacher; she was attractive and exuded intelligence and grace. She watched the whole film, and at the end, she was crying. I just sat there, waited, and wondered. Her words were "I never thought I could understand Shakespeare, but I do now." She had a feeling of revelation. As if to say, *I didn't trust that part of myself.* She was an educated person who had probably spent a lifetime taking a certain posture toward Shakespeare. She was aloof to it and had possibly convinced herself to look down on it. She had been moved to tears because she was both happy with herself and uncomfortable that this was something she might have missed out on at certain points in her life.

Looking for Richard got some recognition, but its failure to thrive hurt me, frankly. It wasn't just a disappointment. It was a life-affecting thing. You can be in a position in life where you're doing somewhat well, and then you experience that rejection and it completely overshadows all your past success. I didn't really address that disappointment at the time, because it's too much to face when it's happening.

Many years later, after I made my switch from New York to LA to be close to my ex and my children, I ended up at a party next door to the house I was renting. The hostess who lived there was a bit of a hotshot in her own right, but I got to know her and she turned out to be a very decent human being overall. There were lots of celebrities and well-known producers high in the pecking order of Hollywood over at her house one night. I met a few of them, and I discovered that no one knew about *Looking for Richard*. Here's a film I wrote, directed, and starred in, with a cast of great British artists and American actors who filled the screen with their gifts. The Directors Guild of America gave me a Best Director award for *Looking for Richard*, and *The New York Times* named it one of the top 10 films of the year. But here at this party, not a soul knew about it. Not only had they not seen it, they never heard of it.

I could be philosophical about that. What was harder to take was that I was there with a friend who had once called the film a masterpiece, and now he wouldn't even admit that he saw it, as if it would somehow compromise him. I wanted to nudge him and say, "Hey, man, speak up! You know the film." But he said not a word, not there, not in that circle of Hollywood. In those places, you go with what's in fashion. It took me a very long time to learn that. I don't demonize it, but I understand it a little better now. I thought maybe I'd get the film cans myself and screen the movie right there in that woman's house, but I had a couple of toddlers at home to deal with at the time.

)(◆)(

AFTER *LOOKING FOR RICHARD*, I DIDN'T DO SHAKESPEARE AGAIN for almost a decade, until I played Shylock in a film version of *The Merchant of Venice* that came out in 2004. I thought its director, Michael Radford, had done some really good films. And its producer, Barry Navidi, came to me with it after he had been working on another project with Marlon Brando and Johnny Depp. I could feel Barry had a good head and an innate understanding of the actor and the art form of filmmaking. He had known Brando well, and he said that Marlon had recommended me to him to play the role of Shylock. How Marlon saw that in me, I'll never know. But when I read the screenplay for the film, I just said, "I see it and I see where I'll go with it. I'll do it." When we realized the time constraints, we got the cast together in New York, where I had a loft space that we could use to rehearse, and we became a close company. We were able to build around the play, interpret it, and find the world we'd be playing in. We were all grateful for that experience, which allowed us the freedom and understanding that you very much need for any film, especially Shakespeare.

I knew that Dustin Hoffman had played Shylock on Broadway and in London, but what stood out most prominently about *The Merchant of Venice* was a stigma that it was perceived as antisemitic. That notoriety dated back all the way to its creation, over four hundred years ago, and has been handed down from there. But we have changed as an audience. There's a way in which the play suits the modern age. We understand the prejudice that Shylock is subjected to when we see it. Many of us can identify with his experience. I am not Jewish, but from my perspective, I saw Shylock as a man who had been relegated to a ghetto, who is abused by bigots. Not only do they mistreat him and spit on him, they steal his beloved daughter away from him, all he had left in the world. And yet, he has a certain dignity about him. He feels a righteousness because of what was done to him. He's not an Iago, not a Richard III, or any of the other villains of Shakespeare. There is a touch of the hero in him. He is a survivor. I thought that our world today had room for that, and that a movie of it would be relevant.

I felt that our *Merchant of Venice* was a pretty good Shakespeare film, and it was supported by the Jewish community. I never felt it was embraced by the powers that be at Sony, who acted fearful of a controversy around the character of Shylock. They were preparing for something that wasn't going to happen—a backlash that never came. They held a premiere for the film at a theater on Third Avenue, which I went to, but you could barely even find it. They were hiding it, for sure. It was very hypocritical, and it upset me. That's when I knew the people releasing the film were not going to support it, but I'm told it did very well and has been one of the most lucrative Shakespeare films.

I would play Shylock again a couple of times. I did it for Shakespeare in the Park, and then I did it on Broadway, both times directed by Daniel Sullivan. What made our production so poignant was a moment when Shylock has his yarmulke thrown to the ground—they rip it off his head, and they put him in the baptismal font and christen him to become a Catholic after he's forced to change his religion. And then after they rip him out of there soaking wet, he goes back to that yarmulke and he picks it up and he defiantly thrusts it on his head. The audience used to cheer. That outburst would more than likely get him killed, and you saw the defiance in him. I thought that was one of the great moments that Daniel Sullivan added to the play and why I wanted to do it.

It took me many months to get to that performance—months of rehearsal, after I did a film of it and after I did it in Central Park. I believe I benefited from all that time I had with it, which allowed me a certain kind of freedom and contributed to my getting nominated for a Tony, which was very rewarding. When I work on things for long stretches, I can find the character within myself.

I would still like to play Shylock again, maybe go to England and do it. Shylock is one of the great actors' roles—it's a role that helped make the reputation of the legendary Edmund Kean. When he did Shylock, people were so stunned they actually ran out of the theater during the performance and into the street to tell people passing by to come in and take a look at this.

I remember that kind of explosiveness when I saw Jonathan Pryce play Hamlet. When he got to the scene where Hamlet is supposed to see his father's ghost, in this production his Hamlet sees his father's ghost *come out of him*. It was an exorcism in that moment that would take you out of your seat. Jonathan would play both parts, with the voice of the father's ghost inside him and coming out of Hamlet's mouth. I saw it with my own eyes and it was Shakespeare to the limit. You could feel the terror permeating the audience. I was mesmerized by seeing how far an actor could go. He didn't need fast cars smashing into others or cinematic explosions. He didn't need a Superman cape. It was all him—he was flying with the words of Shakespeare.

Could you imagine that rehearsal? "Hey, here's an idea: how about we have the part of Hamlet's father played by Hamlet and it comes out of his stomach? He regurgitates him." "*Whoaaah*, I want to try that, man, let's see what happens."

I went backstage and saw Jonathan afterward. I asked him, "How do you do that eight times a week?" He smiled sheepishly and said, "It's okay—we only do it seven."

See what I'm saying? Actors, man—there's nothing like actors. Back then and right now, they are the greatest of humans. I know they call 'em crazy, self-centered, all that stuff. We even accuse them of narcissism. How foul. Are you saying people who have self-interest are narcissists? Give me a break—we all fit that description. They are what they were two hundred years ago, fucking nuts and joyously crazy. Yes, a few more of the elite have joined the crowd of actors, but just remember, they're crazy too.

I ended up getting a Tony Award nomination for doing Shylock on Broadway, and I got to play opposite Lily Rabe, the daughter of Jill Clayburgh. Lily is a wonderful actress, and what a thrill it was to engage with one of the children of my former love. Lily and I did have a bit of a father-daughter exchange when we were working together. It felt like that to me, which was wonderful, and she was too. We lost Jill to cancer during the production, which was such a sad thing to have happen, and we lived through it for the entire run.

12

You Can Always
Buy New Friends

The year 2001 started out on a high note. Beverly D'Angelo and I had fraternal twins, a boy and a girl. I had three kids in all: my two new ones, Anton and Olivia, and my teenage daughter, Julie. What's not to love about that?

Beverly and I had our issues about where to live. Her life was pretty much exclusively in Los Angeles. New York was my home, and I had always wanted to stay there. My psychiatrist warned me not to move to LA. I went anyway.

There I was in my early sixties with a new life in a new city. I had no clue how to navigate Los Angeles. I didn't understand the social scene. I knew I could get back to New York as much as I was able.

In Los Angeles I moved with my two little ones several times, just trying to figure out where to live. We grew out of one rental after the next. Beverly and I were working through the whole gestalt of raising our kids without each other. There were visitations set up, and the kids would stay with one parent or another for a while, until finally we landed on fifty-fifty custody. Even then, my work would take me away from them sporadically. I'm grateful that my kids turned out so well, when you think of what they had to go through. They didn't always get the attention they desired or deserved from me, and though I tried to engage with them as much as possible, once a family is broken, it's always going to be more difficult. As much as I understand that now, I wish I knew it then.

Los Angeles was very different from New York, and a New Yorker anywhere outside of New York is an alien. There was a lot more *interfacing* in Los Angeles; it has a sense of a community, but there are certain rules that one follows depending on which suburb you're in. Beverly Hills is vast, but some of its neighborhoods are like being in a country club—a massive one, where there are parties and dinners, and you sort of fumble your way around in the darkness. At first I was terrified of going out alone, because I would invariably get lost and be unable to find my way back home. But many parts of LA were pleasant and welcoming, and I was fortunate to find people I liked. My good friend Harold Becker and his wife lived in LA, and they both were always more than gracious to me. Harold showed me around the city.

Charlie was living here, too, mainly because the weather was better for his MS, and he and Penny both worked coaching actors. Some of the actors they worked with were well-known while others were still struggling; doing that was always part of their way of life. They lived out in Santa Monica, which I'd learn was far different from where I was in Beverly Hills. I was kind of transient in LA when I first got there. Sometimes I'd make my way to Downtown LA, where I saw a few painters and artists. I wondered what the 1920s and '30s were like in this city. I heard stories and could get little glimpses of the old world, but most of that stuff was gone. What was left were a lot of tall buildings and traffic that made you not want to go anywhere. I started to think to myself, How can I live here?

)I◆)I

LOS ANGELES IS SOMEWHAT PROVINCIAL. IT'S PROVINCIAL LIKE other places where the fundamental identity comes from its work source. And in Los Angeles, the work source is making films. It's an industry town, and the industry is show business. You're never far from the people you work with, and some will make judgments about you not on just the work you do but because of the reputation you may have accumulated over the years.

It took me a while to appreciate the rewards of Hollywood. In certain quarters you had to watch out because you could tell the currency they ran on was gossip. You're just getting the froth, the cream on the top, but there's no cappuccino in that cup. I went to a party maybe twenty years ago for Harold Becker's birthday. I looked at the clock, it was like ten at night, and everybody was gone. I said, "Harold, where did these people go? What happened?"

He said, "Oh, you know, it's Hollywood."

"What do you mean Hollywood? What has that got to do with it?"

He said, "They don't want to be here if it gets to ten. They don't want to get drunk and say the wrong thing to the wrong person."

"Oh, really?" I said.

A few weeks later I was at another party, a post-Oscars event that was in Century City, in an apartment with a panoramic view of the Hollywood skyline. It was a very classy place, and everybody and anybody was there. I was truly enjoying myself, and there were lots of interesting people to talk to. I actually met Oprah Winfrey that night. I was leaving that party with a friend when I noticed a woman I knew—an actress, and quite a good one—holding a drink and crying. I couldn't help saying to her, "What happened? Are you all right?" She stared at me with tearful eyes and said: "I think I said the wrong thing to the wrong person." She might have slighted somebody who could change her life. That could create tension and superficiality. If you're talking to someone and measuring your words, spontaneity could leave the premises. As I looked at this crying woman, I felt for her and thought, That is one strange feeling.

The worst thing is when you offend a critic, and who knows how that happens? I like to stay away from anyone who has the power. If you censor yourself because you don't want to hurt someone's feelings, I could live with that. But when you censor yourself because you don't want to jeopardize a job or a career, well, there goes the human experience. How are you going to make real friends if you're faking it?

I had a run-in once with a guy who ran something big in Hollywood. To call him a producer was to minimize him—he was the head of everything. I had never met him before, because I was hardly ever in Hollywood, and I didn't know who he was. To be totally honest, I never knew who I was talking to in LA, except if I saw them in a movie.

So I met this guy one night when I was out at a restaurant, sowing my oats. I wasn't drinking anymore, but I still had some craziness going on inside me, doing the ol' coin flip. I was on some sort of high, engaging in repartee and surprising myself that I still had that in me past the age of sixty. I just met him off the cuff, didn't know who he was. But I had what turned out to be a hilarious time with this big-time fella, and my appetite for showing off that night was particularly sizable. I wasn't trying, and sometimes not trying is the best way to be. Like Hickey says in *The Iceman Cometh*, "I'd feel free and I'd want to celebrate a little." I enjoyed the guy.

A few days later I got a call from my agent. He told me that so-and-so now wants to meet me in his office way up in the high skies of Hollywood—he was with you the other night, and he thought you were hilarious. I thought, Are you serious? I'm not funny on cue. Just ask my organ-grinder—sometimes I'm just not that way. Why should I meet this guy? I hope he's not looking for a repeat performance.

)X◆)X(

AT THE SAME TIME, I FOUND WAYS TO ENJOY MYSELF IN LA. I HAD friends, and life was okay. I said, I don't want to be here just hanging out. You can only play so much paddle tennis. My life was costing me a fortune—my staff was getting bigger, and I was taking care of two homes, my apartments, and an office, and supporting the households of my children. I was spending three or four hundred thousand dollars a month, which is a lot of moolah, and I wanted to keep active, so I did some films here and there.

I did *Ocean's Thirteen*, which was a franchise, with great stars and a great director, Steven Soderbergh, so I knew I was in good hands. I liked George Clooney, Brad Pitt, Don Cheadle, Matt Damon, and all those guys. It was a really good group of people, and I was very happy. I just didn't know anything about it. Charlie said it was a good script, so I just did my part. I was a man juggling a lot of things. We'd have to run out to Las Vegas for a couple of days of filming, and I would ask, "Can I get back to Los Angeles that same day?" I had the children, and I wanted to get home to them. I thought I had the energy to do it at the time.

I was spinning plates, between taking care of my kids, trying to maintain my work life, and dealing with the standard chaos that has always accompanied me. It was like I was running all the time and about to hit the wall. What can I say about man's tragic fate? I think about what Bertolt Brecht told me on a quiet summer evening as the two of us sat on a love swing. We were slightly high, swinging out there in the middle of the night while there was a party going on in the distance.

He said, "You know, Al, what man's problem is?"

I said, "No, tell me. I want to know."

He said, "He's too durable, he lasts too long."

"Hey, Bertolt, you mind if I steal that one and use it in a book one day?"

He said, "Go ahead. It's not as if you and I actually met. I died in East Berlin while you were still a teenager in the South Bronx."

"Okay, thanks for the contribution. Now can you tell the girl I was sitting with on this love seat to come back? Can you get her back?"

"Sure, kid, I have some writing to do."

As he wandered off I shouted out, "Could you write me a play?" I don't think he heard me.

I think I've gone offtrack some. I guess I need one of them five-hundred-pound gorillas to pull me back in. That's what Charlie used to say to me, way back in the sixties, when we'd be walking the streets of New York, along the sidewalks and bridges, bouncing like a couple of wayward vagabonds who were practicing for a marathon, while spouting Dylan Thomas or Allen Ginsberg or my favorite, "Jingle Bells." He'd say, "We need a five-hundred-pound gorilla to chain you to, because your energy is always on the rise." I have always had high energy, and it's a plus. What I lack in intelligence, I make up for in energy.

After I came to Los Angeles, I still needed to satisfy my own artistic urges and I could feel that need again. So I started making another one of my own films, in the same vein as *Looking for Richard*. This time I set my sights on a play that always intrigued me, and which I had done at Circle in the Square, Oscar Wilde's *Salomé*. I adored Wilde, and this play, and so I set out on a journey that lasted almost ten years to create the film *Wilde Salomé*, which explored the life of Oscar Wilde as I was performing the play *Salomé* onstage at night and filming a version of the play in a studio during the day.

Wilde Salomé says a lot about what was going on in my life at the time, while I was bringing up my kids and adjusting to this new location. Barry Navidi, who produced the film of *The Merchant of Venice*, was now living in LA too. Barry is a wonderful person to work with; he has an openness and knows film. He was also crazy enough to take up with me and my passion for Oscar Wilde. It took me forever to shoot it around LA while I was acting in other films. I was juggling a lot while raising my kids, who actually are in the film as well.

I was fortunate to come across a great actress, Jessica Chastain, who plays Salomé. She was not that long out of Juilliard at the time, and she was a prodigy. As soon as she started her audition, I could see her talent. I turned to the producer Robert Fox and said, "Am I dreaming?" Any doubts about making the film version were over. I knew this was the actress that would play Salomé.

My involvement with *Wilde Salomé* was profound for me. You can think of it as a home movie. But I don't care what anyone says. I was enjoying my romp with Wilde's play and putting a lot of my money in the film. We worked on it for years and screened it privately before ever releasing it. We showed to it Prince Charles, who truly enjoyed it, and we were honored in San Francisco with a day of tribute, called Wilde Salomé Day, along with a special screening at the Castro Theatre. It was a pleasure to make this film that got a little mixed up in the shuffle and may not have had its due. It's on the same spectrum as *The Local Stigmatic*, *Looking for Richard*, and *Chinese Coffee*. They are films that are not about profit—they're not about anything but the event. I like the intimacy; you just put them on a small screen and show them to fifty or sixty people. It's the closest thing to theater.

Beyond what I was spending on *Wilde Salomé*, I was throwing money all over the place because I had it. At least I thought I did. And my accountant kept cheering me on. I was doing what a lot of people do who don't know anything about money and are foolish. One time my seven-year-old daughter had a schoolmate whose father was an actor and needed money. I said, "Okay, what do you need?" I gave him sixty-five thousand dollars. I didn't expect anything back. I would do that a lot. I wasn't doing it because I wanted to show I was generous, I just thought I had a lot to give. To me it was like when you win at Monopoly. This was not real. None of it was real to me. But it is real. I was to find that out.

)X◆X(

I WAS STARTING TO GET WARNINGS THAT MY ACCOUNTANT AT THE time, a guy who had lots of celebrity clients, was not to be trusted.

In 2011, I was sitting in the living room of my rental house in Beverly Hills, looking over my finances, which I rarely did. I pay a ridiculous amount of money to rent some big fancy house in Beverly Hills because I'm always thinking it's just temporary, and I'm going to move somewhere else or do something different. Of course I haven't, and somehow I've managed to rent this same place for twenty years. You don't need to be an accountant to realize that's just a terrible waste of money, but the fact that he wasn't pointing it out should have been a sign.

By this time, when my suspicions had really started growing, my crooked accountant didn't come to see me himself. He rarely ever did; he would always send one of his minions. I'm uncomfortable when I'm around things I don't really feel connected to or know a lot about. I was sitting at a table, looking over the notes, and the minion representing my accountant was sitting behind me. And I said, "This is something. I've got a lot of money."

I hadn't been working that much lately, and I had just taken my family on a trip to Europe. I knew I spent a lot of money because I brought my kids, their nannies, and a couple of other people from LA to London and Denmark and back to LA on a gorgeous Gulfstream 550. When the kids were occupied, I was preparing to play Jack Kevorkian before filming started on *You Don't Know*

Jack. I rented out a whole floor of the Dorchester hotel in London, which became our headquarters, and from there we'd go to whatever sights the kids wanted to check out each day. We flew to Billund, Denmark, where Legos come from, because my son and daughter were really into them. We even stayed at the Legoland hotel, where everything is made of Legos. You haven't lived till you've seen the Mona Lisa made out of Legos. Talk about really going overboard. I was just doing it because it was possible to do and the kids were involved in it.

Now I was back at home in Beverly Hills, sitting there at that table, and I wondered, how did I spend so much money, come back, and have more money than when I left? I thought that was interesting. And I turned to say this to the accountant. I was complimenting him. Is this what it is to make money? I didn't know. I wasn't investing in anything. I looked at the guy and I said, "Wow, that's pretty cool." I noticed a look on his face. It was a look I'll never forget. His right eyebrow lifted. Just a little. As though somebody went over and said, "Can you do that thing you used to do with your eyebrow? Hey, Sam, could you do that again, for me?"

And I thought, It's simple. It's clear. I just know this. Time stopped. *I am fucked. No way out of this one.* His eyebrow went back down, and I said, "Hey, thanks for this." He was a cheery, boyish sort of chap and he took his books and left. What was I going to do now?

I knew something was wrong, but I didn't know how far it went or what had happened. The next day, I went to a lawyer in LA and said, "I think I may be in a lot of trouble. I've just got a feeling." I told him the story. After hearing my tale and looking at a couple of accounts I had, he said, "I've got someone in New York that works for the Rockefellers who I think you should go see." So I went to New York to see this person. His name was Shelby Goldgrab—what a name for an accountant. He had a way of talking that made me very comfortable with him, and I knew he liked me too. And he said, "I want to meet this guy of yours." And he met with my accountant and came back to me and said, "Al, you gotta get out of there. Not only is he a crook, he's an arrogant crook."

I had only known Shelby for about a week or so, but he said, "I like you. I don't want to see you selling pencils in front of Carnegie Hall." I started laughing. I said, "That's a funny image." His face turned serious. He gave me the old Corleone stare. "I'm not joking."

That's when Shelby told me, "Don't worry, Al. You go out there and make more money, and you'll buy new friends." I never forgot that.

I was broke. I had fifty million dollars, and then I had nothing. I had property, but I didn't have any money. In this business, when you make ten million dollars for a film, it's not ten million. Because after the lawyers, and the agents, and the publicist, and the government, it's not ten million, it's four and half in your pocket. But you're living above that because you're high on the hog. And that's how you lose it. It's very strange, the way it happens. The more money you make, the less you have. That's what Marty Bregman told me.

The kind of money I was spending and where it was going was just a crazy montage of loss. The door was wide open, and people who I didn't know were living off me. It was "Come one, come all! Al's got it and he doesn't care!" And even after I had been swindled like that, I still owed gift taxes on all the money I was giving people. Even though I only had two cars, I was somehow paying for sixteen, along with twenty-three cell phones I didn't know about. The landscaper was getting $400,000 a year and, mind you, that was for landscaping at a house I didn't even live in. I don't exaggerate these things. It just went on and on. I wasn't even signing my own checks—the accountant signed them, and I just let them go by. I wasn't looking and he didn't tell me how much I had or where it was going, and I wasn't keeping track of who got what. It was all about: let's keep this dumb actor happy, just keep him working, and we will reap. It wound up this guy wasn't insured, either, so I couldn't sue him to get anything back.

Money was just something that had been coming to me along with everything else that accompanied success. I didn't want to know about it, because I didn't want to feel like I had to learn calculus. I was too old. It would take too much time. And I don't think I could do it.

But I never despaired. I remember saying, "Well, I'm alive." There was something about it that was liberating. In a part of my brain, I felt that I was being taken advantage of by this lifestyle that was all around me. I played into it as though I were a person who had a lot more money than I did. My girlfriend, Lucila, at the time was very supportive, and so were a lot of my friends and people who are close to me. I went into a sort of survival mode, which I can do. I've lived a life that's provided me with the ability to survive. So what do you do? I went to work.

By now, I was in my seventies. I wasn't a young buck, and I was not going to be making the kind of money from acting in films that I had made before. The big paydays that I was used to just weren't coming around anymore. The pendulum had swung, and I found it harder to find parts for myself. I guess it's what happens to all actors—as they age, the parts become fewer. I would have to do what work was available.

I had to change my budget. I had two houses and I sold one of them. I would never do commercials before, but I ended up doing a coffee commercial that Barry Levinson directed me in. It went to Australia, and it repeated there a few times and it made a lot of money. I found out during the filming of that commercial that they had arrested my accountant and charged him with running a Ponzi scheme. He got seven and a half years in prison. It got in the news, but only a bit; it was a different era, and it didn't get quite the attention of Bernie Madoff, which had happened just a couple of years earlier. I tried to keep it quiet too. There's almost nothing worse for a famous person—there's being dead, and then there's being broke.

My seminars were another big find for me. In the past, I used to go to colleges all the time and talk to the kids there, just to get out there and perform for them, in a sense. I'd tell them a little bit about my life and have them ask me questions. I'd bring books on the stage from authors and playwrights and poets I loved. I'd deliver some monologues and recite some poems. I enjoyed doing that. It was a connection with an audience I cared about. It felt good sharing this stuff. It brought me back to the theater. I didn't get paid for it. I just did it.

Now that I was broke, I thought, Why don't we follow this up? There were more places I could go and do these seminars. Not necessarily universities—I knew there was a wider market for this. So I started traveling around. And I found that they worked. Audiences came because I still had popularity. I would show a montage of my work, and then I'd come out and talk to an interviewer and tell stories. It was entertaining, and audiences wanted to hear it. I would do readings of Shakespeare and Eugene O'Neill and others, and do spontaneous question-and-answer sessions. The audience would ask very interesting questions, and I found I enjoyed talking about the past. These seminars paid me well—if I did one a month, I got through the month. It was a way to earn a living.

)(♦)(

BEFORE I WENT BROKE, I WAS DOING FILMS IF I THOUGHT I RELATED to the part and felt I could bring something to it. *Ocean's Thirteen* turned out well. And I did *88 Minutes*, which was a disaster. And then I did *Righteous Kill* with Bob De Niro, which was not good. But I did these things while I thought I had money, so it wasn't like I was doing them for the money. I really thought they could be good.

Jack and Jill was the first film I made after I lost my money. To be honest, I did it because I didn't have anything else. Adam Sandler wanted me, and they paid me a lot for it. So I went out and did it, and it helped. I love Adam, he was wonderful to work with and has become a dear friend. He also just happens to be a great actor and a hell of a guy.

A strange and discordant mix of roles followed. I liked one film I did, *The Humbling*, because I did it with Barry Levinson. It was based on the novel by Philip Roth, who I met at a party in New York. I found Roth there, sitting in a chair, and he was very serious when he looked at me. I said, "Hi, Mr. Roth. I'm Al Pacino." He had a look on his face that was haunting. In a cold, impassive voice, he said, "I. Know. Who you are." I just thought to myself, Well, I'm famous. He's seen me in films. Maybe he saw *The Godfather*, I don't know. But I loved his writing and was a real fan, so I kept spouting to him. I said, "I'm doing a film of your book *The Humbling*. And it's very funny." In that same funereal voice as before, he said, "It's. Not. Funny." I said, "No, I know, it's not really funny. But to get through the drama, sometimes you need a little funny." Again, he said, "It's. Not. Funny." I said, "Sure. Okay. You're right. It's not funny." And I backed out of the room into the street.

He was so grim when he interacted with me that to say it was strange is an understatement. It was only recently that I remembered I met him years earlier. I'd actually had dinner once with Roth and Claire Bloom, just the three of us, in London, sometime in the nineties, when they were still married. Those are the kinds of setups you get into sometimes—someone who knew me, asking, "Oh, you want to meet Philip Roth?" I have no idea what we talked about—I had completely forgotten it. These were two people who I found very interesting, and I loved their work. How could that night be boring? But then fifteen years later I'm saying, "Hey, man, good to meet you," like I didn't recognize him. No wonder he had that look on his face: I was insulting him. How does a normal human being just forget people like that? I don't drink anymore so I don't have that excuse, but I guess sometimes I just check out.

Barry Levinson is my friend and was great to work with on *The Humbling*. We also hired Buck Henry to write it with him. We had great actors, Greta Gerwig and Dianne Wiest, and the wonderful Charles Grodin, who's since passed away. And we did this film for like two million bucks. We were just doing it on the run.

I also did *Manglehorn* because a lot of people were hawking its director, David Gordon Green. He was hot with a certain group in

Hollywood. The best thing about doing *Manglehorn* was going to Austin, Texas, and having dinner with Terrence Malick, who is one of our all-time greatest filmmakers. David Gordon Green was nice to work with, but I wrote him about a hundred emails after I saw the finished film. When I first agreed to do the project, I thought the script had some good stuff in it, especially the way it ended, which was largely why I did it in the first place. But he didn't just change the ending for the film, he completely took out what was in the script so the film now ended in a completely different manner. That led to me writing him over and over about it, but he didn't listen. That happens.

A great thing that came out of making *Manglehorn* was I got to know Harmony Korine, who played a role in the film. Harmony was just plain ol' magic. He just so happens to be the nephew of Joe Chaikin, who had the starring role in the Living Theatre's production of *The Connection*, and who started the Open Theater, a glorious experimental group in Manhattan that thrived in the sixties and seventies. I was a real fan of Joe, and Harmony was mesmerizing. We have a scene together that takes place in a spot that's sort of a cross between a casino and a penny arcade. Harmony started improvising as his character in the film—he went for ten minutes and was out of this world. I was just playing my role, wondering where he was going to land. I felt I was actually listening to James Joyce or watching Robin Williams. I could not believe how this man spouted. I know that footage must be somewhere, but just like the original ending we shot, it didn't end up in the movie either.

I was doing these films for nothing. Here I am, a person who has lost all his money, doing films for nothing when I should have been doing films for something. But they weren't there for me at the time. I did always manage to get offers. Some of these films saw the light of the day and others didn't quite make it. I got opportunities to work with good friends like Fisher Stevens, who I had known for years. Fisher directed me in *Stand Up Guys* and we had fun together; it didn't quite make the grade, though it had potential. Then there was *Danny Collins*, which is one of my favorites and gave me a chance to work again with Christopher Plummer and other actors I've always admired like Annette Bening, Jennifer Garner, and my pal Bobby Cannavale. Dan Fogelman wrote *Danny Collins* with me in mind and is such a sweet, talented guy. We all thought it would have a chance. I certainly enjoyed the experience of making that film and always get a kick when it pops up on TV. There are a lot of films I've done that had a spark and were something we all hoped would catch a little more fire. They may not have reached the heights of some of my other films, but I still like to give them a little nod because they helped support me through the years.

I also ended up doing some really bad films that will go unmentioned, just for the cash, when my funds got low enough. And I sort of knew they were bad, but I convinced myself I could somehow get them up to being mediocre. Then I started putting my own money in those projects—shooting had finished and they were already heavily into postproduction, trying to see if somehow we could clean it up. They'd tell me, "Oh, we can't afford to have another editor." It's okay, I'll pay for it. That's how I started paying for things that I shouldn't have. You'd think I'd learn, but that's just how unconscious I can be. If I'm doing a film, let's at least get it to the level of a C minus, not an F plus. Let's make sure it's not something that gets me sent to film jail.

I KNEW I COULD STILL GO BACK TO BROADWAY AND HIT THE boards. Doing things this way also meant being away from LA and away from my kids. But I couldn't do this kind of theater in LA, and I couldn't find this kind of money off-off-off-Broadway, where I really wished I could be. Oddly enough, when I needed money most is when I agreed to do *The Merchant of Venice* onstage for free, because it was Shakespeare in the Park—the brainchild of the great Joe Papp. I just knew if we could get *The Merchant of Venice* to work it would be destined to go to Broadway. It turned out to be a relatively good run, and I loved being onstage in Central Park every night. I loved doing it there for free, for the people.

I took the Shylock character and changed it to suit what we were doing in the park. I had a great director, Daniel Sullivan, taking me through the rings. The ol' fire in the belly was back. Night after night, I'd show up, go on that stage, and say: tonight, I will play this role, and I will play it without knowing what I will do next. I will say my lines and not know what the other actor is saying next, and the words will come out spontaneously. I will perform moment to moment. I will be alive and ready to engage in that kind of environment. This was going to change my deliveries and get the nerves and the body and the sinews to open up to life— almost like improvisation, only with the great words of Shakespeare.

I failed at that, but that was my reach, and that's what made the fails so exciting. Will I make it? Will I get there? Will I be able to get to the place where I was the night before, when I got a standing ovation? Can I get it again? It's all challenge, challenge, challenge, and that's why I love the theater. It's all in your control and you've got the ball. I can't say that I made it, but here and there it brought a different kind of life to the part—the old Edmund Kean run that I was fantasizing about in my delirium. It's something else out there on that stage, under the stars and the universe and the planets. To think, wow, I got there a couple of times in my life—I came close to the Holy Grail. When the play went from the park to Broadway, all that repetition made my performance better. I got a Tony nomination, but I knew I could have done more and traveled further in that role, and that's what it's all about, the striving. I was pleased when Daniel Sullivan said that the play worked indoors in an even more powerful way.

A couple of years later I was back on Broadway, this time in the stage version of *Glengarry Glen Ross*, and I know I failed. I was working with a great bunch of guys, but I just didn't have enough time to rehearse. In the film, I had played Ricky Roma, while onstage I was playing the character of Shelly Levene. Now I had to learn it all over again. I don't know if I ever really would have gotten to Shelly Levene—maybe if I kept at it for twenty years. This was David Mamet dialogue, and sometimes I would get to a particular speech, not know the words, and use my own. The poor cast had to cope with me doing different things every night, but they were great with me and always landed on their feet. I'm still real close with a couple of them; they are the kind of friends you want to have. The audiences seemed to like it too. The critics are the critics.

I do like those chances you take on that stage. We were deep into the run of *Glengarry*, and there I was playing Shelly Levene, actually dancing in the role—swinging around, doing a little soft shoe from time to time. I wondered where that came from. Later on, after the play's run was finished, I was thinking on it and I realized, hey, my dad was a ballroom dancer. He won prizes for dancing and guess what else? My dad was a salesman, top of the line, like Shelly Levene had once been. So there I was, doing that unconsciously, playing a salesman who can dance. Something was coming through me.

I went back to Broadway again a few years later in another Mamet play. This one, called *China Doll*, had never been performed before and unfortunately was not fully finished by the time we hit the stage. We were never able to turn that second act around. It was essentially a one-man show—there was a second character, played by Christopher Denham, a wonderful actor and a wonderful guy, great to be with and play off. But for almost two hours I'm onstage alone with all these words. Now if I'm doing this play for six months straight, I'm going to learn them—they're going to come and be a part of me. But there was no time for that.

So I'm going to tell you a secret. This is the greatest thing that I have found late in my acting life. Teleprompters. You have teleprompters carefully placed on the stage, providing you with the text. Now it takes a while, but if you know the character and you've worked through it and you understand what's inside you coming out, you start to really free up and get this sucker.

In the old days, they had a guy under the stage who would shout out lines to the actor if they somehow missed a line—they were actually called prompters. It was an old-fashioned device, even in Shakespeare's time. I'm sure even then they would get new line changes the night before. Can't you see it? Some guy onstage up there, saying, "To be, or—" and just stalling till he hears from near the floorboards: "Not to be." Maybe that's how that pause got built in.

So here I am in *China Doll*, and I had them strategically pop teleprompters all over that stage. Now I realized why Marlon had oak tags with his lines put up all around the sets of his films. This was the first time since *The Indian Wants the Bronx* when I really didn't know what I was going to say each night—I would just go out there and see what came to me. Hallelujah, hallelujah, I finally got back there. And I was practically being thrown out to be eaten alive by the press. But I knew I was going somewhere with this part, and after the sixth week and the seventh week and the eighth week, I turned that corner. When the play starts, I'm going into that world, the place I love most, where I don't know what I'm going to say or where I'm going to go next, and somehow I get there. And even though I have the words from the playwright— David Mamet, mind you—coming out of me, they are my own.

What do you say to that, Mr. Stanislavsky? How do you tell that to acting students today? Just go out there and not have a clue where it's going to go, and maybe they can do it too? I had people coming backstage who were shocked by what they'd just witnessed. They were in awe, especially since they had heard such terrible things about the play and my performance leading up to it. There I was, looking at them with a smile, knowing it was working. Well, I didn't always perform to the highest level every night—I knew that too. But maybe twice a week I would really hit it. It was great to see that reaction after the play was so poorly received.

You must understand that I would devour the text, work on it always, over and over again, to understand my character. I was absorbing it through all those weeks of rehearsals, then performing it each night. When I went onstage, it was all somewhere in me, and I threw it away and followed the teleprompters. It was a little easier to just go out there and be free with it.

But it was tough with *China Doll* on Broadway because they had written me off. Sometimes, when you become reputable, you get looked at as a body of work instead of as the thing you just did last week. You get endowed with things you don't really have. Your fame and your gifts as an actor are exaggerated. It makes you want to take a lesson from Marcus Aurelius, the Roman emperor, who had a guy who would stand next to him in his chariot so that when the crowds were cheering for him, the guy would say to him, "Remember, you're only a man. You're only a man."

And sometimes movie stars don't come back to the stage after a failure or two, because it's live and it takes a lot out of you. And while you're getting all this rancor and these raspberries, you're onstage, doing it night after night. On *China Doll* I was nearly eighty and facing all of that. It's like Bob De Niro says in *Raging Bull*, after Sugar Ray Robinson has left him bruised and bloodied but was unable to bring him to the canvas: "You never got me down." I have a part of me that continues to feel that way, and I have to watch out for that sometimes. But I also know how satisfying it can be to succeed in the face of that misjudgment—to say, you're wrong about me, and I will survive—and that was a real motivator for me to get there in *China Doll*. I'm still standing here.

When I was fifteen, back at the High School of Performing Arts, I played the lead role of the producer Sidney Black in our school production of the old Moss Hart play from the 1940s, *Light Up the Sky*, a role Sam Levene first made famous. I think I was able to play that part with a kind of belief I've always tried to aspire to. I was on the tightrope, and I was a butterfly, flying up, up, and away, into that place that I call Nirvana. God gives it to you. God says you can go there. Why? Because you have wings. You don't know you have wings until God brings them to your attention. As Michelangelo said, "Lord free me of myself so I may please you."

We're humans. We're not up there with the gods. We get all that other stuff thrown at us—all the cobwebs come our way. But when that is lifted and you're flying, baby, there's no high like it— at least that I've experienced. So about half of my performances were working, about half were not so much, and some were in the toilet. But I'm only human.

Listen to me now—I'm getting sentimental. I'm saying I'm going to do that great Broadway play in the sky one day. When I was being interviewed on *Inside the Actors Studio*, James Lipton asked me, "What do you think God will say at the pearly gates?" and I said, "I hope He says rehearsal starts tomorrow at three p.m."

13

The Undiscovered Country

It's time for my afternoon walk around the block. They say it's good exercise, and I should be getting more exercise at my age. So I put on my sunglasses, and I plug in a pair of earphones. I'm dressed in a big old overcoat, and I've got white hair all over my face. I'm walking the streets like I'm a polar bear, and it's getting warmer. I am an endangered species. I am at risk of extinction.

I'm walking around thinking about what I can do next. My world is closing in on me; the options are becoming fewer and fewer. What I want to do is make a film adaptation of *King Lear*. I have a producer. I have a director. I have a screenwriter, and a script that we've been refining for a year. To play the lead, I have me. That should be enough. But it's a very ambitious adaptation, and that's going to require money.

Because this is Beverly Hills, I take about ten steps on my walk before I am noticed. A group of people passes by me on the other side of the street, and they recognize me. I have on a baseball cap, sunglasses, earphones. How do you do that? You deserve a trophy. Because, yes, it's Al Pacino, but it's somebody else also.

When my daughter Livvy was about eight, I was driving her and her brother Anton home from school when she said to me, "Dad, are you Al Pacino?" I said, "Well, I'm both. I'm Dad and I'm Al Pacino. Can't you see my two heads? And you got both of them, baby. Both of them are yours."

She laughed and started reading a children's story aloud, and as I was driving along, I thought, This is a good story. And I asked her, "Where'd you get it?" Then Anton spoke up and said, "That's not from a book—she wrote that." That's when I knew my daughter could write. I always knew it, actually.

Now I walk the streets, thinking about having to face the brass, to get a film made. That's where I used to come in with Marty Bregman. He was a facilitator, a hustler, an impresario. But I don't have him anymore. Like the line says, one by one, our old friends are gone.

I'm going to get this movie project done on my own. I feel that fire inside myself, because I know I found something that works for me, finally. And I feel as though I've turned the clock back decades on my life. When you're a certain kind of person, these things keep us going—these passion projects literally keep us alive.

)(◆)(

AS BETTE DAVIS USED TO SAY, "IF THE SCRIPT IS GOOD AND THE director is good, they don't have to pay you." And you know what? She was right. I never got into doing acting for money. Except when

I went broke. Then I got into it. You know I'm a man who has more Golden Raspberry nominations than Oscars.

I wake up in the morning. I went to bed feeling normal. What happened in the middle of the night that made all my bones ache and left me so I can't quite see? I do know that if I wait long enough, like a couple hours, usually, my legs will come back. My left arm will be able to stretch a little. My head will clear. I'll be able to see somewhat better. And it could be my age, which is 103. The first time my eyes did that sort of thing, I was 19 and living in an apartment I had just rented on Eleventh Street and Avenue A. It was a dump in the East Village. I woke up one morning in the middle of the kitchen, because that's where the bed was. I opened my eyes and was looking all around that tiny apartment—looking at my window that faced the street, looking at the bed, looking at the refrigerator, looking at the perennial bathtub in the kitchen, and I thought: How come I can't see? Whatever it was, I hoped it went away, and back then it usually returned to normal pretty soon. But I couldn't see right then, and I still don't. I learned much later in life that I have Fuchs' dystrophy—it's a problem with the eyes that has something to do with your corneas, and it gets progressively worse with age. Nowadays, I get that feeling every time I wake up.

I have to say, I'm losing some weight, I'm feeling better. You'd think I was good-looking or something to dress this badly. I compound it with what little looks I have left. A few years ago, I was doing a show on Broadway when I was running late to the theater where I was performing. Of course those sons-of-bitches got a picture of me with a hood on at the stage entrance. I wasn't even on the curb—I was still in the gutter. I'm bent over and I'm looking up at them, like literally any bagman you've seen on the streets.

I've got these two small shopping bags I'm carrying, and what I've got in them, I'll never remember. People are probably thinking, this fucking guy's a miser. Is that what he's turning into? He's got money in those bags. He cashes those checks and puts dollars in those bags. This is the highest-paid dramatic actor on Broadway. And he looks like that? Equity's going to throw me out of the union.

People come up to me saying, "Oh, can I take a picture with you?" I say, "Sure. Go ahead, all right." They just see that you're famous. They don't see that you look like you've been thrown out with the garbage.

Just the other day, I heard some older famous actor say in passing during an interview on TV, "I'm not interested in looking young." All I wanted to say is, "Because you're not young, dummy." He says he doesn't want to look young? Hey, buddy, you don't have a say in it. You are not young, no matter what you do.

⋊◆⋉

I ALWAYS AVOIDED THAT WORD CAREER. BUT IT SEEMS LIKE IT'S unavoidable. I've had a career.

Part of having a long career in acting means adapting to your age. A lot of actors' careers have been curtailed because of their age. You find them on television—in days gone by, the older stars would go on TV and then get their own shows. Greats like Barbara Stanwyck, Joan Crawford, and Bette Davis all did TV.

I've done some television and had some very fine experiences. I played Roy Cohn in *Angels in America*, written by Tony Kushner and directed by Mike Nichols, two of the best I've ever worked with. I did *Hunters* for David Weil. I played Phil Spector for David Mamet, and I played Jack Kevorkian and Joe Paterno for Barry Levinson. They were all great parts. I got acclaim and recognition for those performances. I even won a couple of Emmys. When I got to know Jack Kevorkian, in preparing to play him, it was a colossal experience for me. I spent time with him in Detroit, and he was up there as one of the top three smartest people I ever met. He was simply the most pro-life person I ever knew—someone who, on the actual battlefield of war, would transfuse the blood from dead soldiers so he could possibly save the living ones. He even tested this experiment on himself, and got hepatitis in the process. He believed in what he did. Jack was a real zealot, the kind that goes right out the window—that's what Jack did and it landed him in prison for eight years.

I loved Kevorkian's wit. It broke my heart, the treatment they gave him. I finally asked him once: "Hey, you went to prison. What was that like? What do you remember of it?" He said, "I remember the snoring." That stopped me dead in my tracks.

I always thought of prison for him like you see in *Birdman of Alcatraz*, with Burt Lancaster whiling away a life sentence in his solitary little cell. I remember seeing Burt Lancaster once in another film, playing the grandpa. I grew up on Burt Lancaster as a swashbuckling actor who could do almost anything, then later in life there he is on-screen as a grandpa, weak, old, and dying. I thought, Is that going to be me one day?

After *The Godfather: Part II*, Lee Strasberg was being seen as an actor and getting a bunch of offers. I remember telling him, "They keep casting you as an old person, but you're young." I meant that he was young in spirit, and he could play other roles that reflected that—but the truth be told, he couldn't. He was older. So he had to play parts that were old men. Probably older than his actual years.

Eleonora Duse, the great star of the nineteenth century, considered the greatest actress, along with Sarah Bernhardt, played Juliet onstage when she was sixty—and Juliet is supposed to be thirteen. Ian McKellen, a great actor, is playing Hamlet on-screen and he's in his eighties and I applaud it. Most people advise that you play Hamlet after you've lived longer and I think Ian will be especially in touch with the wisdom of the play. I believe in what he's doing and look forward to seeing it. But one does have to accommodate oneself, and that is the sad truth.

Now I look in the mirror and I see something looking back at me that looks like an old wolf with a snarl and a mountain of white hair, and I ask, "Is that still you, Al?" Everything is visual.

No matter how slim I get, I've got a great big fat white head of hair right here. That's a dead giveaway. And no matter where I am when the camera snaps, all you see is white hair. And most people who do what we do notice it. I don't think you ever lose your energy. You just lose your looks.

I always wanted to play Napoleon. There was even a time when Stanley Kubrick had me in mind, but that never got off the ground. Then I finally got a script that worked by William Mastrosimone. His script took place in Napoleon's last years, after he's been exiled and has lost all his power, but by then I was too old to play the part. That particular Napoleon was a part I knew I could play—rarely does a written character come along that you would fall into and understand as much as I related to Mastrosimone's text. It's a great role, but all the streaming services passed, telling me that the script was too sophisticated, but I knew it was my age. It's unfortunate I wasn't able to do it, but it's so good that hopefully some other lucky actor will get to play that part.

OKAY, I'M A MAN WHO HAS LIMITED TIME LEFT, LET'S FACE IT. WE all sort of do. But my time is a little more limited. It changes the world for you to have that perspective. You cannot know it at forty-seven. You can try to imagine it, but you can't feel it. And that's what's lonely about it.

I have to think very seriously about my estate now. That means I have to get advice from people who are way smarter than me. Nobody ever left me anything in my life. There was no such thing as a will. There was no such thing as a bank account, either, where I came from. These things just didn't exist in my family.

I was ignorant about what those things meant, unless I happened to do a play about them or read about them in a novel. It was in *The Brothers Karamazov*, I think that's where I read it. Otherwise, I went through life without any thought of such things. I had no sense that if someone dies, you get something. How do you live without that thought in your head? There's a kind of purity to living that way. Death doesn't mean that you're going to get something. All that death means is that you're going to lose someone, and how you feel is relevant to who has passed on. Some are a grain of salt; others feel like you're now missing part of your organs.

I ask myself, how can you be old and not feel old? I don't know how I got here. A lot of people who get past eighty don't know how they got there. Did I really try to eat certain foods or do certain things? I've had a ravaged life. I know that if I would have kept drinking and drugging, I would have been dead twenty-five years ago. Fame and wealth changes everything in your personal life. It requires a certain type of adjustment. I remember way back, when I was going through the mill about fame, Lee Strasberg told me, "Darling, you simply have to adjust." If I knew what I know now, I would have said, "You mean forever? You mean, like, every two or three years, a new adjustment?"

Fame does change your life—this avalanche of stimuli starts coming your way. Some good, some bad, some ugly, and it's difficult for most people to handle. It's why a lot of people turn to drugs and alcohol, to shield themselves from what's coming at them, especially when they're young and going through it. Most really don't have the thick skin that's required to make it through all the lies and assumptions being said about them. It's like Brecht says in his play *In the Jungle of Cities*, "In its natural state human skin is too thin for this world. So men take care to see it grows thicker." Until finally he is bumping into things and not feeling them anymore.

With fame comes money and with money comes lawsuits, but with money also comes access to good doctors, which come in handy if you want to stay alive. I know wealthy people whose best friends are doctors. They make sure they make best friends with doctors. That phone call in the middle of the night: "Hey, Doc, I can't seem to breathe." Or, "my chest is out of control." "I'll be right over," says a sleepy, groggy voice. They say, "No, I'm not asking you to come over. Just what can I do right now?" "How about watching one of your old movies? You've recorded them. Just watch that for a while. And then put your head on the pillow and maybe you'll doze off. And I'll be over in about seven hours."

I discovered in my late seventies that one has to take care of oneself. I had surgery on the carotid arteries in my neck, and the surgeon hit a nerve and I lost the use of one of my vocal cords. The artery was cleared but the vocal cord was paralyzed for about a year. When you're an actor who lives by your voice, that's something you want to avoid. Live theater was out. You need the projection. Without a vocal cord, I was stuck.

One doctor said, "It probably won't come back. We can do implants." I said, "Why do that?" The doctor leaned back, his eyebrows arched, and said, "Hey, man, I gotta eat too," and I thought, I don't want you or anyone to put a mousetrap in my throat. Bye-bye, Doc! I'm staying away from more procedures. Then, about ten months later, my vocal cord miraculously came back. Who did that? Well, the scientists would tell you, and I partially agree with it: I started using my voice anyway. And I think my brain dealt with that, because I had been using my voice my whole life. Finally, the brain must have said, hey, we need some help down there.

I didn't think that using my vocal cord when it was paralyzed was going to get me better. I don't have that kind of medical sophistication. However, I do have the need to perform. I was preparing to do Shakespeare for one of my seminars, where I'd perform Marc Antony's funeral oration from *Julius Caesar*. I was working with a classical composer who scored the scene along with a sound guy who added some effects that made us feel like we were part of a crowd that has gathered in ancient Rome in 44 BC.

Every time I finished doing that speech, I lost my voice for about five hours afterward, but I tried to do it anyway. Sure, my broken voice wasn't what audiences were used to, and I don't quite think my delivery ever got where I wanted to go with it, but it had come back. I think it has something to do with my brain or my prayers to God, either one, take your choice.

All the abuse on your body, the stuff you put yourself through in your younger days comes back to kick your ass. My granddad always used to tell me that. All the times when you were a younger actor, and you were in a scene, and you said, "Go ahead and hit me for real. I can take it." Well, I'm paying for that now.

I look at Tom Cruise, who can jump over the Empire State Building and doesn't even need a cape. He just goes out there and does it. *Wake up, Al*: that guy, Tom Cruise, is twenty years younger than you. I remember twenty years ago, I was running around Riverside Park in Manhattan with two toddlers on my shoulders. But change comes in increments: it's different when you break seventy, and then after eighty it's never the same again. And the way the world perceives you is never the same either.

Still, I want to continue. When the clock stops ticking, I'll stop. And as far as I can tell, my clock is still ticking. I still have the need to do this. Not to direct films, not to go to a monastery and hang out with the monks. I'm not there yet. What I want to do is continue to find that source that I can work through, this character that I can play, this great piece of writing that I can be lucky enough to find.

As long as I feel that, how can I not persist? Like William Blake tells us, if the fool would persist in his folly he would one day be wise. That's what moves me. Appetite is what moves you to go and do whatever you do. It's not just health. It's appetite.

One time my death was reported on YouTube out of nowhere, which was a gruesome sensation. On the other hand, I really did die once. It happened to me at the start of the pandemic, when I had my first round with COVID. I was getting high fevers and becoming dehydrated, so I had a nurse come to my home and put me on an IV to get me fluids. The guy who was administering the needles and running the IV bag was very friendly. I thought, Jeez, I like this guy. It would be a good idea if I could remember his name.

The next thing I knew, I was gone. There was nothing.

Then I opened my eyes, and there were six paramedics in my living room and two doctors, dressed in protective suits that made them look like they were from outer space. There was an ambulance outside my door. My assistant, Michael, had called 911 when the guy who was helping with the IV told him I didn't have a pulse.

I was given monoclonal antibodies, steroids, you name it—all at my house, because there was no way I was going to a hospital, and I meant it. I came through, and in a few days I was up and running. But I believe I experienced death that day.

I still think about it and I shudder. Is this where we go? Nowhere? Nothing? "The undiscovered country from whose bourn no traveler returns," as Hamlet put it? Well, I returned, and I can tell you there was nothing out there. It's over. Socrates talks about death as a dreamless sleep. He says he would be happy if that were the case but even happier if that weren't the case, because look what he would find out—his curiosity would be satisfied. Ever have a night of complete, dreamless sleep? If death is that, I'm happy, but boy, I certainly want a different ending.

I have this recurring fantasy of waking up in my coffin. How about that? It isn't a dream, it's a fantasy. I can think about it anytime I want to—I just don't advise it. Maybe that would be hell:

instead of fire and brimstone and seeing people you know who are merely hot, how about hell in a coffin, alone, and you can't get out? Maybe cremation is the way to go. I haven't made up my mind.

I know my belief in the spirit of God has helped me through things, but I must say I get some solace in something Einstein said that I tend to agree with: "I believe in Spinoza's God who reveals Himself in the orderly harmony of what exists, not in a God who concerns Himself with fates and actions of human beings." As he was about to tip off into neverland, Einstein was supposed to have said to a friend, "See you in the continuum." I hope there is one. The peace I had when I left the earth was kind of amazing, so simple. You're here, then you're not. The real benefit is if you don't have to suffer. It's just over without you knowing it. You would think at least you get a warning—nope. That's what happens, too, when someone gets shot, maimed, or hit by a car.

A lot of people who have had near-death experiences talk about seeing a tunnel and a light at the end. They say what they saw. I don't know, maybe they're lying to get attention. People are funny. Or maybe it has something to do with the mechanics of our brains. When I do the math—Michael calling the ambulance, the doctors getting over here and putting on their space suits—that had to take more than thirty seconds. I probably didn't die. I probably just fainted due to very low blood pressure and am being overdramatic because the nurse said I didn't have a pulse.

Is something meaningful only because you can remember it, or is it meaningful because, in a manner of speaking, you are leaving it? Leaving all the memories you had—leaving everything. I guess if you're lucky, other people will hold on to them for a little while longer, if you have a memorial service or something. But people have to live, they have to go on. One day I'll be gone, but maybe some of the films I was fortunate to be in will remain—maybe there's something to say for that. Maybe that's why some people are always taking pictures on their iPhones. Some want to be remembered. It's called immortality. It's the handprint on the cave, that imprint: they wanted us to know they were there. As I heard it said at someone else's memorial, "You don't have to miss me, just remember me."

)X◆)X

AMERIGO TOT, THE GUY WHO PLAYED MY BODYGUARD IN *THE Godfather: Part II*, was a wonderful artist, a sculptor who knew Picasso. He told me when he went to see him, he put his hand out and Picasso shook it limply. He looked at Picasso and said, "Maestro, you give me such a weak handshake. What is with you?" Picasso looked at him and said, simply, "I need my energy." I really understand that now. That's age. You know why he needed it? Because he used it right to the end. He doesn't want to squander a drop. He gets to that canvas—*whoosh*. He expends it. When Amerigo told this story to me, I understood some of it. But who can relate? Not at the age I was then.

In a strange way I'm more famous now than I ever was—famous in a different way, not so much because of the work I'm doing, but through my associations with various people and my appearing in certain things, and from living in Hollywood. I got lucky. I was in three films in a row that in different ways made a real impact, starting with *Once Upon a Time in Hollywood*. I didn't get paid the big bucks for it, but I was working with Quentin Tarantino, Leo DiCaprio, Brad Pitt, and Margot Robbie, and I did like the part. That's why I did it, but I said to my lawyer, "How do I do this without being paid?" It reminded me of when I had to audition for *The Indian Wants the Bronx*. He said, "You do it." I had a twenty-one-page scene with Leo that we rehearsed together. Leo had a whole monologue that he delivered brilliantly, where he said everything that needed to be said about this industry in 1969. But films have their own rhythms, and the scene turned out to be about two minutes when Tarantino was done with it. I'm not faulting him for it. He had a reason to do it.

I think *Once Upon a Time in Hollywood* is a great film. And the mere fact that I was in it gave me some sort of cachet. And then next comes *The Irishman*. Bob De Niro and Scorsese came to me years before, talking about what they were going to do. And I was all for it. And then finally, it's a script. I go out and do that. I have a huge part. I get a nomination for an Oscar, putting me up against Brad Pitt, Joe Pesci, Anthony Hopkins, and Tom Hanks. I had no problem that night accepting my loser status among those guys.

When I got nominated for *Irishman*, I brought my kids to the Oscars. What's better than that? I was only allowed to have one guest sitting next to me, so my son and my oldest daughter were floating around at the top of the theater, doing their own commentary on the event, which is wicked and funny at the same time. I know those two, and when they get together it's a barn dance. They waved down at us. My youngest daughter loved every second of it and was so happy sitting right next to me in the front with the other nominees. She saw all her favorite actors and singers there, all the names that go right over my head. She'd even jump up and embrace them, she was so effusive. I'll never forget that. It's the only time I felt comfortable at the Oscars.

But I was in that environment again. I was visible. Next thing you know, I'm in *House of Gucci*, which is a hot film with great people like Adam Driver, Lady Gaga, Jared Leto, and my dear friend Jeremy Irons in it. It didn't get the reception that the others got, but it made good at the box office. Plus, it was directed by one of the all-time greats, Ridley Scott, who I really took to, someone so gifted and so much fun to work for.

)X(◆)X(

WRITING THIS WHOLE BOOK, I'M FINDING OUT A LITTLE MORE about myself. I'm starting to see this person who is, in a word, *anarchic*. Charlie used to call me "a wild square." I'm actually seeing that now.

Objectively, I never knew what the fuck I was doing. It's that simple. I went from one thing to another. I'll never learn, and that's my problem. Or my gift. I don't learn things. I'm the first one to raise my hand high and say, "I don't know." Who wants to wallow in the pretense of knowing everything? What knowledge? What do I know, that I can sit with a pipe and expound on? I'm not Socrates.

I'm an actor. It's what I do, and occasionally I'm lucky enough to find roles that I'm suited for, and I get the chance to express something and do a good job and feel as though I created something. There's still opportunity for that. That boy I was, that little fourteen-year-old kid at the High School of Performing Arts who broke through that door in the play *Light Up the Sky*, that was an absolutely living, breathing thing that I did, and I did it without any knowledge of what I was doing, not even knowing that it was a form of expression, and it was marvelous. And when I did Strindberg's *Creditors*, it gave me a sense of my relationship to the world. I felt my reach opening up to other realms through the prism of acting. Through this discovery—and it *was* a discovery—it's a little bit deeper than I can explain, frankly. I'm trying to get as close to it as I can, because it changed my life. That's how profound it was. I had this epiphany. It didn't mean that I was a great actor or anything. I just thought that this is what will keep me alive.

The last Tony I won was for *The Basic Training of Pavlo Hummel*. The night after I got the award, I performed in the play and Charlie was in the audience. At the end of the show, I saw him and I asked, "Well, Charl, what did you think?" He said, "Wow, you acted like a real Tony winner." It cut right through me. He was saying I didn't play the character, I played winning the Tony, which is close to showing off. It was just like when I was a kid, and I mentioned to my grandfather that I had told on a fellow student misbehaving in class, and my grandfather said to me, "So you're a rat, huh?"

You can get a lot of money now for teaching these master classes about acting on the internet. I never went near it, because I don't know what I can say to any actor that would be of service—because like a lot of things in life, it's so personal. If I had to, I would suggest you just do it over and over again till it gets inside you somehow. Hopefully it does, but to be as honest as I can be,

most of the time, it won't. I'd also mention that it may sound simple, but it's the truth: believe in the story you're telling as though
it were really happening. In the end, I can relate to the inscription
on ol' Charles Bukowski's gravestone: Don't try. I really think I
know what he means.

14

Who Speaks of Triumph? To Endure Is Everything

In the 1990s, I was a guest at a big event, an award show for the Directors Guild, and I was assigned to give a speech about Francis Ford Coppola. There we were in the middle of this great hall with its high ceilings and high-class décor, and I saw another man my age, working as a busboy or a waiter. He was pushing a cart that was loaded with plates, and he had a uniform on, a sort of mini tuxedo that was a requirement for the job. I didn't know what his title was, but I did know his name: he was an old friend from the South Bronx named Marty-P. And as soon as I saw his face, all I could think of was the last time I saw him. It was more than forty years earlier—we were around eleven or twelve years old, and I was staring up at that same face, younger and full of fear, while I shouted at him, "Jump! Jump! Come on, we gotta go!" as he had to leap from a storefront rooftop as fast as he could before the cops could get us.

Marty-P and I had been standing with the rest of the gang on a store rooftop. These rooftops were relatively low to the ground, much lower than the tenements, and the access was easier. We enjoyed the freedom up there and we hung there like pigeons, a little smoke, a little drink. However, Cliffy had just thrown a water balloon that was the size of a sack of potatoes. It hit a passing police car solidly on its hood—*pow!*—and we had to quickly jump off the roof to get away from those cops. Marty-P seemed to be having trouble making the leap, and I was screaming at him to take the plunge, which he finally did. Once we escaped to the nearest alleyway, we were gone—they'd never find us.

Now here we were, staring at each other in this ballroom together, these two kids from the block. We had come to positions in life that were far apart—I was this famous actor and he was a busboy, but it didn't change how we related to each other, and why should it? He wasn't Cliffy or Bruce or Petey, but he did stir up these memories in me.

Today I find myself caught up in that time in my life, and I can't stop going back to those early days. I never imagined I'd still be looking back on these events, let alone that more and more I'd imbue them with such positive energy.

For instance, there was a time, sometime in the seventies, when I was talking with Lee Strasberg in his beautiful apartment on Central Park West, where on Sundays he would play for us a recording of a Toscanini rehearsal or Sarah Bernhardt performing *Phèdre*, or the first recording of Caruso in 1907. In the midst of this, out of nowhere Lee said to me: "I've been thinking about my old neighborhood where I grew up, down under the Manhattan Bridge on the Lower East Side. Would you like to visit there with me?" I said, "Sure. Whenever you'd like."

We never did it. He passed away before it happened. Now I,

too, get the feeling that there's something back there for me in my old haunts, in the South Bronx.

There's a strange sensation you start having at a certain age: your memories flash in front of your eyes without asking permission. Recently, I was tempted to go back to my old neighborhood, but I finally thought, There's nothing left of it anymore that resembles what I grew up in. The world I'm talking about is not going to happen again.

All that survives of that place, that era, that frame of mind are these stories. Maybe that's the reason I wrote this book. I want to go home. These memories keep bringing me back to a place where I enjoyed being. I look back at that life and I think I was so lucky. There was a satisfaction to that life. There was hope in that life. In my mind, I go back to those Bronx streets as they were in my youth, and I look at those stores, and those people. I see the boys I grew up with, climbing up on top of the big girders that spanned the front of the 174th Street Bridge, overlooking a patch of the Bronx River. There we were, our legs dangling off those girders above the entrance to the bridge as the drivers passed underneath, looking up at us and assuming that these boys are completely crazy. You have to know how dangerous that was. My mom used to take me to that same bridge when I had whooping cough. She was told it was important for me to get near the water. I think they meant the ocean, but all we had was the Bronx River.

I can see myself sorting fruit at this market on the corner of Bryant Avenue and 174th. I was twelve or thirteen and going to school, but my mother wasn't working at the time, so on weekends I had to help earn some money. Cliffy and the rest of the guys would pass the fruit store when they were on their way to the

Dutchies or some other misadventure, and they'd whistle at me and shout, "Hey, Sonny Boy! Throw us an apple! What are you doing in there, man? Come out with us!"

The guy who owned the fruit store would notice my friends hollering out to me. The kids I ran with bothered him. One day the guy took me aside and said, "I want to talk to you about something." He pulled over one of those crates that the fruit would come in, he took out a big pencil and started drawing something for me. It was a map that showed a path that split in two directions. As I was looking at his drawing, he said to me, "You see, this is life. And here, where it splits, there is this path and there is *that path*." And he put a sort of ominous emphasis on "that path." He said, "I see you walking down that path. That's the wrong path."

It was like he'd become the Pat O'Brien character from some film in the 1930s, the boring old street priest who tells James Cagney to straighten up and fly right or he'll end up in the electric chair. All I wanted to do was shove an apple in his mouth and go back to separating the lettuce from the cucumbers. He was a working person, which was fine and he meant well, but he was now telling me how to live and I'm twelve and a half years old. I'm just trying to get through the day. I'm looking at the clock until it's time that I can go meet my friends who you reject, out there where there's life and fun, and—guess what?—a fucking future. I ain't gonna die holding a piece of rotting fruit in my hand while you pontificate about how sweet life can be if I just do what you say. Fuck you and the pineapple crate you came in on, buddy. Of course I didn't blurt that out; I just gave him the ol' A-OK nod, like most kids would, but I did think it, and then I quit, and I was back out there with my mongrel friends.

Sonny Boy

I think about my past, and I can't come up with anything that could possibly explain how I ever ended up here, where my life is today. It had to be luck. Close calls here, close calls there. My grandmother used to say, "Sonny Boy is a lucky boy," out of nowhere, and my grandfather would say, "The kid's got personality." These are the things you remember.

I knew I wasn't going to get stuck in some fruit store on Bryant Avenue or some other odd job I did to get by. I was looking up at that El that sang to me every time I walked to it. Trains that are up in the sky—my God, what an invention. When you are up in the front of that train, in the first car, standing next to where the motorman sits, right there at that big bay window, you see everything. You are up in the air, above everything, looking down at the streets and the scatterings of people below. You became the train, and as you'd come out of the tunnel, you'd see the air and the earth, and you'd see the South Bronx spread out in front of you like some great big flag. You are flying. I would think, wait, where are we? Oh, there are the old tenements. And there are the clotheslines— I never forget the clotheslines. There are all those kids running around down there. You could hear the cry of their joys and the echo. I knew I was coming back into my town, and I would be flush with memories. I would look at it the way you would look at an old friend you loved—it's a place where I belonged but became separated from, and no longer recognize it like I once did.

When you're young, you're not into memories—you talk about yesterday or the day before. You're creating them as you live. Me, I've got plenty of memories, and I don't need old structures or physical artifacts to put me in touch with them. Sometimes it's a sight or a sound or a scent; sometimes all it takes is a sensation. I'll

345

just feel cold, and all of a sudden, I'm nineteen or twenty years old again, shivering and shaking in a Manhattan boardinghouse on Tenth Avenue, because I had just been walking alone in the freezing snow. My room there was up a few floors and it was tiny, yet it had a window where I could look out to see people on Tenth Avenue, coming and going in the snow, and that little window with its view made it kind of appealing. But the coat I was wearing had gotten soaking wet, head to toe. Like all my clothes, I had picked it up in a thrift shop for a couple of bucks. I couldn't have been wetter or more tired, and my secondhand clothes were leaking and falling apart. The steam radiator in my room had gone berserk, showering the bed with condensation and leaving me with no heat. I got into my wet bed, put my wet coat over my wet head, and outside the snow kept coming down, soon to turn into sheets of ice as the night kept getting colder and colder, making for slippery roads, car crashes, and slush along the sidewalk. Forever wet, inside and out, as those thoughts made their way into my head, I fell asleep.

The next morning I woke up alive but dizzy. I was freezing and shivering hysterically. I knew I had a fever. I knew I had to go to the hospital. I got myself to the emergency ward at Bellevue, and I waited forever at their clinic, a twenty-year-old wreck.

I was brought into an exam room, still shivering, where a nurse held up some pills and tried to explain to me that I had to take one every four hours. She was making big, exaggerated gestures and slowly enunciating. "Four. Hours," she said with her four fingers right in my face. The more she did this, the dumber I became. I thought, Was there a school somewhere that teaches them how to do this? I imagined a clinic where they hired Marcel

Marceau, the great pantomime artist, to explain to the patients what the nurse was trying to tell them. She probably thought I didn't speak English, and I was following her lead. This was New York, the melting pot, and she was used to people coming in from all over. If you were poor like me, you went to the clinic.

Then a doctor came into the room and examined me. He said, "You have a virus of your cerebrum."

And I said, "A what?"

He said slowly, "You. Have. A head cold."

I said, "A head cold?"

He looked at me in silence, and I looked at him, and he said, "Stick your head under the radiator."

I said, "Under the radiator?"

He said, "You ever think about going to the outpatient clinic we have here at Bellevue?" It was a notorious nuthouse. "You need to talk to somebody. You're a little high-strung."

I thought, Talk to who? I'm dying here.

However, I didn't go to the outpatient clinic, but I did go to my cousin Mark's apartment in the West Bronx under the El on Arlington Avenue. My cousin Mark and the girlfriend he was living with took care of me and put me on a couch while I nursed a 104-degree temperature. I was there for a few days until I recovered. I don't know why I didn't go to my grandmother's place. I guess I went to Mark's because he lived closer to Manhattan. I love my cousin like a brother.

It seemed I always needed someone to take care of me. Many years later, in the period when I was doing David Mamet's *American Buffalo* on the East Coast, the great movie star Elizabeth Taylor was also doing a play on Broadway, and I became fast friends

AL PACINO

with her. We would hang out, just enjoying each other's company. She was a great actress with a gentle heart, and she got to know some of the people in my life, like Jim Bulleit and Jimmy Hayden. We would talk about everything. I would always ask her about Richard Burton, who she'd been married to twice, and who was my favorite actor along with Marlon; sometimes she'd indulge me and sometimes she'd brush me off. She was a regular person and a walking, talking treasure.

Once we went out to dinner together, me, her, and Jimmy Hayden, at some posh restaurant. I knew Jimmy had a real eye for her. Elizabeth's bodyguard had gotten married a few weeks earlier, and we all went to the wedding. Jimmy spent the night trying to get real close to her, dancing and prancing. He was a lady's man. Now as we sat in that posh restaurant, I was looking at the huge diamond ring Elizabeth wore on her middle finger, and she was looking at the bandanna I wore wrapped around my head. She finally said to me, "Al, would you please take that thing off your forehead?" And I said, with my South Bronx delivery, "When you take off that big shiny rock you got on one of your digits. It's blinding me." We laughed, and I took off the bandanna, but she never touched the ring.

Sometime in the early 2000s, I visited her at her house in LA, which was staggeringly beautiful. As I looked at its walls, which were decorated with paintings by Renoir, Matisse, and Picasso, I thought, What a place to live. Imagine having that every day when you wake up, just feeling that inspiration. When she was in New York, she'd come over to my place in the country, and I'd make spaghetti for her. A friend of mine told me she ran into Elizabeth Taylor in LA and she asked about me. "How's Al doing? Is he okay? He said he needed to get someone to help him out." My friend re-

plied, "I think he did. I think he's got someone working for him."
"Good," she said, "because that boy needs all the help he can get."
How right she was. Long before I had any friends who were famous, I found people who tried to help me make my way.

)(◆)(

IT'S STAGGERING TO ME THAT THESE THINGS REALLY HAPPENED TO
me, and I can't even prove it anymore. There's no more 34th Street
East, the movie theater where I watched that masterpiece *The Red
Shoes* maybe a hundred times while I worked there as an usher. I
felt like a shadow in that theater, and I enjoyed it. They put that
monkey suit on me, which I didn't like, but I stood in the dark and
looked up at that screen. The Rugoff theaters were turning movies
into cinema, catering to a higher-class audience. They mainly
hired guys for ushers and girls for cashiers. You just had to be relatively nice-looking to be hired as an usher, that was the requirement. If you were someone who was intermittently in and out of
it, like I was, you just did what they told you to do. I could operate
the flashlight and stand in one place. Sounds easy enough, but I
would still get fired from these places pretty regularly.

Outside of these jobs I continued to try to act and to audition
for roles. Charlie came with me one time to the Hudson Playhouse
in Greenwich Village, where I had been called back for not just one
but two plays. I had already gone to read for them before, and both
directors liked me the first time, so I thought at least I'll get one of
the parts. There was a little hope. But somehow I didn't get either,
and that's what actors go through.

It was springtime, so Charlie just hung outside and waited for me while I gave my auditions. I came out the door, and he looked at me and said, "The big ol' rejection, eh?" I just shrugged my shoulders and told him I didn't get either one, so we started walking west toward the Hudson River. Charlie turned to me and said, "Al, you don't seem bothered." I told Charlie, "It's their loss," and he seemed happy. He said, "Al, you got moxie." Moxie must be in my survival kit. How else would I have it? You don't go to a store and buy it.

Where I really needed moxie was in the old days, when my mother would send me out to the store to go get her Kotex tampons. Somehow they seemed larger back then. I remember going to the druggist for her when I was ten or eleven years old, and there were a few people around in the store. The guy who ran it had seen me around from time to time, bopping in and bopping out, and he said, "What do you want?" Very calmly and quietly, I said to him, "You know, every once in a while I feel a little moody. And then sometimes, I just don't know what it is, I start to feel pain, and I look down there and there's blood there. They told me to go get some Kotex for it." He glared back at me and said, "You gotta get out of here. You know we don't need wise guys." I thought we'd share a laugh, one guy to another. But he wasn't a guy, he was a pharmacist, and I was an eleven-year-old wiseass. I did get the Kotex though.

While I worked as an usher, I took it upon myself to recommend friends for jobs. I even got Charlie hired as an usher at Carnegie Hall of all places. We had arrived. Okay, I was still only an usher, but this was Carnegie Hall. I remember I had a huge crush on a cute lesbian girl who worked there. I don't know whatever happened with her, but I really liked her, though she didn't seem to have any interest in me. So there's Charlie in a tuxedo looking like a master of ceremonies, he could be a maître d' at a restaurant or giving out Oscars at the big ceremony. The man had majesty. He worked one day there and turned to me and said, "I think I'm too old for this." He was gone.

I tried to hang in there. One night, they had a Jamaican music concert, and I was seating people way up in the balcony of Carnegie Hall. Of course I was seating people in the wrong rows. I always felt, who cares where you sit when you go to the movies or a play or a concert? You're in the theater, you're going to see or hear it. What does a couple of inches mean, behind or in front of somebody? It's all built on a slope anyway. If you want to do the math, you're inches away from the row in front of you. In the last row, in some ways, you have a better seat.

So I said, why not let them go first come, first serve? But this was Carnegie Hall, and these people had tickets. That was the point. They had tickets they paid for, and the tickets had their seat numbers on them. And they started kvetching. Pretty soon they started hitting one another. I thought, Wow, what did I start? What I started was my demise and a mini riot, because they fired me on the spot there too. And I wanted to see that Jamaican concert.

I was gone, pounding the streets again, looking for another usher's job. By that time, I knew what I wanted to be, an usher—no, no, an actor. You would think I would be down in the dumps because I'd been fired so much. Or that I might be anxious, worrying about where I would find the next job. But I was always sure that one would come along—the jobs were just something to eat by, and they would keep coming while I pursued my vocation. And New York City gave me so much to support that dream.

I don't have memories like that today. I don't remember anything that vividly now, and not because I'm suffering from some kind of dementia. Yes, I'm still living, but living in a much more predictable ambiance. Thank God for my kids—I love them so much, as you can tell, and I'm glad they have lives of their own. An actor has his own life too. That's why for me work has always been life—something that opens the door and allows the spirit to come out. A world I can visit, where the imagination has switched on and life becomes once again what it was: discovery, delight, ecstasy.

Why are these things still so vivid to me? It's not that I don't have conflicted feelings about this time in my life. I was often alone for long periods. Of course I had Charlie and Penny and their little daughter, but the rest of my life was lonely. Charlie used to call me "Lonesome Pine." There I was, walking the city late at night, doing my monologues from O'Neill and Shakespeare on the dark, silent streets, usually in back of warehouses. New York gave me the cool nights and the gift of empty streets to practice on. My audience was the stars and the buildings and the cars parked nearby. If anyone walked past, they would have thought I was crazy; if animal services drove by they'd have netted me like a stray dog. Then I'd get home to my room somewhere in the stratosphere of Manhattan island, alone again, and I'd ponder what the next day would bring. It always did bring something. Perhaps a new encounter, another usher job, or a trek downtown to Washington Square, where Charlie and I would sit and have Chock full o'Nuts coffee on some bench in that park in the middle of winter. Maybe I'd sleep on the stage at the Actors Gallery, like I did when

Sonny Boy

I was performing in *Creditors*, and Charlie would meet me there in the morning. It was okay. It was all okay.

)(◆)(

THEY HAVE THAT EXPRESSION, "YOU CAN'T LOOK BACK." WELL, I look back and I love it. I love what I see. I love that I existed. I look at this little baby, my son Roman, who has recently come into my life, and I say, wow, look at you. It just gives me a chuckle every time I look at him. When he was three or four weeks old, I would think, what does he know about anything? There he is, sitting there. Nobody's touched him, in the way of influencing him. He's just there. So he's got everything going for him. He's like a little Buddha. It takes a while for the face to change. That mask that we all eventually get, where does that come from? Maybe it comes from all the clichés that are thrown at us growing up, the delusions and illusions, the screwing and unscrewing of light bulbs. Be a good boy, be a good girl. And you see that in the infant. It's not just a little human being—it is a canvas that's going to be painted on. It's so fresh, and alive and new. The world will paint its face on the specimen we all are.

I saw him just the other day, and now he's four months old. Now this little baby is talking, really going at it. I couldn't believe how much he was talking. Not saying a word, just baby babble, but talking like he really wanted to say something. I thought, He's trying to reach me. He's talking to me, and he's telling me about where he came from. He's saying to me, "Dad, there's a place I've been and it's great. It's a place you're going to go to soon and you'll see how great it is. I can't talk but I just want to get it out. Because soon

I'll learn how to speak words and I won't remember anymore." He's trying to make me feel better, and I want to tell him thanks for letting me know that it's going to be okay. Thanks, kid.

I wonder how much my little son will come to understand all of this. When I try to explain what it was like growing up in the South Bronx to young people, I feel like I'm describing Oliver Twist's London to them, or Thornton Wilder's Grover's Corners, or that small town in Texas from *The Last Picture Show*. And it's not really the Bronx I'm describing, much less New York City; it's a tiny, provincial world, its own little community. I didn't know anybody's business a couple of streets over, on Vyse Avenue, or Longfellow. What I knew was our block. This was the world of Marty-P jumping off the storefront roof before the police could catch him; the world of Philly, if you remember him, sitting silently outside in a chair with his mother next to him, all because some bully had called him a rock; of great big Hymie, sent off to live in a home and never seen again; of Steve and whatever had happened to him at the bus depot; of that strange man in the suit who walked around saying, "You don't kill time—time kills you." We didn't try to process these characters or make sense of them. They were just fixtures on our block and every small town has its share of them. This was Anywhere, U.S.A.

An entire universe existed under the El at the White Plains Road line, a short walk from my house. Right there was the barbershop where my grandfather brought me as a little boy to get my hair cut, and I would need a box to sit on in the barber's chair because I wasn't big enough. From that chair, if I looked up and to my left, I could see the El flying by, taking people to and from our little neighborhood. Just across the street, under that El, was a little diner where my mother would take me when she brought me with her to the movies in the early 1940s, at the age of four or five. I can still remember the warmth of that luncheonette, with its tiled walls of blue-and-white checkerboard, the melancholy songs that came out of wartime emanating from the radio, and the pretty girl working the counter, the one with the white ribbon in her blond hair and the blue bow on her apron, looking at me with a big smile. Just a few doors down was the Dover Theatre on Boston Road, where my mother and I would see our movies. My mother was everything to me then. Somehow she always knew when something was about to happen.

)X◆X(

CLIFFY ALREADY SEEMED TO BE MOVING OFF IN ANOTHER DIREC-tion, as young as the age of thirteen, as drugs came into his life. To name just one incident, a bunch of us were walking past a shoe store in our neighborhood when out of nowhere Cliffy kicked open a glass display case on the sidewalk in front of the store. He just smashed it in and all hell broke loose. We all sped away in different directions as Cliffy took off with a pair of sneakers. There just happened to be a cop car right across the street when he did it. The next thing you knew, we were running from those cops and Cliffy was behind me, laughing and grabbing at the back of my shirt, holding me and slowing me down so I couldn't get away. I never knew if he did it in a fit of excitement and energy or if he was just high. By the time the cop car caught up to us, Cliffy was rolling around the ground laughing while I stood there with my hands up in the air, and they marched us back to the scene of the crime.

After that ordeal, I started to question what I was getting myself into. We all got into a lot of trouble for that little escapade. Luckily, some of the neighborhood people pooled their money to pay for the display case that Cliffy smashed. I thought to myself at the time, That's the last of that stuff—that's vandalism and that's a crime. That was on another level. It was a shock and something about it made me feel uncomfortable, I guess.

Meanwhile, I still didn't know yet that there was a whole world beyond this neighborhood. That day would come, a couple of years later, when Anton Chekhov came to town. For now, we had no awareness that we were poor or that we lacked anything. We had each other; we were on top of the world, as James Cagney said in *White Heat*. We didn't think of ourselves as having nothing. It wasn't even a question in our minds.

My friends and I had the whole world, as far as we knew. What else would you call hanging on the corner and trying to harmonize? Or talking about girls? Or scheming about what we'd do tonight and where'd we go tomorrow? Or getting excited about the Yankees winning the pennant—after all, Yankee Stadium was right there in the Bronx? Or trying to convince the cop on the beat to get us some Sneaky Pete, the kind of alcohol that rips your stomach apart, like you were drinking airplane glue? Or hoping to overhear one of those wise old teenagers talk about his cryptic sexual escapades, which always made our ears shoot up? We didn't have sex education in school, we learned it in the streets by hearsay. Life was ours. Let's do something! Let's go somewhere! Let's take the subway and go downtown, or just walk and strut. Just stay away from any of those display cases that Cliffy seemed violently drawn to.

When it was late spring or summertime and the sun went

down, we couldn't play stickball anymore. That was when it was time to go out and find some trouble, some adventure. Maybe there'd be a Boy Scout meeting at one of the junior high schools that we could interrupt, shake it up a bit and get chased through the hallways by the custodians. We'd zip around and duck into the darkened classrooms, just looking for a place to hide. These schools were vast, two or three stories with classrooms everywhere, and they felt luxurious to us. Tell me, is there anything more exciting than getting chased? I ain't gonna run now, my legs don't move like that anymore. But back then, it was like we were tight ends doing somersaults over the goal line and life was passing the football to us.

There I am with my friends in the vacant lots closest to 174th Street, where we'd always end up at the day's end, waiting for the half mass of light to turn into darkness. We're messing around, wondering what's up, what's next. My friends want me to go off with them to somewhere else. But not for me, not this night. Cliffy and Bruce and Petey were ready to go, and a couple of other guys with them, but my mom was calling. Our windows didn't face the street, so I'd hear my mother from the roof of our tenement. She'd be up there, calling out to me, "Hey, Sonneeeeeee, get up here, you haven't eaten, come upstairs, I have supper." Her voice came off the roof and echoed everywhere.

Cliffy would give me that look that was a mix of pity and envy. No one was ever calling from the roof for him, or Petey, or Bruce, or any of the other guys. He'd shrug and say something like, "If you gotta go, you gotta go," and the guys would peel off and recede into the coming dark.

I wanted to be with them, and wish that we'd have gotten together again and that life would have gone on forever, because it was paradise. I think it might have been the love we came to have for one another, and we had each other's backs. But those guys went way before their time. They all died of drugs; Bruce was found on the floor of a motel room off the parkway, his body lying next to a duffel bag.

By the time he died, I had already made it as an actor. I got word of Bruce's funeral service while I was working, so I headed out to his burial at a barren cemetery in the Bronx. I arrived there on a cold, cloud-covered day in January. There, alone on a hill, no one else around for miles, was Bruce's mother and another woman, possibly her friend or Bruce's aunt, the two of them just staring down at Bruce's body in a box. I ran up to his mom, who I remembered from way back, when she used to bring young Bruce his little jar of chocolate milk, in front of all of us, right there in the street. We'd have to stop whatever we were doing at the time to watch her do this and declare, "Brucey needs his milk." We never wondered why she needed to do it. I guess when you're six or seven there are a lot of things you don't bother to question. When I saw his mother now standing by her son's grave, I gave her a hug. Of course, she was distraught and crying, and it had been years since I had seen her.

But the older woman with his mother—she could have been an aunt or a cousin—was so eloquent as she spoke about Bruce at his graveside. What she said was not generic rhetoric; it was perceptive, and it was so spot-on that it threw me. Bruce was someone I grew up with, who would have my back if anyone tried to be a tough guy with me, who I had directed in the comedy revues we put on in the café theaters of Greenwich Village in the sixties. What this woman was able to say about him was the blatant truth.

It could only be expressed by someone who was smart enough and old enough to understand life, and to understand a guy like Bruce. I thought that I knew him, and with just a couple of sentences she showed me that I didn't, not on that level. It was so full of wisdom that I shuddered. I was certainly in awe of it.

Petey and Cliffy went down hard a little earlier. Petey was just nineteen when he went the way of the gutter with a needle in his arm. I didn't see it happen. The news came to us through some dirty-faced punk from his drug crowd who said with a smirk, "He was greedy, man. Greedy people die."

Of course there's Cliffy, who was so smart and full of feeling, and he just got stopped in life. There are people who die later on, after they've achieved something and they can't live with it, but he went before he could even get there. It's heartbreaking, because he was capable of so much, and he didn't deserve to just be written off. I didn't see Cliffy go either; I heard about it from the streets, like with Petey. It was the needle again and I wished I'd gotten the chance to memorialize Cliffy in some way.

One of Charlie's poems touched on who Cliffy was to me— Charlie had written it about a soldier he knew, named John, who had been killed by a fellow officer in a fragging incident. I imagined I would take that poem, change the name, and put it on Cliffy's gravestone one day. The poem is called "John Is Dead":

> evil
> was a coloration
> through the very air
> he strove.
>   a zone

a conflagration of haunts
a belladonna drag
through the slums
     his quest
aimed always
     at the frozen hour.

lost in the lonely dews
of his birth and death
his nocturne
as grey as ashes
now.

on no face
reads the news
no one bows his head

so, i take
          this time
and place
          to say:
rue of the moon
sorrow of the cold clay:

John is dead.

The poem says John, but in my mind I hear Cliffy. There were
a lot of people like Cliffy, and there will always be people around

like him—to awaken life, to be destructive in life, and if you're not careful, to be destructive to you also. But I loved him. I understand he never meant to hurt anyone. I got to learn more, later in life, and to make that lucky turn away from Cliffy's fate. But I still feel it. I feel the hurt, I feel the waste, I feel it all.

I remember when Cliffy threw that rock aimlessly and hit that squirrel. He never thought he'd hit it, but he did, and Cliffy flung himself to the ground, praying to God for forgiveness, bawling his eyes out and then holding a ceremony to bury that little animal.

He was a guy who was always there when you needed it. You always had the feeling that any one of those friends would give their life up for you. I guess it's like soldiers in a foxhole—that strange collective that happens. Not to compare us with soldiers fighting on a battlefield, of course, but we faced our own danger and we provided protection for each other. Like I said when they took my baseball glove, that wouldn't have happened if I had Bruce or Cliffy or Petey there. It's not in the head, it's in the body and heart. It's not superficial, it's born out of trust and love, because the world was better when we were together. The whole world existed in us. We were alive in the real sense of the word, rich and alive with life.

I never got to eulogize any of these friends until now, so maybe this is a good spot to give you one more poem from Charlie's canon, called "When I Die."

> when I die
> I'll die here
> within these tenements

and still the moon
and a woman alone
with blue-cold hands
will high-stake white sheets
to the Winter sky

the dawn will come
and fugitive figures
will issue from doorways
like whispers.

across the alleyway
there'll be a shadow of birds
like sudden gravel
thrown against the wall.

more people will come
into the streets
speed by—
criss cross—
hurry on—

the end of a scarf
will dissolve in the wind.

As for all the others in our little gang, I can only guess what happened to them. Sometimes I think, why didn't I end up that way? Why am I still here? Was it all luck? Was it Chekhov? Was it Shakespeare? Was it meeting Charlie for the first time? Or how about my granddad, or my mom up on that roof, calling down, "Sonny Boy, you haven't eaten anything, there's supper on the table"? What keeps us going? Where does that come from, survival? Perhaps it's the memories, as the great Charlie Laughton told me once. He was eighty-four at the time, paraplegic from MS, and only had the use of one of his arms. He pointed at his heart and said, "Al, you're right here. Don't worry about me. I got my dreams at night, I got my memories, and I got my imagination. I'll be okay."

Another thing that Charlie said to me at the end of his life was "You're a miracle, Al. You're a miracle." Who has that said to them? I didn't believe that, of course. But I knew what he was saying. My whole life was a moon shot.

This life is a dream, as Shakespeare says. I think the saddest part about dying is that you lose your memories. Memories are like wings: they keep you flying, like a bird on the wind. If I'm lucky enough, if I get to heaven perhaps I'll get to reunite with my mother there. All I want is the chance to walk up to her, look in her eyes, and simply say, "Hey, Ma, see what happened to me?"

Acknowledgments

Of course, I want to thank Dave Itzkoff for his commitment and energy. His considerable help and persistence got me to turn corners I never would have turned. I owe him a lot. Scott Moyers, our editor, is such a stand-up guy with deep integrity and intelligence. He stood by us as I moved in my ponderous and mind-changing, toss-up ways. I'd drive anyone crazy, but Scott and Dave hung on and stayed with it. I want to thank Mollie Glick and Josh Lieberman at CAA, whose encouragement and steadfast purpose got me through this. Writing is not my first language—I needed all the help I could get and I certainly got it. I have to give special mention to Michael Quinn, who was there hands-on, making a colossal contribution to this book, along with bearing with my oddities, including my temperament and my innate desire to lie down till it passes. Also, I want to thank my friends and family who gave me feedback on various chapters they graciously read for me. They gave me the kind of support I needed to put some of this stuff out there. I had the essential wake-up call from all of these devoted people, and without their contributions there would be no book.

Credits

Insert 1

p. 1: (top and bottom) Courtesy of Mark Scarola

p. 2: (top and bottom) Courtesy of Mark Scarola

p. 3: (top) ARCHIVIO GBB/Alamy Stock Photo, (bottom) Courtesy of Mark Scarola

p. 4: (top and bottom) Courtesy of Mark Scarola

p. 5: (top) Courtesy of Mark Scarola, (bottom) NYC Department of Records and Information Services, NYC Municipal Archives Collection, Bronx 1940s Tax Photos

p. 6: (top and bottom) Courtesy of Mark Scarola

p. 7: (top and bottom) Courtesy of Mark Scarola

p. 8: (top) [X2010.7.2.5573] Museum of the City of New York, (left) Courtesy of Mark Scarola, (right) Michael E. Avedon

p. 9: (top and bottom) Fred W. McDarrah/MUUS Collection via Getty Images

p. 10: (top) Friedman-Abeles, copyright © NYPL, (bottom) Film Publicity Archive/United Archives via Getty Images

p. 11: (top) Steve Schapiro/Corbis via Getty Images, (bottom) Silver Screen Collection/Getty Images

p. 12: (top) Imago/Alamy Stock Photo, (bottom) Courtesy of Giovannina Jennifer Bellino

p. 13: (top) Steve Schapiro/Corbis via Getty Images, (bottom) Ron Galella/Ron Galella Collection via Getty Images

p. 14: (top) Paramount Pictures/Courtesy of Getty Images, (left) Jack Mitchell/Getty Images, (bottom) Photo 12/Alamy Stock Photos

p. 15: (top) CBS Photo Archive via Getty Images, (bottom) Steve Schapiro/Corbis via Getty Images

p. 16: (top) Film Publicity Archive/United Archives via Getty Images, (middle) Sunset Boulevard/Corbis via Getty Images

Insert 2

p. 1: (top) Ron Galella/Ron Galella Collection via Getty Images

p. 2: (top) Donald Cooper/Alamy Stock Photo, (bottom) Columbia Pictures/Sunset Boulevard/Corbis via Getty Images

CREDITS

p. 3: (top) Courtesy Everett Collection, (middle and bottom) Courtesy Everett Collection

p. 4: (top) Jack Buxbaum/J. F. Kennedy Center, (bottom) ©Warner Bros./Courtesy Everett Collection

p. 5: (top) Pictorial Press Ltd./Alamy Stock Photo, (bottom) Steve Schapiro/Corbis via Getty Images

p. 6: (top left) Ron Galella, Ltd./Ron Galella Collection via Getty Images, (top right) ©Touchstone/Courtesy Everett Collection, (bottom) Anita and Steve Shevett, copyright © NYPL

p. 7: (top) New Line Cinema/Sunset Boulevard/Corbis via Getty Images, (bottom) PictureLux/The Hollywood Archive/Alamy Stock Photo

p. 8: (top) United Archives GmbH/Alamy Stock Photo, (bottom) HAL GARB/AFP via Getty Images

p. 9: (top) Getty Images, (bottom) ©Warner Bros./Courtesy Everett Collection

p. 10: (top) Album/Alamy Stock Photo, (bottom) Lawrence Schwartzwald/ Sygma via Getty Images

p. 11: (top) Christopher Polk/FilmMagic, (bottom) Everett Collection Inc./Alamy Stock Photo

p. 12: (top) Will Ragozzino/Patrick McMullan via Getty Images Patrick McMullan, (bottom) Copyright © Salome Productions LLC

p. 13: (top) WENN Rights Ltd./Alamy Stock Photo, (bottom) Moviestore Collection Ltd./Alamy Stock Photo

CREDITS